SOCIETY FOR NEW TESTAMENT STUDIES
MONOGRAPH SERIES

GENERAL EDITOR
MATTHEW BLACK, D.D., F.B.A.

27

JESUS OF NAZARETH IN
NEW TESTAMENT PREACHING

JESUS OF NAZARETH IN NEW TESTAMENT PREACHING

G. N. STANTON

Lecturer in New Testament Studies
University of London King's College

CAMBRIDGE UNIVERSITY PRESS

Published by the Syndics of the Cambridge University Press
Bentley House, 200 Euston Road, London NW1 2DB
American Branch: 32 East 57th Street, New York, N.Y. 10022

© Cambridge University Press 1974

Library of Congress Catalogue Card Number: 73-92782

ISBN: 0 521 20465 8

First published 1974

Printed in Great Britain
at the University Printing House, Cambridge
(Brooke Crutchley, University Printer)

TO MY WIFE

AND TO THE MEMORY OF MY BROTHER

CONTENTS

PREFACE

I am deeply grateful to the many people who have assisted me in various ways while this book has been in preparation.

I owe a particular debt to Professor C. F. D. Moule, who supervised my work on an earlier draft which was submitted to the University of Cambridge in 1969 as a thesis for the Ph.D. degree. Professor Moule has not only assisted and encouraged me in many ways, but has set me an example of Christian commitment and of careful and thorough scholarship which I shall always value.

Dr A. H. McDonald, Fellow of Clare College, Cambridge, and sometime University Lecturer in Ancient History kindly read a fuller draft of the material on Greek and Roman biographical writing and made a number of helpful suggestions.

I must also thank colleagues and students at Princeton, New Jersey, Cambridge and London who listened patiently to parts of the material in this book and made valuable and constructive criticisms.

My brother Murray took a keen interest in the progress of my work and looked forward to the appearance of this book. He died on 13 May 1972, while serving as a medical missionary at Ahmednagar, India.

My wife's love and patience have been an enormous encouragement, both during my studies in Cambridge and during the preparation of this book.

JUNE 1973   G.N.S.

ABBREVIATIONS

AJT	*American Journal of Theology*
ATR	*Anglican Theological Review*
BJRL	*Bulletin of the John Rylands Library*
BZ	*Biblische Zeitschrift*
CBQ	*Catholic Biblical Quarterly*
comm.	commentary
E.T.	English translation
ETL	*Ephemerides theologicae Lovanienses*
EvT	*Evangelische Theologie*
ExT	*Expository Times*
HTR	*Harvard Theological Review*
JBL	*Journal of Biblical Literature*
JQR	*Jewish Quarterly Review*
JR	*Journal of Religion*
JSS	*Journal of Semitic Studies*
JTS	*Journal of Theological Studies*
KD	*Kerygma und Dogma*
LQHR	*London Quarterly and Holborn Review*
NovT	*Novum Testamentum*
NRT	*Nouvelle Revue Théologique*
NTS	*New Testament Studies*
RB	*Revue Biblique*
RGG	*Die Religion in Geschichte und Gegenwart*, 3rd edition, ed. K. Galling (Tübingen, 1957ff.)
RHPR	*Revue d'Histoire et de Philosophie Religieuses*
SJT	*Scottish Journal of Theology*
ST	*Studia Theologica*
TB	*Tyndale Bulletin*
ThLZ	*Theologische Literaturzeitung*
TR	*Theologische Rundschau*
TWNT	*Theologisches Wörterbuch zum Neuen Testament* I–IX, ed. G. Kittel and G. Friedrich (Stuttgart, 1933–73)
TZ	*Theologische Zeitschrift*
VT	*Vetus Testamentum*
WD	*Wort und Dienst*
ZNW	*Zeitschrift für die neutestamentliche Wissenschaft*
ZTK	*Zeitschrift für Theologie und Kirche*

Note. Full bibliographical details are given in the first footnote reference to each title; the page on which these details are given is indicated by italics in the Index of Authors.

INTRODUCTION

There is a deeply rooted conviction that the Christian message is bound up with the life and character of Jesus of Nazareth. Today some professing Christians find that an intellectual understanding of God and experience of God's activity raise hosts of awkward questions; nevertheless they cling tenaciously to the conviction that by reading the gospels' accounts of the life of Jesus we gain our clearest understanding of God. Did not the Johannine Christ say, 'Anyone who has seen me has seen the Father' (John 14: 9)? Most Christians accept that the gospel message is spelt out *in nuce* in the life, teaching and suffering of Jesus of Nazareth.

For many Christians, the Christian life involves attempting to emulate the kindness and goodness of Jesus. Stories of the 'gentle Jesus, meek and mild' are still prominent in Christian education of the very young. Missionary preaching in non-Christian societies frequently takes the character of Jesus as its starting point; Mark's Gospel, not a Pauline epistle, is usually the first book to be translated. Many who reject Christian convictions about Jesus would acknowledge that Jesus is a classic martyr figure: he went about doing good and healing people, but his intentions were misunderstood and he was rejected and put to death.

In sophisticated scholarly circles we find the same continued fascination with the character of Jesus. Motifs such as 'Jesus as the Man for others' and, indeed, the humanity of Jesus in general, feature prominently in the work of many contemporary systematic theologians.[1] But this interest in the earthly life of Jesus is completely at odds with the conclusions of many New Testament scholars who insist that there was no close relationship between early Christological proclamation and the life and character of Jesus. The earliest post-Easter claims about Jesus were not influenced by the church's interest in or memory of the sort of person Jesus showed himself to be in his teaching,

[1] See R. Slenczka's wide-ranging discussion, *Geschichtlichkeit und Personsein Jesu Christi. Studien zur christologischen Problematik der historischen Jesusfrage* (Göttingen, 1967).

actions, and relationships with others, but by expectations of an imminent *parousia* which were deeply influenced by apocalyptic.

In this apparent impasse the following questions – the questions with which this book is concerned – are relevant. Was the primitive church interested in the life and character of Jesus? If so, when and in what context did this interest arise?

These questions are, of course, not new. They are worthy of consideration not only for the *theological* reasons just mentioned, but because they touch on several sensitive areas of current New Testament scholarship; in particular they necessitate a fresh examination of some of the assumptions of form criticism which have long been considered as closed issues.

R. Bultmann and K. Barth vigorously attacked the older liberal scholars who made an accurately reconstructed account of the life and personality of Jesus the very heart of the Christian message.[1] For both Bultmann and Barth not the historical Jesus but the proclaimed Christ of the kerygma is central. R. Bultmann repeatedly insisted that the primitive kerygma was not concerned with more than the mere *Dass* of the existence of Jesus of Nazareth.[2]

The emergence of form criticism was closely allied to this theological position. R. Bultmann and M. Dibelius (together with K. Schmidt and M. Albertz) pioneered form critical study of the gospels. Although differing in emphasis and detail, they argued that the gospel traditions could be related closely to the needs and interests of the early church – and reports of the past life of Jesus were neither of interest nor of use to the primitive church. Both accepted that the kerygma was

[1] The details need not be repeated here. For a recent survey, see J. Roloff, *Das Kerygma und der irdische Jesus* (Göttingen, 1970), pp. 9–39.

[2] See R. Bultmann, 'Die Bedeutung des geschichtlichen Jesus für die Theologie des Paulus' in *Glauben und Verstehen* I (Tübingen, 1933), 188ff. [E.T. in *Faith and Understanding* I (London, 1969), 220ff.]; 'Das Verhältnis der urchristlichen Christusbotschaft zum historischen Jesus' in *Sitzungsberichte der Heidelberger Akad. Wiss., Phil.-hist. Klasse* (1960) [E.T. in *The Historical Jesus and the Kerygmatic Christ*, eds. C. E. Braaten and R. A. Harrisville (Nashville, 1964)]; and Bultmann's final comments, 'Antwort an E. Käsemann' in *Glauben und Verstehen* IV (Tübingen, 1965), 190ff.

all-important; the gospel traditions were developed in its light and used as a supplement: they proclaimed Jesus as the Risen and Exalted Christ. Until quite recently the basic principles of form criticism went unchallenged.

But the theological conclusions drawn from form critical study of the gospels did not all win the day. Bultmann's attempt to drive a wedge between Jesus of Nazareth and the primitive kerygma was modified by a number of his former pupils and challenged by many other scholars. E. Käsemann's 1953 lecture, 'The Problem of the Historical Jesus', sparked off the so-called 'new quest' for the historical Jesus.[1] A flood of literature continued unabated for a decade.[2] Two themes dominated the discussion: the question of continuity between the Christ of the kerygma and the historical Jesus, and the adequacy of an existentialist view of history in connection with the problem of the historical Jesus.[3] Discussion tended to become repetitive and boring and, not surprisingly, scholarly interest moved elsewhere. The 'new quest' might have been expected to lead to a vigorous reappraisal of some of the basic tenets of form criticism – but with few exceptions this did not happen.

More recently the vexed question of the role of traditions about Jesus in the early church has come to the fore again. Scholars who are in broad agreement with Bultmann's theological position have taken the point that if only the *Dass* of the historical existence of Jesus was part of the kerygma, the eventual emergence of the gospels is a puzzle; for, however the traditions behind the gospels were used, the gospels look very much like lives of Jesus, admittedly of a rather special kind.

The problem is frequently solved in terms of the development of the early church: interest in the sort of person Jesus was is often considered to have been a late and even illegitimate

[1] 'The Problem of the Historical Jesus', in *Essays on New Testament Themes* (E.T., London, 1964).

[2] See the well-documented surveys by J. M. Robinson, *Kerygma und historischer Jesus* (Zürich, 2nd ed. 1965), pp. 11–86, and W. G. Kümmel, 'Jesusforschung seit 1950', *TR* **31** (1966), 15–46 and 289–315.

[3] N. Perrin, *Rediscovering the Teaching of Jesus* (London, 1967), pp. 226f.

3

development of the primitive kerygma. The earliest Christians were so captivated by the Risen Christ and expectation of his *parousia* that past events of his life were of little or no interest. Only as hopes of an early *parousia* faded did the early church begin to look back to the life and character of Jesus, a process which it is alleged reached its zenith in the writings of Luke.

A number of detailed explanations of the reasons behind the emergence of the gospels, with their apparent concern with the 'biography' of Jesus, have been offered. E. Käsemann insists that the gospels as such, as opposed to the traditions which they contain, reflect not the most primitive preaching, but a late development; they are a reaction to early Christian *Enthusiasmus* which at least partly overlooked the earthly Jesus.[1] G. Ebeling suggests that the final separation of Gentile and Jewish Christianity may have led to the necessity of speaking graphically about the earthly life of Jesus; cultured Hellenistic circles would have grasped a 'biographical' presentation of Jesus more readily.[2] U. Wilckens believes that Hellenistic Christians, including Paul, propagated a 'Christ kerygma' but knew almost nothing about the teaching and ministry of Jesus, which remained the preserve of Jewish Christians in Palestine. The resurrection was central in both 'branches', but only at a later stage did traditions about Jesus penetrate the Hellenistic churches.[3] Somewhat similar views have been set

---

[1] 'Sackgassen im Streit um den historischen Jesus', *Exegetische Versuche und Besinnungen* II (Göttingen, 1964), 47. [E.T. 'Blind Alleys in the "Jesus of History" Controversy' in *New Testament Questions of Today* (London, 1969), p. 41.]

[2] *Theology and Proclamation* (E.T., London, 1966), p. 133. Cf. M. Dibelius, *Gospel Criticism and Christology* (E.T. London, 1935), pp. 76f. The customary distinction between the Hellenistic and the Palestinian church is not entirely satisfactory; there is increasing evidence which confirms that Hellenistic culture had penetrated Jewish life earlier and much more deeply and extensively than formerly was considered likely.

[3] This situation arose, Wilckens suggests, because the Hellenists in Jerusalem were from the first an almost completely autonomous group: 'Tradition de Jésus et Kérygme du Christ: La Double Histoire de la Tradition au Sein du Christianisme Primitif', *RHPR* **47** (1967), 1–20; cf. also 'Hellenistisch-christliche Missionsüberlieferung und Jesustradition', *ThLZ* **89** (1964), 518ff. S. G. F. Brandon proposed a similar hypothesis in his *The Fall of Jerusalem* (London, 1951).

out by P. Vielhauer[1] and S. Schulz.[2] W. Schmithals goes still further: gospel traditions remained virtually unknown or 'apocryphal' right up until the time of Justin Martyr; outside the synoptic gospels there are very few traces of the use of gospel traditions in the New Testament documents or in the Apostolic Fathers.[3]

Some of the above scholars assume too readily that the small amount of material which has come down to us from some parts of the early church (from the Q community, for example) can be used to reconstruct the *whole* theological outlook of that community. This is a dangerous argument from silence which assumes that what we do not know about or what has been lost never existed!

Although a 'development' theory seems to account for the apparent gulf between the synoptic gospels and the epistles, the evidence is often over-simplified. The variety of suggested turning points indicates that it is difficult to locate any one development which was sufficiently dramatic or deeply influential to bring the past life and character of Jesus into the centre of the Christian message for the first time.

One example may be mentioned briefly. Interest in the past of Jesus is often linked to the adjustment made necessary by the so-called delay of the *parousia*.[4] But it is not easy to locate the beginning of its effect on the early church, if indeed it did cause quite the upheaval often envisaged. While some gospel traditions probably were modified under the influence of the delay of the *parousia*, traditions relating to the life and

[1] 'Ein Weg zur neutestamentlichen Christologie?', *EvT* **25** (1965), 70f.

[2] 'Die neue Frage nach dem historischen Jesus' in *Neues Testament und Geschichte* (Festschrift O. Cullmann), eds. H. Baltensweiler and B. Reicke (Zürich and Tübingen, 1972), pp. 33ff.

[3] 'Paulus und der historische Jesus', *ZNW* **53** (1962), 145ff. (Cf. also E. Haenchen, 'Die frühe Christologie', *ZTK* **63** (1966), 145–59.) W. G. Kümmel correctly notes that W. Schmithals has grossly exaggerated his case: 'Jesus und Paulus', *NTS* **10** (1963–4), 176 (now reprinted in Kümmel's collected essays, *Heilsgeschehen und Geschichte* (Marburg, 1965), p. 452).

[4] See, for example, H. Conzelmann, *The Theology of St Luke* (E.T. London, 1960), p. 186 and M. Dibelius, *From Tradition to Gospel* (originally published 1919, E.T. London, 1934; reprinted 1971), p. 298.

character of Jesus were not suddenly created as soon as the church began to shed its apocalyptic outlook. The differences between the strata of the gospel traditions and the individual gospels have to be pressed beyond the evidence in order to fit a theory of a sharp reversal of emphases. Did the delay influence Mark's decision to write a gospel? There is plenty of precedent for a community having both a strong apocalyptic outlook and written documents! As will be shown, the most commonly suggested *volte-face* in the early church's attitude to the life of Jesus, Luke's Gospel, does not mark the appearance of a new and unique attitude.

The various theories of development all assume that, on the one hand, initial preaching of the gospel looked something like the main theological themes of the New Testament epistles, and, on the other hand, that at any given period the theological outlook of the church can be established with some certainty by tracing the traditio-historical and redaction critical development of the gospel traditions and of the gospels. The *Sitz im Leben* of gospels and epistles tends to be all but equated, and since their theological perspectives differ so markedly, a 'development' theory seems to be unavoidable. Some of these assumptions will be called in question in the course of this book.

H. Riesenfeld, B. Gerhardsson and T. Boman have taken a very different approach. They do not point to a development or a reversal of emphasis, but claim that the gospel traditions, which are very much concerned with the earthly life and teaching of Jesus, remained a quite separate entity from the kerygma. Riesenfeld insists that missionary preaching was never the *Sitz im Leben* of the gospel traditions, for they were 'holy tradition' not to be readily mentioned by mouth.[1] Gerhardsson places a great deal of weight on Jewish methods of transmitting tradition (the relevance of which has been severely criticised) and argues that the gospel traditions originate in the setting of Jesus' careful instruction of his disciples.[2] But if the teaching of Jesus was largely confined to the disciples and if the gospel traditions originated as 'new torah' and as 'holy tradition', it

[1] 'The Gospel Tradition and its Beginnings', *Studia Evangelica* 1 (1959), 43–65.
[2] *Memory and Manuscript* (Lund, 1961).

would be difficult to account for the end result of the ministry of Jesus, and the traditions would be much more clearly oriented to his teaching than in fact they are.

And, as will be emphasised later, Jesus' actions and teaching are inseparable: taken together they are 'message', not only in the setting of a teacher–pupil relationship, but also in terms of Jesus' opponents and uncommitted enquirers. Jesus' words were not merely words of instruction, or even words of revelation, but proclamation of God's kingly rule. The gospel traditions not only tell us what Jesus did and taught, but indicate, in various ways, what sort of a person he was; their deeply 'personal' perspective marks them off from comparable Old Testament and rabbinic material.

T. Boman points to the significance of the results of recent study of techniques of transmitting folk lore tradition and argues that the kerygmatic tradition proclaimed by the apostles was quite separate from the gospel traditions which were recounted by a special group of narrators who were subject to the apostles and prophets.[1] This is a fascinating suggestion, but it is difficult to find evidence for the existence of narrators as a special group in the early church.

Many scholars have denied that the early church was un-interested in the past of Jesus and have urged that Christian converts must have wanted to know about the life and character of the One now proclaimed as Lord, the One to whom they had committed their lives.[2] This point has been made several times, but there have been few detailed examinations of the evidence.[3] Some writers associate the early church's interest in the story of Jesus with the need to know about the example

[1] *Die Jesus-Überlieferung im Lichte der neueren Volkskunde* (Göttingen, 1967).

[2] See, for example, T. W. Manson, *The Sayings of Jesus* (London, 1937), p. 10; A. M. Ramsey, 'The Gospel and the Gospels', *Studia Evangelica* I (1959), 35ff.; L. Malavez, 'Jésus de l'histoire et l'interprétation du kérygme', *NRT* **91** (1969), 785ff.; L. E. Keck, *A Future for the Historical Jesus* (London, 1972), pp. 109 and 134.

[3] More detailed studies include P. Althaus, *The So-Called Kerygma and the Historical Jesus* (E.T., Edinburgh, 1959); R. A. Bartels, *Kerygma or Gospel Tradition... Which Came First?* (Minneapolis, 1961); C. F. D. Moule, 'Jesus in New Testament Kerygma' in *Verborum Veritas* (Festschrift G. Stählin), eds. O. Böcher and K. Haacker (Wuppertal, 1970), pp. 15–26; J. Roloff, *Das Kerygma*.

Christians ought to follow.[1] But while the 'imitatio Christi' and 'following Jesus' motifs cannot be eliminated from primitive Christianity, they did not play a central and influential role which might account for the form of the gospel traditions.

There are references to the example of Christ in the epistles, but since ethical instruction and exhortation are very much part of their purpose, such references are surprisingly few in number. Paul refers directly to the imitation of Christ twice (1 Cor. 11: 1 and 1 Thess. 1: 6); in both cases he links his own example to that of Christ. ἀκολουθεῖν is found quite frequently in the gospels, but, with the partial exception of 1 Peter 1: 21 and Rev. 14: 14, it is not used outside the gospels to refer to following Jesus.

Nor is the example of Jesus deeply embedded in the gospel traditions themselves.[2] The relationship between Jesus and his disciples and the 'following Jesus' traditions are very different from the rabbinic teacher–pupil relationship, where the pupil eventually hopes to take the place of his teacher and to continue the transmission of tradition by gathering a group of pupils around him. Jesus did not encourage his disciples to follow his example in an ethical sense; rather, the traditions speak of a relationship of commitment to Jesus in which Jesus himself takes the initiative, and they spell out the resulting implications and requirements of discipleship.[3] Mark 8: 34 and the similar Q logion (Matt. 10: 38 = Luke 14: 27) might be considered as partial exceptions, but even here it is not so much a question of following the ethical example of Jesus, as of being prepared to share his fate.[4]

M. Dibelius underlined the importance of preaching in the early church and related the development of the gospel traditions very closely to it.[5] He insisted that Christian missionaries did not relate the life of Jesus; the gospel traditions

---

[1] So, for example, A. M. Ramsey, 'The Gospel and the Gospels', Studia Evangelica I, 40.

[2] The terminology of the epistles, especially μιμέομαι and μιμητής, is not found in the gospels. Cf. H. D. Betz, Nachfolge und Nachahmung Jesu Christi im Neuen Testament (Tübingen, 1967), esp. pp. 4 and 27.

[3] Cf. E. Schweizer, Erniedrigung und Erhöhung bei Jesus und seinen Nachfolgern (Zürich, 2nd ed. 1962), pp. 7ff. and 19.

[4] A. Schulz, Nachfolgen und Nachahmen (Munich, 1962), pp. 197ff. and 265.   [5] From Tradition to Gospel.

were used in preaching, but they were secondary to the proclamation of the salvation which had come about in Jesus Christ and were used to confirm that proclamation. The traditions behind the gospels and, indeed, the emergence of written gospels are undoubtedly to be related to preaching in the early church; but the chapters which follow advocate a very different understanding of the extent to which the gospel traditions and the gospels themselves intend to portray the life and character of Jesus.

C. H. Dodd also linked the gospel traditions and the gospels to the preaching of the early church, but, unlike M. Dibelius, he saw the gospel traditions not so much as supporting or illustrating proclamation of the Risen Christ of the kerygma, but as a historical report of the facts of the ministry of Jesus.[1] Dodd's position has been attacked from many angles; some steps in his argument are no longer tenable and others must be modified considerably. As has often been observed, Dodd's rigid distinction between kerygma and didache is an over-simplification of the New Testament evidence,[2] as is his view that the kerygma assumed one constant pattern in the early church. But Dodd's critics have often missed the wood for the trees; there is more to be said for his understanding of the nature and purpose of the gospel traditions than some have allowed.

This book argues that there is plenty of evidence which, taken cumulatively, indicates that the early church was interested in the life and character of Jesus and that the primary (though not the only) *Sitz im Leben* of that interest was the missionary preaching of the church. This is a most unfashionable view and the weighty objections which can be brought to bear against it, especially on form critical grounds, obviously must be taken very seriously indeed. Although some of the assumptions of form criticism will be challenged, the basic insights of the form critical method will be appealed to frequently.

Merely to mention the character of Jesus of Nazareth is to

[1] *The Apostolic Preaching and its Development* (London, 1936) and 'The Framework of the Gospel Narrative', *ExT* **43** (1931–2), 396–400.

[2] For a recent discussion, see R. C. Worley, *Preaching and Teaching in the Earliest Church* (Philadelphia, 1967).

raise in many quarters the ghosts of liberalism. There is a deep-seated fear of 'psychologising' Jesus, and a suspicion that any concern with the character of Jesus inevitably turns the clock back to nineteenth-century attempts to reconstruct the 'inner life' of Jesus and make Jesus as an appealing personality the centre of the Christian message. Neo-positivism is the new giant in the land. Awareness of the course of the history of theological discussion in the twentieth century is itself sufficient safeguard against hasty conclusions; but in any case the evidence must be considered on its merits and not merely in the light of past debates. As will be shown, interest in personality and the way an individual differs in his psychological make-up from other individuals is a modern phenomenon not to be confused with character portrayal, with which the ancient world was certainly familiar.

Before turning to the question of method, some of the more important terms used must be discussed briefly. 'Preaching' and 'Jesus of Nazareth' (or simply 'Jesus') are chosen deliberately instead of the more usual 'kerygma' and 'historical Jesus'. The latter terms have been used in so many ways by recent writers that confusion rather than clarity has often resulted.[1] 'Preaching' refers to the content of the message proclaimed by the early church, without in any way denying that proclamation was a dynamic activity and no mere recital of past events. 'Preaching' is normally used to refer to initial evangelistic preaching, though obviously this is not to be distinguished completely from preaching to committed Christians within the Christian community.[2] The interest of the early church in the life of Jesus, rather than that of the modern historian or theologian, is considered; hence the terms 'Jesus of Nazareth' or 'Jesus', not 'historical Jesus', are used. Before the modern historian can reconstruct the teaching and activity of the historical Jesus, he must determine the extent

[1] W. C. van Unnik notes that J. M. Robinson distinguishes two meanings for 'historical Jesus', G. Ebeling four! 'Jesus the Christ', *NTS* **8** (1961–2), 103.

[2] As C. F. D. Moule correctly notes, 'However often the gospel is repeated to the already evangelised, it still remains likely that its initial form will be distinctive, so that this initial form cannot be deduced from subsequent (partial) repetitions alone.' 'Jesus in NT Kerygma', *Verborum Veritas*, p. 24 n. 16.

to which the gospel traditions and the gospels were intended
to set out the life of Jesus. If the early church had a stake
in the story of the life and teaching of Jesus, the gap between
the Jesus of the gospels and the historian's Jesus is likely to
be much less wide than many have maintained.[1]

Luke–Acts forms the starting point. Many will readily
concede that, of all the New Testament writers, Luke has the
keenest interest in the life of Jesus. But as there is no agreement
either on the reasons for this, or on the extent to which he
is distinctive in his approach, his methods are examined in
some detail.

Has material which the modern historian might use to
reconstruct aspects of the life and character of Jesus survived
against the primary intention of the gospel traditions? This
question can be answered only by establishing the interests
and needs of the early church. Reconstruction of any aspect
of the life and faith of the church solely from the 'forms'
of the traditions themselves is always exposed to the dangers
of a circular argument: it is all too easy to allow a particular
view of the needs of the church to influence judgement of the
Sitz im Leben of various parts of the tradition, or *vice versa*.[2]
This difficulty arises in all form critical study of the gospels.
It is acknowledged by R. Bultmann, who notes that, whereas
M. Dibelius investigates the history of the synoptic tradition
from a study of the community and its needs, he himself
proceeds from an analysis of individual elements of the
tradition.[3]

Can the dangers of a circular argument be minimised? In
an attempt to do this, the second and third chapters of this
book concentrate on the relevant New Testament evidence
apart from the gospel traditions: pre-Lucan traditions in Acts,
and such evidence as there is of the importance Paul attached
to the life and character of Jesus.

Any attempt to ask about the extent and *raison d'être* of
interest in the character of Jesus must meet two main objections:
kerygmatic, not historical interest lies behind the preservation
and transmission of the traditions; the gospels are not bio-

[1] This is discussed further in the Conclusions.
[2] Cf. F. G. Downing, *The Church and Jesus* (London, 1968), pp. 104f.
[3] *The History of the Synoptic Tradition* (E.T. Oxford, 1963), p. 5.

graphies, but reflect faith in the Risen Christ. The gospel traditions are considered against the background of comparable material from the ancient world in order to clarify their perspective without reading the evidence in the light of pre-conceptions about what was possible or not possible in the early church. This method cannot produce conclusive results, but it does provide a strong hint that the assumption that the gospels and the traditions on which they are based cannot have been intended to sketch out the life and character of Jesus is quite arbitrary.

CHAPTER I

JESUS OF NAZARETH IN MISSIONARY PREACHING: LUKE'S VIEW

The Lucan writings are of particular importance for our attempt to show that some kind of an account of the life and character of Jesus formed an integral part of the early church's preaching – especially its initial evangelism. For the speeches in Acts provide the only explicit New Testament examples of missionary preaching and it is generally agreed that Luke has a richer and more carefully drawn character portrait of Jesus than the other evangelists – though, as we shall see in the next chapter, the significance of this is much debated.

The speeches in the early chapters of Acts, especially Acts 10: 34–43, have been used to elucidate the relationship between primitive preaching and the life and character of Jesus in three quite different ways.[1] In his very influential book, *The Apostolic Preaching and its Development*, first published in 1936, C. H. Dodd insisted that while the speeches were not *verbatim* reports of Peter's words, they represented the *kerygma* of the church at an early period. Primitive preaching included reference to the past events of the ministry of Jesus, and it is from this preaching, ultimately, that our gospels derive. Dodd went on to argue that Mark conceived himself as writing a form of *kerygma*: his Gospel may be regarded as based upon an expanded form of the middle, or historical, section (p. 47).

The Gospels of Matthew and Luke do, after all, fall well within the general scheme of the *kerygma*, though they subtly alter its perspective. It is, however, in the Fourth Gospel that we return to the main line of development which runs through Mark from the original preaching...It is surely clear that the fourfold Gospel

---

[1] For surveys of the literature on the speeches, see U. Wilckens, *Die Missionsreden der Apostelgeschichte* (Neukirchen-Vluyn, 1961), pp. 7ff.; E. Haenchen, *Die Apostelgeschichte* (Göttingen, 15th ed. 1968), pp. 13ff. [E.T. *The Acts of the Apostles* (Oxford, 1971), pp. 14ff.]; J. Schmitt, art. 'Prédication Apostolique' in *Supplément au Dictionnaire de la Bible*, VIII (Paris, 1972), cols. 251–73.

taken as a whole is an expression of the original apostolic Preaching (pp. 54f.).

Quite independently, M. Dibelius argued that the speeches in the opening chapters of Acts were partly based on primitive material and provide important indications of the way gospel traditions were used and understood in the early church. Dibelius argued that missionary preaching was the cause and preaching the means of spreading abroad that which the disciples of Jesus possessed as recollections.[1]

But these views have been strongly attacked by a number of recent writers who have claimed that any earlier traditions Luke may have used in compiling the speeches have been thoroughly assimilated to his own theological perspective. The prominence of reference to Jesus, especially in Peter's speech to Cornelius in Acts 10, arises from Luke's own concern to place the past ministry of Jesus at the centre of his understanding of the Christian message.[2] On this view, Luke is the first New Testament theologian to make a historical report about Jesus the focus of Christian proclamation. U. Wilckens' thorough study of the speeches has been very influential in recent scholarship. E. Haenchen bluntly states that Wilckens 'has proved against Dibelius and Dodd that Peter's speeches in the first part of Acts do not contain any old pattern of Jewish-Christian missionary preaching'.[3]

H. Riesenfeld and T. Boman have defended a third very different approach. They claim that missionary preaching was not the *Sitz im Leben* of the gospel traditions. Traditions about the ministry of Jesus and kerygmatic proclamation of him

---

[1] 'The Speeches in Acts and Ancient Historiography', completed in 1944, first published in 1949; E.T. in *Studies in the Acts of the Apostles* (London, 1965), pp. 165f. and 184; *From Tradition to Gospel* (originally published 1919; E.T. London, 1934; reprinted 1971), pp. 13 and 22. C. H. Dodd and M. Dibelius differed widely in their interpretation of many parts of Acts; their agreement on the significance of the speeches for the origins of the gospel traditions is thus all the more striking.

[2] The following may be noted, though they differ in detail: E. Haenchen, *Apostelgeschichte*; U. Wilckens, *Die Missionsreden*; C. F. Evans, 'The Kerygma', *JTS* **7** (1956), 256ff.; J. T. Townshend, 'The Speeches in Acts', *ATR* **42** (1960), 150–9. This general approach owes a good deal to H. Conzelmann's *The Theology of St Luke* (E.T. London, 1960).

[3] *Acts*, pp. 129f. (Cf. *Die Apostelgeschichte*, p. 682.)

remained separate entities, even in Luke's own day. The absence of 'synoptic' traditions about Jesus from the speeches is stressed by Boman, while Riesenfeld denies (without giving reasons) that Peter's speech in Acts 10 suggests that the gospel tradition could have been expanded from such rudiments into its later fulness.[1] Both fail to recognise that the speeches are not intended to be more than very brief summaries of the main themes of the preaching. Many of the speeches are so brief that if they had been delivered *verbatim*, the attention of the audience would hardly have been caught before the preaching was completed! In addition, their suggested alternative settings of the gospel traditions in the early church are far from convincing.[2]

I take the point made by Dodd's critics: even in the early chapters of Acts, Luke's own theological perspective is much in evidence. As Dibelius correctly noted, the speeches are intended by Luke to indicate how the gospel should be preached in his own day.[3] But I do not accept that the references to Jesus in some of the early speeches have been composed by Luke as summaries of his own gospel; this argument is developed, with special reference to Acts 10: 34–43, in chapter 3.

The strikingly similar structure and content of the early speeches in Acts have often been noted. But no less significant is the consistent pattern which emerges from an examination of all the passages in Acts which refer to the content of missionary preaching.

Peter's opening speech on the day of Pentecost is particularly important in the overall design and theological perspective of Acts.[4] The ministry of Jesus is mentioned briefly at the beginning of the second section of Peter's speech (Acts 2: 22–3). Peter reminds his audience about Jesus, even though he assumes that they either know about or have seen the evidence of God's action through Jesus.

---

[1] H. Riesenfeld, 'The Gospel Tradition', *Studia Evangelica* i (1959), 50; T. Boman, *Jesus-Überlieferung*, pp. 37ff., 43 *et passim*. Again there are very considerable differences in detail.

[2] See above, pp. 6f.　　　　　[3] *Studies*, p. 165.

[4] This is one of the main conclusions of R. F. Zehnle's recent study, *Peter's Pentecost Discourse: tradition and Lukan reinterpretation in Peter's speeches in Acts 2 and 3* (Nashville, 1971).

The speeches must not be considered in isolation from the surrounding narratives. Once this is recognised, it becomes clear that the primary reason for the reference to the mighty works and wonders and signs of Jesus in 2: 22 is to be found in the link which was seen between the Joel prophecy (2: 19), the ministry of Jesus (2: 22), and the wonders and signs done through the apostles (2: 43). This is also why the Joel citation is continued beyond the point immediately relevant to the main theme of Peter's speech.

In the first part of his speech, Peter has sought to make the extraordinary events of Pentecost intelligible to his audience. This apologetic note is continued in 2: 22; it was necessary to remind the audience of the wonders and signs in the ministry of Jesus in order to show that the events of Pentecost – and also the raising of Jesus from the dead – should not have caught them completely by surprise.

Even though the hearers know about Jesus of Nazareth, Peter refers very briefly to his ministry to show that God was at work in his actions and that the significance of his ministry was closely bound up with the resurrection, the exaltation of Jesus and the outpouring of the Spirit. Acts 2: 22 lies at the very heart of this speech. It is in no way related to Lucan or pre-Lucan biographical interest in the ministry of Jesus; it is an exposition of part of the preceding Joel citation.

The second speech (3: 12–26) is still set in Jerusalem; the καθὼς αὐτοὶ οἴδατε of Acts 2: 22 still applies, so there is no need to sketch out the life and character of Jesus. But there are some indirect references to the character of Jesus. Acts 3: 13–15 consists of a series of strong antitheses. God's action in glorifying Jesus is contrasted with the Jews' action; Jesus is παῖς but is glorified; τὸν ἅγιον καὶ δίκαιον is contrasted with ἄνδρα φονέα (v. 14); Jesus is ἀρχηγὸν τῆς ζωῆς but is killed; and finally God's action in raising Jesus from the dead is contrasted with the killing of Jesus. These strong antitheses leave no doubt that even though these expressions are christological, there is reference to the sort of person Jesus was. In order to emphasise the guilt of the Jews the speech not only stresses that they killed Jesus but reminds them of the character of Jesus. The second half of the speech also contains an indirect reference to Jesus. The prophecy of Deut. 18: 15ff. that God

16

would raise up a prophet like Moses has been fulfilled in the preaching and teaching of Jesus (Acts 3: 22–3).[1] Once again these references to the character of Jesus are very closely bound up with the central themes of the speech.

The two speeches at Acts 4: 8–12 and 5: 29–32 stress the rejection of Jesus (in both cases with reference to scripture), but do not make any other comment on his ministry. This is not surprising. The speeches are extremely brief and are still set in Jerusalem where knowledge of the crucifixion of Jesus, the preceding events and even the character of the one crucified can, Luke believes, simply be assumed.

With the next reference to missionary preaching, the setting has moved beyond Jerusalem to Samaria (8: 5); Luke does not give a summary of the content of Philip's preaching, but the reader knows full well what ἐκήρυσσεν τὸν Χριστόν means – it certainly includes reference to the actions and teaching of Jesus. Luke is slightly more explicit in 8: 12: Philip proclaims good news περὶ τῆς βασιλείας τοῦ θεοῦ καὶ τοῦ ὀνόματος Ἰησοῦ Χριστοῦ.

This is the first of several examples of Luke's use of βασιλεία in Acts as a summary of the content of the Christian message. For Luke, Jesus' teaching about the Kingdom is part of the Christian message – but βασιλεία in Acts includes more than the teaching of Jesus; the Kingdom proclaimed by Jesus has been manifest in his ministry, and it will be seen again when he comes in the future.[2]

Luke uses βασιλεία to sum up Paul's preaching in the synagogue at Ephesus (Acts 19: 8). In Paul's farewell speech to the Ephesian elders at Miletus, his earlier preaching at Ephesus is recalled and summarised as proclaiming the Kingdom (Acts 20: 25). And then in the closing verses of Acts, which are almost as important for Luke's theology as are the closing verses of Matthew's Gospel for Matthean theology, βασιλεία is used twice in summaries of Paul's proclamation to the Jews in Rome (28: 23, 31).

In each case there is little doubt that Luke uses βασιλεία

[1] Cf. C. H. Dodd, *Apostolic Preaching*, pp. 40 and 53. Admittedly Acts 3: 22f. comes awkwardly in the structure of the speech. On this, see E. Haenchen, comm. *ad loc.*

[2] So also H. Conzelmann, *The Theology of St Luke*, p. 124 n. 1.

as a shorthand way of referring to the entire Christian proclamation – and that includes reference to the life of Jesus.
This is disputed by E. Haenchen in his commentary at 28: 23.
Haenchen allows this meaning for 19: 8 and 20: 25, but argues
that, because at 8: 12; 28: 23, 31 Kingdom is mentioned
'along with the events of Jesus', in these passages βασιλεία
refers to the future coming of the Kingdom at the *parousia*, of
which 14: 22 speaks. But this observation is surely quite beside
the point. Unlike all the other Kingdom passages in Acts
(outside chapter one), 14: 22 does not refer to evangelistic
preaching, but to the second visit of Paul and Barnabas to
Lystra, Iconium and Antioch; the local Christians are encouraged and strengthened and given the firm assurance that
it is through tribulations that they must enter the Kingdom of
God. Here Kingdom clearly has only a future sense. But in
all the other passages in an evangelistic setting, although the
future aspect is included, Luke is using 'Kingdom' as a convenient way of summarising Christian proclamation.

Philip's preaching to the Ethiopian eunuch is referred to as
εὐηγγελίσατο αὐτῷ τὸν Ἰησοῦν (8: 35) – but the starting point
is Philip's insistence that Jesus is the one referred to in Isa. 53:
he was rejected, denied justice and put to death. Once again
reference to the life of Jesus is linked to scripture and is an
integral part of missionary preaching.

Luke's narrative of the conversion of Cornelius, the Roman
centurion, at Caesarea is a central part of his whole design
in Acts. In chapter 8 the reader is given broad hints as to the
content of the proclamation, but in 10: 34–43 a full summary
is given; a relatively detailed account of Jesus of Nazareth
forms the starting point of the proclamation to Cornelius and
those gathered in his house.[1]

---

[1] The literature on the Cornelius narratives is listed by F. Bovon,
'Tradition et Rédaction en Actes 10, 1 – 11, 18', *TZ* **26** (1970), 22f. n. 1.
On the relationship of the speech to the rest of Acts 10 and 11: 1–18, see
E. Haulotte, 'Fondation d'une Communauté de Type Universel: Actes
10, 1 – 11, 18' in *Recherches de Science Religieuse* **58** (1970), 63–100.

Is Peter's speech to Cornelius evangelistic?

U. Wilckens has recently proposed a novel interpretation of Acts 10 which runs directly counter to the argument of this book. He claims that unlike the preceding speeches, these verses are not evangelistic; the people in the house of Cornelius have already been converted by the direct intervention of God before Peter speaks. Luke's much more detailed reference to the life of Jesus is not an example of the content of missionary preaching but an indication of his own understanding of what a gospel is. Luke has 'transformed the schema of a missionary sermon into the formal schema of a gospel, as he understands it... Luke shows here that in fact the *Gattung* of "gospel" is a secondary transformation of the kerygma; the contents of a gospel are to be seen as an expansion and arrangement of primitive kerygmatic material.'[1]

Wilckens' starting point is M. Dibelius' analysis of Acts 10: 1 – 11: 18. Dibelius resolves apparent discrepancies between Peter's speech and its context in the Cornelius narratives in Acts 10 and 11 by claiming that, as in the case of the other speeches, this speech has a fixed scheme and is a literary composition of Luke designed to show his readers 'what Christian preaching is and ought to be'.[2] Wilckens believes that his own analysis of the preceding speeches proves that they have a much closer relationship to the particular situation of the audience; the speech cannot be severed from its context as easily as Dibelius suggests.[3] Dibelius noted that the literary phrase at the beginning of 10: 37, ὑμεῖς οἴδατε, could scarcely be appropriate to Cornelius, who knows a little about the Old Testament, but nothing about Jesus Christ.[4] Wilckens, on the other hand, takes this phrase as an indication that Cornelius has already understood and accepted the kerygma before Peter begins to speak.

Wilckens insists that as the speech does not follow precisely

---

[1] *Missionsreden*, p. 69. On Wilckens' approach to the speeches in general, see J. Dupont's review article in *RB* **69** (1962), 37–60 [now reprinted in *Études sur les Actes des Apôtres* (Paris, 1967), pp. 133ff.]; J. Rohde, *Rediscovering the Teaching of the Evangelists* (E.T. London, 1968), pp. 202ff.

[2] *Studies*, pp. 109ff. and 165.   [3] *Missionsreden*, p. 65.

[4] *Studies*, p. 111.

the same pattern as the earlier speeches, the differences must be accounted for. Considerably more prominence is given to the ministry of Jesus; these verses contain a short 'history' of Jesus with emphases so similar to Luke's Gospel that they are intended to be a summary of it.

The immediate context in Acts confirms that it is through the direct and decisive intervention of God, not through an evangelistic sermon, that Cornelius is converted. Wilckens underlines the discrepancy between 10: 44 (the Spirit fell on those present while Peter was still speaking) and 11: 15 (the Spirit was given as Peter *began* to speak); he also points to the absence of any reference to repentance or conversion.[1]

From these observations Wilckens concludes that these verses are not intended by Luke to be an example of evangelistic preaching; they are catechetical in intention, as is Luke's Gospel.[2] The more detailed reference to the ministry of Jesus is not an indication that traditions about Jesus were used in missionary preaching – even in Luke's own day.[3]

This hypothesis is strikingly original, but it is unconvincing; the validity of some of the key points may be challenged.

(*a*) Would Luke have considered that a God-fearing Gentile centurion in Caesarea would have known nothing about the ministry and death of Jesus? Does ὑμεῖς οἴδατε therefore indicate that Cornelius is converted before Peter speaks?[4]

Caesarea is not envisaged by Luke as a city far removed both from the earliest missionary expansion of the church and from the ministry of Jesus. The narrative of Acts strongly

[1] *Missionsreden*, p. 67.

[2] U. Wilckens, 'Kerygma und Evangelium bei Lukas. Beobachtungen zu Acta 10: 34–43', *ZNW* **49** (1958), 236. This article, published before *Missionsreden*, contains a more detailed discussion of the hypothesis.

[3] Wilckens seems to be slightly confused about the implications of his hypothesis. On the one hand Peter's speech to Cornelius (and Luke's Gospel) is not evangelistic, but 'Katechese'; on the other hand 'hat Lukas – erst Lukas – die synoptische Tradition als zentralen, beherrschenden Teil christlicher Predigt formal mit der kerygmatischen Tradition verbunden. Die Predigt, durch die man zum Glauben an Jesus als den Christus kommt und im Namen Jesu das Heil empfängt, ist in ihrem entscheidenden Zentrum historischer Bericht von Jesus von Nazareth.' *Missionsreden*, pp. 206f.

[4] Some writers have suggested that ὑμεῖς οἴδατε is intended to refer to the readers of Luke's own day.

implies that Philip had preached and founded a Christian community in Caesarea (Acts 8: 40 and 21: 8). Saul was taken to Caesarea in order to flee from the Hellenists, possibly to be protected by Christians there.

Luke was well aware that Caesarea was the capital of the Roman province and that, even though it was a thoroughly Gentile city, there were close ties between Jerusalem and Caesarea.[1] He probably knew that Caesarea lay very near one of the main routes between Galilee and Jerusalem,[2] and that Caesarea, Pilate's capital, was not isolated from Galilee, Herod's territory.[3] In addition, Luke believed that knowledge of the events of Jesus' ministry and death was widespread; Paul, in Caesarea, assumes that Agrippa knows about the origins of Christianity.[4] Hence Luke simply took it for granted that Cornelius would have heard something about Jesus of Nazareth. Wilckens does not mention that Peter's sermon was preached at Caesarea; Luke mentions Caesarea at 10: 1 and again at 10: 24, as if to stress the location.

Wilckens completely by-passes Acts 2: 22 (καθὼς αὐτοὶ οἴδατε) which is similar and relevant to the interpretation of ὑμεῖς οἴδατε in Acts 10: 37a, and refers instead to Pauline parallels where Christian communities are reminded about matters Paul had already stressed. But the situation in Acts is quite different: as at 2: 22, Peter assumes that his audience is slightly familiar with the story of Jesus, and therefore gives a résumé of it, stressing its significance.

Wilckens' interpretation of ὑμεῖς οἴδατε must be rejected.[5] Why, then, is there more detailed reference to the ministry of Jesus in Acts 10? The consistent structure and content of the speeches in Acts 1–13 have often been observed. But the extended reference to the ministry of Jesus in Acts 10 is not the only place where the pattern is broken.[6] Acts 14: 15–17

---

[1] Acts 12: 19; 21: 10; 23: 33; 25: 1, 13.

[2] This road may well have been the most popular route between Galilee and Jerusalem. Cf. E. Stauffer, *Jesus and His Story* (E.T. 1960), pp. 47f.; G. Dalman, *Sacred Sites and Ways* (E.T. London, 1935), pp. 221ff.

[3] Luke 3: 1, 23: 12 and Acts 4: 27.   [4] Luke 24: 18f.; Acts 26: 26.

[5] So also H. Conzelmann, who suggests that ὑμεῖς οἴδατε is simply a stereotyped formula: *Die Apostelgeschichte* (Tübingen, 2nd ed., 1972), *ad loc.*

[6] Pilate is mentioned only at 3: 13 and 13: 28. Reference to fulfilment of the scriptures is missing from 5: 30–2. Jesus as future judge is found

and 17: 22–31, in which Paul proclaims the living God, the Creator, are quite unlike the speeches in the earlier chapters. The reason for this is obvious: Paul is speaking to a Gentile audience with little or no knowledge of Judaism. Similarly in Acts 1–13, the nature and location of the audience have determined which aspects of the missionary proclamation required emphasis or elaboration. In chapter 10 the ministry of Jesus is mentioned more fully because Jerusalem is no longer the setting and because such knowledge as Cornelius the God-fearing Roman centurion has needs to be supplemented.

(b) Wilckens stresses the parallels between the prologue of Luke's Gospel and Peter's speech: both emphasise a definite succession of events and the role of eye-witnesses; in neither case is it a question of initial proclamation.[1] But the role of eye-witnesses is emphasised in most of the earlier speeches in Acts which Wilckens accepts as evangelistic.[2] However καθεξῆς (Luke 1: 3) is interpreted, it is hardly an important characteristic of Peter's speech in Acts 10. Wilckens claims that the speech is a *historia Jesu*, but even if the events mentioned are taken to imply chronological order, the chronological details are so meagre that such chronological order as there is can be said to lie behind all four gospels.

Can we be as sure as Wilckens is that Theophilus knew and had accepted the kerygma before Luke wrote to him and that he provides a parallel to Cornelius? Theophilus is in a similar situation to Cornelius: both know something about Jesus, but need to be told more, before they can be expected to accept the kerygma. There are similarities between Peter's speech and Luke's Gospel, but to suggest that neither is evangelistic in intention is to take a one-sided view of the evidence.

only at 10: 42. The brief speeches in Acts 4 and 5, although they include the 'core' emphases, do not contain all the points found in the longer speeches; for example, there is no mention of witnesses in 4: 9–12.

[1] *Missionsreden*, pp. 68f.

[2] Acts 2: 32; 3: 15; 5: 32; 13: 31. Admittedly 10: 39 refers specifically to the ministry of Jesus, whereas other references to witnesses are linked to the resurrection; but in 2: 22, and in the other speeches in Jerusalem, Peter assumes that his whole audience has witnessed at least some of the events of the ministry and death of Jesus.

(c) Serious objections must also be raised against Wilckens' view that it is through the direct and decisive intervention of God, not through an evangelistic sermon, that Cornelius is converted. The discrepancy between 10: 44 and 11: 15 does not support this conclusion. Would Luke have waited until 11: 15 to bring out God's direct intervention? In any case, 11: 14 contradicts Wilckens' point, for it assumes that Peter's speech was evangelistic (ῥήματα...ἐν οἷς σωθήσῃ). Peter's opening remarks (10: 35) indicate that Cornelius has been obedient to such light as he has, and imply that he will be given the greater light of the gospel, not that he is already converted.

There is a much more plausible reason why the outpouring of the Spirit is advanced by Luke from 'even before the end' of Peter's speech (10: 44) to an early stage (11: 15): to make more explicit the parallel between Pentecost and the 'Gentile' Pentecost.[1] The suddenness of the descent of the Spirit is emphasised in 10: 44, recalling the suddenness of the outpouring of the Spirit at Pentecost (2: 2);[2] 11: 15 takes both points a stage further with, admittedly, a different turn of expression, but this in no way alters the character of Peter's speech.[3]

(d) Although Wilckens constantly stresses the close relationship between the speeches and their immediate context, he fails to discuss the implications of the reference to baptism in 10: 47–8. If Peter's speech is not evangelistic, but is catechetical,

---

[1] Some writers have sought to alleviate the difficulty by noting that the idea of 'beginning' in the phrase ἐν δὲ τῷ ἄρξασθαί με λαλεῖν (11: 15), need not be taken literally, as ἄρξασθαι may be an example of a Semitising redundant auxiliary (e.g. F. F. Bruce, *The Book of Acts* (London, 1956), p. 235 n. 13). But this is probably an over-simplification. Luke frequently avoids the Marcan usage of ἄρχομαι where the distinctive meaning has almost disappeared, and he uses ἄρχομαι with an infinitive much more rarely in Acts than in the Gospel; in the few passages in Acts, 'there is no reason to doubt a distinct sense of inception'. The usage is, in any case, attested in Greek literature outside the New Testament and need not be traced to Semitic influence. J. W. Hunkin, 'Pleonastic ἄρχομαι in the New Testament', *JTS* **25** (1924), 394.

[2] This is in contrast to the pattern found in the preceding chapters, e.g. 8: 17 and 9: 17.

[3] H. Conzelmann correctly notes that in both passages the intention is the same: to underline the divine initiative. Comm. *ad loc.*

and if it is followed by the baptism of the catechumen, one might have expected it to show clear signs of the sort of catechetical material found in the epistles, whether in the context of baptism or not.[1]

(e) By arguing that Cornelius was already converted before Peter spoke, Wilckens implies – or at least his hypothesis requires – that the gift of the Spirit followed the conversion of Cornelius and Peter's 'didactic' preaching. No doubt one could argue that the outpouring of the Spirit in 10: 44 was an extraordinary event and hence tells us little about Luke's *ordo salutis*. But if Luke intended to indicate that Peter's speech in Acts 10 was catechetical, and that the speeches in Acts were a pattern for preaching in his own day (as Wilckens and Dibelius argue), then one might have expected the *ordo salutis* to be in some sense normative. Since the gift of the Spirit is so important in the preceding chapters, no discussion of Acts 10 can by-pass the relationship of the gift of the Spirit to conversion and baptism. Both Wilckens and Luke would be unhappy with the implication that the gift of the Spirit is distinct from conversion, but this is the logical conclusion which must be accepted if we allow that Cornelius was converted before Peter spoke.

Wilckens suggests that the baptism of Cornelius was a catching up on the part of man of what God had already accomplished directly in the gift of the Spirit, stressing that there is no mention of the repentance and conversion of Cornelius at the end of the speech.[2] How can this be accounted for? His acceptance of Peter's words about forgiveness and belief in Jesus Christ (10: 43b) is taken for granted in the gift of the Spirit – for the gift of the Spirit is the mark of God's acceptance of the Gentiles and of his forgiveness of Cornelius. This is made clearer in 11: 14–18. The angel tells Cornelius that Peter will declare to him a message (λαλήσει ῥήματα 11: 14) by which he will be saved. The same phrase is used in 10: 44 (ἔτι λαλοῦντος τοῦ Πέτρου τὰ ῥήματα) immediately

---

[1] See, for example, E. G. Selwyn, *The First Epistle of St Peter* (London, 1946), pp. 363ff., and P. Carrington, *The Primitive Christian Catechism* (Cambridge, 1940).

[2] *Missionsreden*, p. 66. Cf. J. D. G. Dunn, *Baptism in the Holy Spirit* (London, 1970), pp. 80ff.

before the mention of the gift of the Spirit. In 11: 17 belief in Jesus Christ is implicitly mentioned as the ground for the gift of the Spirit. The gift granted to the Gentiles is both the Holy Spirit and repentance unto life: these are not distinct actions of God, but are mutually inclusive.

The same point is made in 15: 7–9. Here Peter mentions that God has ordained that from his lips the word of the gospel should be heard by the Gentiles; τὸν λόγον τοῦ εὐαγγελίου is a reference to the only example of Peter's preaching to Gentiles Luke has given – Acts 10: 36–43.[1] Peter's speech before Cornelius is not catechetical 'gospel type' material, but Peter's τὸν λόγον τοῦ εὐαγγελίου is evangelistic![2]

There can be no doubt that for Luke, God's gift of the Spirit marked his acceptance of Cornelius' repentance and his conversion. Wilckens' hypothesis leads to insuperable difficulties as soon as the relationship between Peter's message, the conversion of Cornelius, the gift of the Spirit, and his baptism is considered and as soon as the later references to the Cornelius episode (11: 14–18 and 15: 7–9) are brought to bear on the interpretation of chapter 10. These wider considerations, ignored by Wilckens, make it clear that Luke intended Peter's speech to be regarded as evangelistic.[3]

As in the earlier passages, Jesus Christ is proclaimed. On the grounds of Cornelius' acceptance of Peter's proclamation of Jesus Christ, the Spirit is given signifying God's acceptance of his faith. The fuller references to the ministry do *not* mean that Luke has replaced evangelistic with catechetical material. The greater emphasis on the pre-crucifixion events arises from

[1] The same phrase is used to refer to Peter's proclamation as at 10: 44 (15: 7 ἀκοῦσαι...τὸν λόγον = 10: 44 τοὺς ἀκούοντας τὸν λόγον). In 15: 7 τὸν λόγον is qualified – the Gentiles are said to hear from the lips of Peter τὸν λόγον τοῦ εὐαγγελίου καὶ πιστεῦσαι. τὸν λόγον τοῦ εὐαγγελίου recalls the opening of Peter's speech in 10: 36, τὸν λόγον ...εὐαγγελιζόμενος εἰρήνην.

[2] 15: 8 and 9 are linked closely together: Peter is not referring to a series of events, but is saying the same thing in a different way. God bore witness to the Gentiles by giving them the Holy Spirit, who cleansed their hearts: these acts showed that God did not discriminate between Jew and Gentile.

[3] So also F. Bovon, who rejects Wilckens' hypothesis. 'Tradition', *TZ* **26** (1970), p. 42 n. 70.

the differing circumstances. This speech confirms that, at least in Luke's day, reference to the life and character of Jesus was an integral part of the preaching of the early church.

Paul's preaching to the synagogue at Pisidian Antioch (Acts 13: 16–41) is Luke's next example of initial proclamation. The following points about Jesus are made. God brought to Israel a Saviour, Jesus, of the posterity of David (verse 23), and he sent a message of salvation through Jesus.[1] Before the coming of Jesus, John had preached a baptism of repentance to all the people of Israel, and had announced that he was not the promised one and was unworthy to untie the sandals of the one who would follow him (verses 24–5). Jesus travelled from Galilee to Jerusalem, accompanied by a group who became his witnesses to the people after he was raised from the dead (verse 31). Jesus was innocent; the rulers and inhabitants of Jerusalem could charge him with nothing deserving death – they had not recognised him, yet they had asked Pilate to have him killed (verses 27ff.). There are obvious similarities to Peter's speech to Cornelius in Acts 10, but in Acts 13 there is a much fuller account of John the Baptist and of the accusations against Jesus, yet no mention of Jesus' healing ministry. As in Acts 10, one can hardly speak of the references to the ministry of Jesus as a chronological outline, but there is at least some material closely woven into the whole speech, which answers the questions, 'Who was Jesus? What did he do?'

Luke indicates that Paul's missionary activity at Thessalonica was, at first, very similar to that at Pisidian Antioch. Paul's preaching is summarised: 'This Jesus, whom I proclaim to you, is the Christ' (Acts 17: 3); the preaching about Jesus is once again linked to the scriptures. A full account of the content of the preaching is unnecessary – sufficient examples have already been given.

At Beroea the word is received eagerly and its correspondence with scripture is mentioned yet again (Acts 17: 11); as we shall see, ὁ λόγος is another of Luke's shorthand ways of referring to proclamation about Jesus.

---

[1] This interpretation of verse 26 is confirmed by the link between ὁ λόγος τῆς σωτηρίας and verse 24 ἤγαγεν τῷ Ἰσραηλ Σωτῆρα Ἰησοῦν.

Whenever evangelistic preaching is in view, and whenever knowledge about the story of Jesus cannot simply be assumed, initial missionary preaching, at least as far as Luke is concerned, included reference to Jesus. The apparent exceptions, as it were, prove the rule. Stephen's speech in chapter 7 is hardly evangelistic; the speeches at Lystra and Athens are intended to be vigorous attacks on idolatry – 'pre-evangelism' rather than proclamation of the life, death and resurrection of Jesus in the context of scripture. Paul's speech to the Ephesian elders at Miletus (Acts 20: 18–35) is not initial proclamation – it recalls Paul's method of encouraging and exhorting the readers of his epistles; the speech almost seems to be a Pauline epistle in miniature.[1] It is thus not surprising that there is no reference to Jesus! And yet when Paul's earlier preaching at Ephesus is recalled, it is summarised, as we have seen, as 'preaching the Kingdom'. In addition, Acts 20: 35 seems to indicate that Luke believed that some sayings of Jesus formed part of Paul's initial preaching.[2] The Pauline speeches in the final chapters of Acts are of a different character again – they are Paul's defence of his own actions and are not primarily evangelistic.

What is the significance of this evidence? Whether or not the speeches in the opening chapters of Acts contain pre-Lucan tradition, Luke's own conviction that missionary preaching must indicate who Jesus was is striking. The very much fuller reference to the ministry of Jesus in Acts 10: 34–43 than in the earlier speeches was noted by both C. H. Dodd and M. Dibelius. Dodd suggested that the speech before Cornelius represents the form of the kerygma used by the primitive church in its earliest approaches to a wider public.[3] Dibelius, on the other hand, noted that the life of Jesus was not mentioned in all the speeches in Acts 1–13 and concluded that reference to the deeds of Jesus was not essential, but quite incidental in missionary preaching; it was included only for illustration and

---

[1] Paul's defence of his conduct (20: 18), reference to his humility (19), boldness (20), his readiness to surrender his own life for the sake of the gospel (24), his reminder that he earned his living by his own labours (34), all recall Paul's autobiographical references in his epistles.

[2] J. Blank, *Paulus und Jesus: eine theologische Grundlegung* (Munich, 1968), p. 64.   [3] *Apostolic Preaching*, p. 28.

to provide examples.[1] By examining evidence from the whole of Acts, we have shown that Dodd's view is much preferable – at least, this is how Luke saw matters.

Luke's use of ὁ λόγος both in Acts and in his Gospel provides further confirmation that he saw reference to the life and character of Jesus as an integral part of the Christian message. In Acts, especially in chapters 4–19, Luke frequently sums up the content of the proclamation as ὁ λόγος, ὁ λόγος τοῦ θεοῦ or ὁ λόγος τοῦ κυρίου, phrases which are used almost synonymously. Luke understood these phrases in terms of the evangelistic addresses to which he attaches so much importance. Luke summarises Peter's speech to Cornelius (10: 36ff.) as ὁ λόγος (10: 44, cf. 10: 36; 11: 1), and ὁ λόγος τοῦ εὐαγγελίου (15: 7). Paul's speech in chapter 13 is referred to as ὁ λόγος τοῦ θεοῦ (13: 46) and ὁ λόγος τοῦ κυρίου (13: 48, 49). Both speeches include a sketch of the ministry of Jesus, even though they are but summaries.

The phrase ὁ λόγος τοῦ εὐαγγελίου (Acts 15: 7) is particularly significant, for Luke's avoidance of Mark's εὐαγγέλιον (especially Mark 1: 1) is sometimes linked to his alleged intention to write a biography of Jesus.[2] This phrase, however, refers to Peter's speech to Cornelius, a speech which, as we have seen, was intended by Luke to be evangelistic. Acts 10: 36ff. cannot be interpreted as a secondary transformation of the kerygma into catechetical material.[3] Who Jesus was and what happened during his ministry is very much part of the preaching. 'Kerygma' and 'historical foundation' cannot be separated in this speech.[4] This speech indicates that Luke wished to show the readers of his day that an account of the life and character of Jesus was part of the preaching of the church – and always had been. Luke's avoidance of εὐαγγέλιον is not an indication of a different attitude to the past of Jesus of Nazareth; Luke simply prefers

[1] *Tradition*, pp. 22ff.

[2] E.g. G. Bornkamm, art. 'Evangelien', *RGG* II, col. 764; S. Schulz, *Die Stunde der Botschaft* (Hamburg and Zürich, 1967), p. 284.

[3] U. Wilckens, *Missionsreden*, p. 69.

[4] Wilckens interprets Acts 10: 36ff. in line with H. Conzelmann's view of the purpose of Luke's Gospel: *Theology of St Luke*, p. 11. But the distinction between 'kerygma' and 'historical foundation' is not one Luke would have drawn.

εὐαγγελίζεσθαι and ὁ λόγος, which he uses in essentially the the same way as Mark's εὐαγγέλιον.[1]

Theophilus is in the same position as Cornelius: neither is a committed Christian, but both have heard something about Jesus and the Christian message. Both men are referred to at crucial points in Luke's two books. Luke's aim is to present Theophilus (and his wider circle of readers) with the same message that Peter proclaimed to Cornelius: the Word of God.

The prologue to the Gospel also uses λόγος to refer to the content of the proclamation,[2] and essentially the same content is envisaged by Luke in the report of the αὐτόπται (1: 2), in the narratives which have already been compiled (1: 1), and in his own account (1: 4). In each case the content can be summarised as ὁ λόγος (1: 2).[3]

While κατηχέω (Luke 1: 4) can be taken to refer either to 'reports' about the Christian message or to specific doctrinal instruction,[4] the evidence of Acts 10 and Luke's use of ὁ λόγος confirm the former more general meaning.[5] Luke did not intend his account of Jesus of Nazareth to be a historical basis undergirding the truth of the Christian proclamation to

[1] εὐαγγέλιον also occurs in Acts 20: 24. Cf. Conzelmann, *Theology of St Luke*, p. 221 n. 1. In his commentary on the Gospel (London, 1963), p. 35, G. B. Caird suggests that Luke prefers the verb because it carries definite associations from its use in the Old Testament.

[2] Cf. G. Klein, 'Lukas 1: 1–4 als theologisches Problem', *Zeit und Geschichte* (Festschrift R. Bultmann), ed. E. Dinkler (Tübingen, 1964), p. 204.

[3] H. Flender argues that Luke sees the story of Jesus from two very different angles, the historical and the kerygmatic; the prologue highlights only the historical angle. But the use of ὁ λόγος, which is a very important Lucan word, proves embarrassing and has to be dismissed as 'ambiguous': *St Luke, Theologian of Redemptive History* (London, 1967), pp. 65f.

[4] See the full discussion of the prologue by H. J. Cadbury in *The Beginnings of Christianity*, ed. F. J. F. Jackson and K. Lake (London, 1922ff.), II, 489–510, where he rightly warns against drawing too much from its phraseology. C. H. Talbert takes Theophilus as a representative of Christians who have been instructed but who are now disturbed by false teachers and teachings: *Luke and the Gnostics* (Nashville, 1966), p. 56 n. 15.

[5] The commentators are divided. Cf. G. Klein, 'Lukas 1: 1–4', *Zeit und Geschichte*, ed. E. Dinkler, pp. 213f., and H. W. Beyer, art. 'κατηχέω', *TWNT* III, 640.

which Theophilus had already committed himself. Luke's Gospel is evangelistic in intention, even though its fullness and length mark it off from any form of initial preaching likely to have been known in the early church.[1]

Important conclusions have emerged. The content of the speeches in Acts is very closely related to the circumstances of the hearers. Whenever evangelistic preaching is mentioned (whether or not details are given), and whenever knowledge about the life of Jesus cannot simply be taken for granted, missionary preaching included reference to Jesus. Luke, at least, would be most unhappy with Bultmann's famous *Dass*: for Luke, the life and character of Jesus is part and parcel of the message of the church and is especially important in initial evangelistic preaching.

[1] *Contra* H. Conzelmann, *Theology of St Luke*, p. 11.

CHAPTER 2

LUKE'S PRESENTATION OF JESUS IN HIS GOSPEL

Luke, it is now frequently argued, looks back to the life and character of Jesus in quite a new way, not so much as the historian or the most skilled writer among the evangelists, but from his own particular theological perspective. Luke has made a biography of Jesus central in his interpretation of *Heilsgeschichte*;[1] Luke has written the first life of Jesus.[2] Only at this late stage in the development of primitive Christianity does the life and character of Jesus play an important role in the message of the primitive church. Luke's theological achievement is often criticised and viewed as a corruption or distortion of the primitive kerygma.[3] R. Bultmann, for example, suggests that Luke has surrendered the original kerygmatic sense of the Jesus tradition and has historicised it.[4]

[1] H. Conzelmann, *The Theology of St Luke*, esp. pp. 193ff. See also, among many others, S. Schulz, *Die Stunde der Botschaft* (Hamburg, 1967), pp. 235ff.

[2] Earlier writers frequently saw Luke as a biographer. See, for example, E. Renan, *Life of Jesus* (E.T. London, 1867), p. 25. The more recent use of the term 'biography' seems to stem from M. Dibelius: see, for example, *Gospel Criticism and Christology* (E.T. London, 1935), p. 54. E. Käsemann's description of Luke's Gospel as 'the first life of Jesus' is now widely accepted; 'The Problem of the Historical Jesus' in *Essays on NT Themes*, p. 29. See also, for example, W. Marxsen, *Mark the Evangelist* (E.T. Nashville, 1969), p. 16; G. Bornkamm, art. 'Evangelien, synoptische', in *RGG* II, col. 764; H. Flender, *St Luke*, p. 167.

[3] See the full discussion in U. Wilckens, *Missionsreden*, pp. 193ff.; E. Haenchen, *Apostelgeschichte*, pp. 682ff. (E.T. pp. 130ff.); E. Lohse, 'Lukas als Theologe der Heilsgeschichte', *EvT* **14** (1954), 256ff.; W. G. Kümmel, 'Luc en accusation dans la théologie contemporaine', *ETL* **46** (1970), 256–81. As an interesting example of the change of theological perspective some have seen in Luke's Gospel, see H. D. Betz, *Nachfolge and Nachahmung im NT* (Tübingen, 1967), p. 40. Betz argues that only in Luke does the 'following Jesus' motif refer to the earthly Jesus; in Matthew, Mark and John it refers to the exalted Lord.

[4] *The Theology of the New Testament* II (E.T. London, 1955), 117.

Does Luke's Gospel represent a new understanding and presentation of the traditions about Jesus as 'biographical'? Does Luke view the life and character of Jesus from a completely new theological perspective? The distinctive features of Luke's presentation of Jesus in the passion narratives are clarified in the opening section of this chapter. For M. Dibelius, among others, contends that a new way of estimating the tradition of the life of Jesus quite unlike that found in other parts of the New Testament can be found here: the passion becomes a martyrdom, Jesus a hero, and Luke's narrative an edifying description of a noble character.[1]

I   JESUS IN THE
LUCAN PASSION NARRATIVE

Since Luke undoubtedly used some parts of Mark's passion narrative and yet constructed a narrative which differs considerably both in details and in overall impact, the distinctive features of Luke's approach to the life and character of Jesus can be isolated at least as readily in chapters 22 and 23 as elsewhere in the gospel.[2] Luke, it is often claimed, has rewritten Mark's account with a conscious desire to minimise

[1] M. Dibelius, *From Tradition to Gospel* (E.T. London, 1934), p. 300.

[2] Differences in content, literary style, vocabulary and order are so extensive that it is extremely difficult to envisage Luke's passion narrative as a revised and expanded edition of Mark, written from Luke's own distinctive point of view; there are good reasons for believing that Luke possessed an independent passion narrative which he frequently preferred to Mark. But our argument does not depend on this hypothesis; where necessary, source-critical decisions are defended.

The case for an independent narrative has been presented (with important differences) by several writers and it has yet to be refuted in comparable detail. See H. Schürmann, *Der Paschamahlbericht, Lk 22, (7–14) 15–18* (Münster, 1953); *Der Einsetzungsbericht, Lk 22, 19–20* (Münster, 1955); *Jesu Abschiedsrede, Lk 22, 21–38* (Münster, 1957), cited as I, II, III respectively; F. Rehkopf, *Die lukanische Sonderquelle* (Tübingen, 1959) (on Rehkopf, see H. Conzelmann in *Gnomon* **32** (1960), 470f.); G. Schneider, *Verleugnung, Verspottung und Verhör Jesu nach Lukas 22, 54–71* (Munich, 1969); D. R. Catchpole, *The Trial of Jesus* (Leiden, 1971), esp. pp. 153–220; V. Taylor, *The Passion Narrative of St Luke* (Cambridge, 1972). See also P. Winter, 'The Treatment of his sources by the Third Evangelist in Luke 21–24', *ST* **8** (1954), 138ff.

the tragedy, replacing it with pathos.[1] M. Dibelius goes even further:

Luke is the first evangelist to interest himself in the human qualities of Jesus...Luke endeavours to present a picture of Jesus in a biographical sense, and that, among other essentials, required proof of piety, even in the presentation of the Son of God and Lord of the Church. Luke thinks in terms of biography...Luke's construction of the story bears a close resemblance to that of a martyr legend.[2]

Has Luke consciously turned the passion traditions into an edifying biographical account? M. Dibelius' widely accepted assessment of Luke's passion narrative as an account of a martyrdom and as a conscious attempt to emphasise the high human qualities of Jesus rests on a very flimsy basis.[3]

The struggle of Satan against the martyrs is said to be an important aspect of the late Jewish presentation of a martyrdom.[4] At the very beginning of his passion narrative Luke adds to Marcan material the comment that Satan entered into Judas called Iscariot (Luke 22: 3). This is almost certainly a phrase from oral tradition, not from Luke's own hand; the motif is also found in John 13: 2, 27. In any case, the clearest Jewish parallel, Asc. Is. 5: 1, is probably not pre-Christian.[5] The motif plays no part in 2 and 4 Macc., nor does it seem to have been present in early rabbinic martyrdoms which are also cited as possible parallels to the passion narratives.[6]

[1] Cf. M. Kiddle, 'The Passion Narrative in St Luke's Gospel', *JTS* **36** (1935), 273.

[2] *Gospel Criticism*, pp. 54f.

[3] *Tradition*, pp. 199ff., 300f. As examples of the widespread acceptance of Dibelius' view, see S. Schulz, *Stunde*, pp. 289f.; H. Flender, *St Luke*, pp. 17f., 54; J. Schreiber, *Theologie des Vertrauens* (Hamburg, 1967), pp. 57f.; C. H. Talbert, *Luke and the Gnostics*, pp. 71ff.; more cautiously, H. Conzelmann, *Theology of St Luke*, pp. 81ff., 88f., 200 n. 4, 217 n. 2. Cf. also R. H. Lightfoot, *History and Interpretation in the Gospels* (London, 1935), pp. 176ff.

[4] E.g. H. W. Surkau, *Martyrien in jüdischer und frühchristlicher Zeit* (Göttingen, 1938), pp. 90ff.

[5] Cf. D. S. Russell, *The Method and Message of Jewish Apocalyptic* (London, 1964), p. 59.

[6] Cf. Surkau, *Martyrien*, pp. 34ff.; J. Downing, 'Jesus and Martyrdom', *JTS* **14** (1963), 279ff.; H. A. Fischel, 'Martyr and Prophet', *JQR* **37** (1946–7), 265ff. and 363ff.

M. Dibelius and H. Surkau both point to Luke 22: 43 and argue that the appearance of the angel in answer to prayer and the 'strengthening' of the martyr are typical,[1] and they defend the authenticity of the longer reading. But the textual evidence is much more finely balanced than they allow. If the verses are Lucan and if the appearance of the angel is a martyrological motif, one might have expected verse 43 to have followed verse 44, for the strengthening angel does not resolve the martyr's struggle and enable him to face death joyously, as in other Jewish martyrdoms; the agony and the bloody sweat still follow.

M. Dibelius and H. Surkau both note that the conversions of opponents and of the unprejudiced by means of the attitude of the martyr are 'proofs very typical of a martyrdom' and are features of Luke's narrative. Surkau refers to the impression Jesus made on Pilate, again citing Asc. Is. as a parallel.[2] But Luke does not include Mark's ὥστε θαυμάζειν τὸν Πιλᾶτον (Mark 15: 5), to which Matt. 27: 14 adds λίαν, nor anything comparable to the additional material on Pilate and his wife introduced by Matthew. While the 'daughters of Jerusalem' pericope is more relevant, it is included primarily because of the eschatological sayings in 23: 28–31. Surkau, citing a striking parallel from the account of the martyrdom of R. Hananiah ben Teradyon to Jesus' promise to the penitent thief (Luke 23: 39–43), argues that even though this account is later than Luke's Gospel, the motif is common in rabbinic accounts of martyrdoms.[3] But there is no parallel in the Maccabean literature with which Luke and his readers are much more likely to have been familiar.

As we shall argue shortly, the difference between the centurion's response in Mark and that in Luke is less decisive than is often suggested; there is no evidence to suggest that Luke has altered the Marcan confession and so introduced a martyrological motif not found in Mark. M. Dibelius refers to the crowd which 'strikes its breast and goes home, frightened by the martyr's blameless suffering'.[4] The crowd is convicted by Jesus, but not, as in later apocryphal literature, converted.

---

[1] Dibelius, *Gospel Criticism*, p. 61; Surkau, *Martyrien*, p. 93.
[2] Surkau, *Martyrien*, pp. 94ff.; Dibelius, *Tradition*, p. 202.
[3] *Martyrien*, pp. 98f. [4] *Tradition*, p. 203.

But this is not a typical martyrological motif in Jewish literature, for there is no parallel in the Maccabean accounts, nor, apparently, in rabbinic literature.[1]

M. Dibelius notes that the prayer for the executioners is characteristic of a martyrdom. But even if the longer reading in 23: 34 is genuine, it does not suggest that Luke has altered Mark's account into a martyrdom, for there are no Jewish parallels.[2] Nor are there any Jewish parallels to Luke 23: 46, although the motif becomes common in Christian martyrological literature, beginning, of course, with Stephen.[3]

Is Luke's account of Stephen's martyrdom modelled on Jesus' passion, indicating that Luke intended to present Jesus as the proto-martyr?[4] The differences between the two accounts are more striking than the agreements. The charge brought against Stephen (Acts 6: 14) is very similar to that brought against Jesus in Mark 14: 58 (cf. Mark 15: 29; Matt. 26: 61 and 27: 40; John 2: 19), but this logion is not found in Luke's Gospel. Although Stephen's final words do recall the final words of Jesus, there is no close parallelism. Acts 7: 60 and Luke 23: 34 do not have a single word in common; Stephen's prayer does not include the motif of ignorance which occurs elsewhere in Acts.[5] The preceding words, 'Lord Jesus, receive my spirit', are not a mere echo of Jesus' words. Unlike Jesus' similar words (Luke 23: 46), they are not Stephen's final cry. Luke seems to take pains to avoid suggesting that Stephen is re-enacting the first great martyrdom.[6] Only at a later stage, as in the account of the martyrdom of Polycarp, do we find

[1] Neither Surkau, *Martyrien*, nor H. L. Strack and P. Billerbeck, *Kommentar zum Neuen Testament aus Talmud und Midrasch* (Munich, 1922ff.) cite parallels.

[2] 'In den jüdischen Martyrien pflegen die Märtyrer ihren Richter nur zu beschimpfen', Surkau, *Martyrien*, p. 97. Cf. Dibelius, *Tradition*, p. 203.

[3] *Contra* Dibelius, *Tradition*, p. 203. See H. von Campenhausen, *Die Idee des Martyriums in der alten Kirche* (Göttingen, 1936), p. 58 n. 5, and cf. Surkau, *Martyrien*, p. 85.

[4] So Talbert, *Luke and the Gnostics*, p. 76. Talbert argues unconvincingly that Luke intended his emphasis on martyrdom to be understood as his reply to Gnostics who refused to undergo suffering or martyrdom for the faith.

[5] Acts 3: 17; 13: 27; 17: 27, 30. Cf. Conzelmann, *Theology of St Luke*, pp. 88f.

[6] *Contra* Surkau, *Martyrien*, pp. 117ff.

similarities between a Christian martyr's death and the narratives of the death of Jesus drawn out explicitly.

The other gospels contain almost as many martyrological motifs as Luke.[1] The motif of the astonishment of the judge before the accused is found in 2 and 4 Macc., in Mark 15: 5b but not in Luke. Matthew and Mark include an expression traditionally used for the death of Jewish martyrs – δοῦναι τὴν ψυχήν (Mark 10: 45; Matt. 20: 28), but it is not found in Luke.[2]

Luke has not turned the passion narratives into an account of a martyrdom. Although some martyrological motifs can be traced in his narratives, M. Dibelius has exaggerated the distinctive contribution of Luke.[3] The whole tone of the Maccabean narratives bears little resemblance to any of the gospel narratives: there the endurance and patience of the hero is set out as an example,[4] and the sufferings are described in a way foreign to Luke, as well as to the other evangelists. The gospels' portraits of Jesus are quite contrary to the joyful courage of Jewish and Christian martyrs and the serenity of Socrates; no miracles counteract the mocking and scourging of Jesus, nor do miracles make it extremely difficult to kill him.[5] Luke was not influenced by the conventional martyr figure of Jewish literature to a significantly greater extent than the other evangelists.

Nor has Luke consciously redrawn the Marcan portrait of

[1] D. W. Riddle, *The Martyrs: A Study in Social Control* (Chicago, 1931), singles out not Luke, but John, as the most thoroughgoing account of a martyrdom among the Gospels. Cf. also D. W. Riddle, 'The Martyr Motif in the Gospel according to Mark', *JR* **4** (1924), 397ff.; J. Downing, *JTS* **14**, 279ff., appeals to Matthew and Mark as frequently as to Luke.

[2] F. Büschel, art. 'δίδωμι', *TWNT* II, 168. Luke's nearest equivalent is 22: 19.

[3] Surkau, *Martyrien*, develops the points made by Dibelius, giving references to the Jewish literature where possible. But although he is in broad agreement with Dibelius, he concludes (p. 100) that Dibelius has contrasted Luke's account with Matthew and Mark too strongly.

[4] Cf. 2 Macc. 6: 27f.

[5] Cf. H. Fischel, 'Martyr and Prophet', *JQR* **37** (1946–7), 373, 383. K. L. Schmidt shows that the passion narratives do not belong to any literary *Gattung*, but rest on living popular tradition: 'Die Stellung der Evangelien in der allgemeinen Literaturgeschichte', ΕΥΧΑΡΙΣΤΗΡΙΟΝ (Festschrift H. Gunkel), ed. H. Schmidt, II (Göttingen, 1923), pp. 78f.

Jesus from a new 'biographical' perspective, replacing the stark tragedy of Mark with an emphasis on the nobility of Jesus' character and his high human qualities generally. There is no sign of the 'novelising' tendencies of the Matthean additions to Mark's account. Surprisingly, Luke is even less interested in precise chronology than Mark: only once does Luke include a chronological reference which has no equivalent in Mark (Luke 22: 59), but in no fewer than eight passages Luke either does not have an equivalent chronological note or has a less precise expression.[1]

As soon as particular passages are examined, it becomes clear that Luke's alterations spring from such a variety of motives that it is rash to generalise about his intentions. Take, as an example, the final words of the crucified Jesus in Mark and in Luke. At first sight Luke's 'Father, into your hands I commit my spirit' (Luke 23: 46) is so much 'milder' than 'Eloi, Eloi, lama sabachthani' (Mark 15: 34) that it does suggest an attempt to arouse feelings of pity or sadness as part of an interest in the human qualities of Jesus. But Luke has almost certainly preferred to retain his source at this point, a quotation of Ps. 31: 5, the evening prayer of pious Jews;[2] Mark's references to Elijah may well have been considered unintelligible to Luke's readers.

The divergent comments of the centurion in Mark and Luke provide a further warning against hasty generalisations. Luke's centurion confesses, 'Certainly this man was innocent' (23: 47), while in Mark the response is 'Truly this man was Son of God' (15: 39).[3] Is the centurion in Luke simply responding to the patience and courage of Jesus? Is only a 'psychological miracle' intended?[4] Luke and Mark are not as far apart as is often suggested. In both gospels the introduction to the centurion's words has a similar force. In Luke, as

[1] Cf. Mark 14: 1 and Luke 22: 1; Mark 14: 12 and Luke 22: 7; Mark 14: 17 and Luke 22: 14 (Lucan phrase is less precise); Mark 14: 30 and Luke 22: 34; Mark 14: 37 and Luke 22: 46; Mark 14: 43 and Luke 22: 47a; Mark 15: 25 – Luke does not even give a hint as to the length of time Jesus suffered on the cross; Mark 15: 33 and Luke 23: 44.

[2] See H. von Campenhausen, *Die Idee des Martyriums*, p. 58 n. 5.

[3] Cf. Wis. Sol. 2: 18, εἰ γάρ ἐστιν ὁ δίκαιος υἱὸς θεοῦ, where the main points of both the Marcan and Lucan versions are found side by side!

[4] Dibelius, *Tradition*, p. 195.

clearly as in Mark, it is primarily the death of Jesus which elicits the centurion's response. Luke's ἰδών...τὸ γενόμενον is less precise than Mark's ἰδών...ὅτι οὕτως ἐξέπνευσεν, but if Luke had wished to stress that the centurion was merely impressed by the patience and courage shown by Jesus on the cross, he would have used τὰ γενόμενα, as in the inferior reading of R, θ, and a few codices. In verse 48 there is an explicit reference to the impression made by the whole cruci-fixion scene – all the multitudes who assembled to see the sight, when they saw τὰ γενόμενα, returned home beating their breasts. A comparison with Matt. 27: 54 shows how close Mark and Luke are to each other: in Matthew the centurion and those guarding Jesus are frightened into confession by the accompanying events and not, as in Mark and Luke, by the death of Jesus.

Luke's inclusion of ἐδόξαζεν τὸν θεόν, which has no parallel in Mark, is not intended to be a weak expression of amazement on the part of the centurion.[1] This is a favourite Lucan expression; in eight of the nine times δοξάζω is used in Luke's Gospel τὸν θεόν is the object, but the expression occurs only once in Mark. The Lucan usage denotes a believing response, usually by the person concerned in a miracle of Jesus. If Luke simply wished to state that the centurion was impressed by the suffering of an innocent man, why did he use a term reserved elsewhere for response to a miracle of Jesus?[2] Mark's expression is stronger, but in both cases there is a believing response, however incongruous this may seem to be.[3]

While both the 'cause' of the centurion's response (the death of Jesus, not his patient suffering) and the end result (believing

---

[1] C. F. D. Moule points out to me that δοξάζειν τὸν θεόν is used, in good Hebrew idiom, for acknowledging that God is in the right – as when a penitent admits his wrong and gives God the glory. It is thus, association-ally, very close to ὁμολογεῖν.

[2] Conzelmann (*Theology of St Luke*, p. 88), following Dibelius (*Tradition*, p. 203), suggests that in Mark the centurion is a Gentile, whereas in Luke he is a man moved by a martyrdom. But surely Luke's centurion is just as much a Gentile as Mark's.

[3] The difference between Luke and Mark is often accounted for as arising from Luke's preference for his non-Marcan source. See, for example, K. H. Rengstorf, *Das Evangelium nach Lukas* (1956) and W. Grundmann, *Das Evangelium nach Lukas* (1966), *ad loc.*

response, not amazement) are thus broadly similar in Mark and in Luke, the centurion's words do differ significantly. Luke's δίκαιος is neither more obviously martyrological than Mark's υἱὸς θεοῦ, nor is it linked to any intention to underline the excellent human character of Jesus. It is part of the motif of 'innocence' which Luke brings out clearly in the passion narratives, and which almost certainly is an aspect of his wider intention in both the Gospel and Acts to stress the 'innocence' (in Roman eyes) of followers of Jesus.[1]

There are even some passages in which Luke's narrative is less likely to 'arouse emotions', and is less 'interesting' than Mark's account.[2] Luke's equivalent of Mark's Gethsemane scene is perhaps the clearest example. This pericope includes a major textual *crux* (Luke 22: 43–4). Without these verses Luke's account is extremely brief and unadorned, but even if the longer text is retained, Luke's account misses much of the 'emotional' tension of Mark's narrative. Luke's account comes from his own independent tradition, although Marcan influence is likely at 22: 39–40a and 46b.[3] Luke's non-Marcan source largely accounts for the difference between the two narratives, but Luke was aware of the Marcan material at some point, and has deliberately rejected the longer, more vivid and 'emotional' Marcan account. Luke has not allowed any trace of Mark's καὶ ἤρξατο ἐκθαμβεῖσθαι καὶ ἀδημονεῖν (14: 33) or the dramatic words of Jesus περίλυπός ἐστιν ἡ ψυχή μου ἕως θανάτου (14: 34) to intrude into his narrative. Only after Jesus has resolved to accept his Father's will (22: 42) does the strengthening angel appear and the intense agony begin. No hint of the nature of the 'more earnest' prayer of verse 44 is given. On the other hand Mark portrays Jesus as distressed, troubled and sorrowful *before* praying ἀλλ' οὐ τί ἐγὼ θέλω ἀλλὰ τί σύ (Mark 14: 36b). Later Mark explicitly mentions

[1] See Conzelmann's discussion, *Theology of St Luke*, pp. 138ff.; also G. D. Kilpatrick, 'A Theme of the Lucan Passion Story and Luke 23: 47', *JTS* **43** (1942), 34ff.

[2] Cf. Dibelius, 'The oldest story seeks neither to be interesting nor to arouse emotions', *Gospel Criticism*, p. 62.

[3] Luke retains the non-Marcan tradition in the 'core' of his pericope, but was less reluctant to use Mark's account as his introduction (39–40a) and conclusion (46b). Further examples of this method of redaction are given below.

that when Jesus left the disciples for the second time, he prayed the same words (verse 39), thus underlining the tension which is sustained throughout the Marcan pericope.

Some of the usual explanations of Luke's tendencies are inadequate. While it would be rash to suggest that few passages in Luke 22 and 23 are closely related to an interest in the character of Jesus, there is no clear evidence that Luke is portraying Jesus from a new perspective as part of his attempt to link the character of Jesus to the message of the church for the first time.

Luke's passion narrative is very different from Mark's, and the differences must be accounted for. They can be partly explained as arising from his preference for his non-Marcan traditions – Marcan material, whether strongly revised by Luke or not, is much less prominent than in other parts of the Gospel. But this explanation by itself will not do, for Luke has placed his own stamp on the traditions he has used. By paying close attention to Luke's redaction of his sources, a more precise estimate of his distinctive contribution is possible.

Luke's distinctive approach

Luke has carefully woven together Marcan and non-Marcan traditions – and it is precisely in this process that his own hand can be seen most clearly. Luke's superior abilities as a literary artist emerge from an examination of the way in which he has constructed his passion narratives; a number of closely related methods can be observed.

(a) Luke separates Jesus from the disciples or from others, thus narrating much more vividly what Jesus did. The opening passion pericope provides a good example of Luke's redaction of Marcan material; at 22: 8ff. Luke alters Mark's account in order to shift the initiative from the disciples to Jesus. In Mark the disciples ask where *they* are to prepare for the Passover (14: 12); in Luke some of their words are found on the lips of Jesus (22: 8b) and he initiates the preparations by commanding them to go to prepare the Passover – only then do they ask Jesus where they are to go to do this. This is not a haphazard alteration, but part of a pattern found elsewhere in Luke 22 and 23. Jesus is 'separated', as it were, from the disciples, and is pictured as much more vividly in control of the situation than in Mark; the redaction is primarily stylistic, not theological.

In the Last Supper scene Luke does not include the two Marcan references to the group eating (Mark 14: 18, 22); attention is constantly focussed on Jesus:

Mark 14: 17, 18a	Luke 22: 14
καὶ ὀψίας γενομένης ἔρχεται μετὰ τῶν δώδεκα καὶ ἀνακειμένων αὐτῶν καὶ ἐσθιόντων...	καὶ ὅτε ἐγένετο ἡ ὥρα, ἀνέπεσεν, καὶ οἱ ἀπόστολοι σὺν αὐτῷ.

Luke replaces the Marcan plural ἀνακειμένων by ἀνέπεσεν, thus avoiding Mark's inclusion of Jesus with his disciples.[1] The disciples are almost an afterthought, and are placed firmly in the background; they do not occupy the centre of the stage until verse 23. Luke carefully presents the preparations (22: 8b) and the Supper itself as initiated, sustained and dominated by Jesus.

The introduction to Luke's equivalent of the Gethsemane scene, which links the whole section of 'farewell words' with the following narrative, provides a further striking example of his method. Even though Luke 22: 40b–46 come from a non-Marcan source, vv. 39 and 40a are a Lucan redaction of Marcan material.[2] In the latter verses Jesus dominates the

---

[1] J. Jeremias disagrees with H. Schürmann's analysis of Luke 22: 14 as a Lucan redaction of Mark 14: 17, noting that Mark and Luke have only one word in common, καί. But Schürmann includes Mark 14: 18a in his comparison and is able to offer other plausible reasons for Lucan redaction: *The Eucharistic Words of Jesus* (E.T. London, 2nd ed. 1966), p. 99 n. 1; H. Schürmann, I, 104ff. This passage should be added to H. J. Cadbury's list of passages where Luke uses the singular instead of Mark's plural for Jesus and his companions, thus focussing attention on the chief actor, Jesus: *The Style and Literary Method of Luke* (Cambridge, Mass., 1920), p. 165.

[2] The evidence is as follows: (a) καὶ ἐξελθὼν (ἐξῆλθον in Mark)...εἰς τὸ ὄρος τῶν ἐλαιῶν is taken from Mark 14: 26, Mark's link between the Supper and Gethsemane. Γεθσημανί is dropped because of Luke's well-known aversion to Semitic names. Hence the basis of the verse is Marcan. (b) κατὰ τὸ ἔθος is Lucan (Luke 1: 9; 2: 42; 22: 39) and is not found elsewhere in the New Testament. It is introduced by Luke to refer to 21: 37 and to explain how Judas knows the place where he will betray Jesus. (c) While πορεύομαι is not confined to the Lucan writings, it is found

41

narrative while the disciples fade into the background. With the words ἠκολούθησαν δὲ αὐτῷ καὶ οἱ μαθηταί Luke separates Jesus from his disciples and thus vividly pictures him as leading the disciples. In Mark there is no differentiation between Jesus and his disciples: Mark simply records καὶ ἔρχονται.

Luke uses, but deliberately alters, the Marcan 'framework' which surrounds the Supper. At the beginning of the preparations for the Supper (22: 8), and at the conclusion of the sayings after the Supper and the introduction of the next scene (22: 39–40a), Luke writes with a particular understanding of Jesus in mind. Luke's redaction is completely consistent with the non-Marcan traditions he welds together: both present a portrait of Jesus which is quite distinct from that found in Mark. No longer is Jesus, as it were, *primus inter pares*, he is now simply *primus* – but ὡς ὁ διακονῶν (22: 27). Luke has carefully 'separated' and contrasted Jesus and the disciples.

Luke's account of the arrest also concentrates attention on Jesus. Apart from 22: 52b and 53a, Luke here follows a non-Marcan source.[1] In the Marcan pericope Jesus does not speak until 14: 48; Judas, not Jesus, dominates the first part of Mark's account. But in Luke the reverse is the case. Whereas Mark 14: 45 focusses attention on Judas as he moves up to Jesus, Luke 22: 47–8 directs attention to Jesus.[2] Mark has no equivalent to the powerfully dramatic saying of Jesus, which contrasts Jesus and Judas in 22: 48. Here Luke's source, not his redaction of Mark, provides a more vivid account dominated by Jesus.

there much more frequently than elsewhere. In Mark it occurs only at 16: 10, 12, 15 and as a variant at 9: 30! The combination ἐξελθὼν ἐπορεύθη (or in the plural with a different tense) occurs only once outside Luke–Acts (at Matt. 24: 1, where the subject is placed in the middle). But see Luke 4: 42 (Lucan rationalising chronological redaction of Mark); Luke 13: 31 (L); Acts 12: 17; 16: 36; 20: 1 and 21: 5. There is thus a strong case for regarding the phrase as Lucan. (*d*) In v. 40a Mark's λέγει is changed by Luke to εἶπεν. F. Rehkopf notes 15 examples of Lucan alteration of Mark to εἶπεν (ον, αν) αὐτῷ (αὐτοῖς): *Sonderquelle*, p. 93. (Cf. H. Schürmann, I, 88f.; H. J. Cadbury, *Style*, pp. 168f.) While this is a feature of both Luke's non-Marcan source and Lucan redaction of Mark, the latter is more likely as Luke 22: 40a continues the same differentiation of Jesus and the disciples, and is closely linked to verse 39.

[1] See Rehkopf, *Sonderquelle*, pp. 31–82 for a detailed study of the sources of this pericope.　　　　　　[2] So also Rehkopf, *Sonderquelle*, p. 42.

Luke's reference to Simon of Cyrene at 23: 26 is a redaction of Mark 15: 20b–21.[1] Luke has added the significant phrase ὄπισθεν τοῦ 'Ιησοῦ thus showing that Jesus walks in front of those accompanying him. This is confirmed by the introduction to the next pericope ἠκολούθει δὲ αὐτῷ πολὺ πλῆθος (23: 27a). Again Jesus is separated from those who are with him by a deliberate redaction of Mark.

One further example of this method may be noted. The criminals barely enter the Marcan crucifixion scene. In Luke they appear at a much earlier stage; they are led away with Jesus (23: 32). Luke suggests that Jesus was the first to be crucified: ἐκεῖ ἐσταύρωσαν αὐτὸν καὶ τοὺς κακούργους...(23: 33). Yet again Jesus is separated and contrasted with those who are with him; Luke's narrative is much more vivid, even when the same events are being recorded.

(b) Luke's methods of grouping material also reveal his literary abilities and result in greater clarity. The Last Supper scene provides an example of an alteration which might be taken as theologically motivated, but which, on closer inspection, is a stylistic improvement. As Luke 22: 21–3 is basically Marcan,[2]

---

[1] The evidence may be shown briefly: (a) The agreement between Mark and Luke in the rather strange words ἐρχόμενον ἀπ' ἀγροῦ is striking. (b) Luke has replaced Mark's ἐξάγουσιν with ἀπήγαγον because, unlike Mark, his previous scene does not take place in a building. (c) In Mark, the soldiers who have just mocked Jesus lead him out to be crucified and then press Simon into service. Luke deliberately retains the same crowd throughout chapter 23 and hence replaces Mark's ἀγγαρεύουσιν, which has distinct military connotations. (Cf. Matt. 5: 41, the only other occurrence.) Luke used the more appropriate ἐπιλαβόμενοι, which he also uses a number of times in Acts with a crowd as subject of the verb. (Cf. Acts 16: 19; 17: 19; 18: 17; 21: 30.) (d) Luke reduces Mark's two sentences to one by using a participial construction, in accordance with his well-known preference for participles. (Cadbury, Style, pp. 132ff.) (e) Alexander and Rufus disappear in Luke and in Matthew, as they are no longer known to readers. (f) Examples of Lucan redaction of Marcan material at the beginning of a pericope which has non-Marcan material as its 'core' have already been given. On this, see Rehkopf, Sonderquelle, p. 84 n. 3. There is a strong cumulative case; Luke's version is very probably redaction of Mark.

[2] Schürmann, III, 3–21. Contra Rehkopf, Sonderquelle, pp. 7–30 and 83f.; but see now, H. Schürmann, 'Protolukanische Spracheigentümlichkeiten' in Traditionsgeschichtliche Untersuchungen zu den synoptischen Evangelien (Düsseldorf, 1968), p. 214 n. 34.

Luke has deliberately placed the announcement of the betrayal after the words of institution, making it clear that Judas participated in the Last Supper, thus heightening rather than lessening the tension of the occasion.[1] A theologically motivated alteration might have worked in the opposite direction and emphasised that Judas was not present at the climax of the Last Supper.[2]

The sayings of Jesus which are grouped together after the Supper are obviously intended to be a particularly important part of Luke's Gospel; Luke shows himself to be a literary artist by the way in which he presents his material. The collection of sayings is an artificial construction, which recapitulates the past events of the ministry and prepares for the future. Jesus and the disciples are contrasted in 22: 15ff.; this is continued in verses 21-38. Jesus has expressed his eagerness to eat with the disciples, but one of them will betray him. The disciples dispute among themselves, while Jesus refers to himself as the one who serves. By implication Jesus expects the disciples' desertion (verse 31); they will be sifted by Satan. Their disobedience is exposed, for they were not commanded to buy swords.[3] The difficult two concluding words of Jesus (verse 38) can be interpreted as the final disappointment of Jesus with the disciples. They are contrasted in a subtle and yet striking way; the authority of Jesus is stressed over against the obtuse and confused disciples. Jesus, even as the 'one who serves', is the one who says, 'as my Father appointed a kingdom for me, so do I appoint for you...'. Through the grouping of these sayings Luke portrays Jesus vividly, even though the sayings themselves barely reveal Luke's hand.

(c) Closely related both to Luke's careful 'separation' of Jesus and those around him and his grouping of material in order to contrast Jesus and the disciples, is his method of indirect characterisation. In the narrative of Peter's denial, Luke contrasts Peter and Jesus by including the comment not found in

[1] See Rehkopf, *Sonderquelle*, pp. 3f., for various other suggested reasons.

[2] Jeremias suggests that the Marcan order is less likely to be original, as it tends to make things easier, possibly under the influence of the eucharistic liturgy which introduced the exclusion formula before the eucharist: *Eucharistic Words*, p. 98 n. 4.

[3] P. S. Minear, 'A Note on Luke 22: 36', *NovT* **7** (1964-5), 133.

Mark, 'and the Lord turned and looked at Peter' (22: 61a) – words which almost certainly stem from Luke's own hand;[1] the contrast is underlined by the two uses of ὁ κύριος to refer to Jesus, the only occurrence of κύριος in the passion narratives. In Luke it is not the crowing of the cock, as in Mark, which first leads to Peter's penitence, but the impression made by the penetrating glance of Jesus. In chapter 23 there are a number of further examples of vivid portrayal of Jesus either by contrasting him with others or by noting their reaction to him. For example, although Luke's pericope about Barabbas (23: 18ff.) is similar to Mark's, there is a biographical sketch of Barabbas both at the beginning and at the end of the pericope. In verse 25 Luke presents a striking contrast between Jesus and Barabbas; this is quite deliberate, for Luke repeats almost word for word what has just been said about Barabbas.[2]

Luke's method of indirect characterisation is also seen in the formulation of the more detailed charges preferred against Jesus at 23: 2, 5 and 14. These details are not found in the other gospels. They provide a summary of the ministry of Jesus as seen through the eyes of his opponents. By listing accusations which are obviously incorrect, Luke points indirectly to the true nature of the ministry and character of Jesus and thus reveals not only his literary skill, but also his intention to present Jesus as misunderstood and innocent. The accusations stem from Luke's hand and not from non-Marcan tradition, and thus confirm that his stylistic abilities result in a clearer characterisation of Jesus.[3]

At a number of places in the passion narratives Luke has

---

[1] See Schneider, *Verleugnung*, pp. 91ff. for a detailed discussion.

[2] Cf. also Luke's redaction of Mark in the Joseph of Arimathea pericope (Luke 23: 50–6); Luke contrasts Joseph and those responsible for Jesus' death, and includes a character sketch which goes beyond the bald facts stated in Mark.

[3] Luke's own hand is indicated by the following evidence: (*a*) There is an interesting parallel to ἤρξαντο δὲ κατηγορεῖν (23: 2) in Acts 24: 2, ἤρξατο κατηγορεῖν ὁ Τέρτυλλος where the context is similar – the high priest's spokesman accuses Paul before Felix. (*b*) διαστρέφω also occurs in Acts 13: 8, 10 and 20: 30, all in a context of turning from the faith. The only other occurrence is Luke 9: 41 (= Matt. 17: 17, addition to Mark, possibly from Q). (*c*) τὸ ἔθνος, used of the Jewish people, is a favourite Lucan expression not used by Mark or Matthew (6 times in Acts; Luke 7:

directed the attention of the reader to Jesus and allowed other participants in the drama of the passion to fade into the background. Luke's hand can often be discerned; this trait cannot be dismissed as a coincidence due to Luke's non-Marcan source. Luke separates Jesus from others, not in order to present Jesus in splendid isolation, but to characterise him in contradistinction to those with whom he comes in contact. The disciples, Judas, Peter, the Sanhedrin, Pilate, Herod, the crowd, Barabbas, the daughters of Jerusalem, the two criminals, the rulers, the soldiers and the centurion all enter the stage for varying lengths of time and respond to Jesus in different ways. All are contrasted with Jesus and yet are influenced by him in some way. Luke focusses attention on the chief actor by this method of indirect characterisation rather than by his own direct comments or even by the words of Jesus – except in the Last Supper scene. While Luke may or may not have been aware of literary methods of characterisation used by Hellenistic writers, his use of contrasting characters, his careful concentration on Jesus, his rearrangement of his

5 is from Luke's hand, as a Lucan narrative is added to the Q dialogue at this point). (d) The phrase φόρον δοῦναι is found only at Luke 20: 22 and here. At Luke 20: 22 Luke has altered Mark's Latinism, κῆνσον (also in Matthew) to φόρον. 20b and 26a are intended by Luke to refer to 23: 2. τοῦ ἡγεμόνος refers to Pilate (cf. 3: 1). The use of φόρος in Luke 20: 19–26, which prepares for 23: 2, points to Luke's own hand. (e) αἴτιον as a noun is found only in Pilate's three declarations of the innocence of Jesus (23: 4, 14, 22) and at Acts 19: 40. (f) καθ᾽ ὅλης τῆς Ἰουδαίας and ἀρξάμενος ἀπὸ τῆς Γαλιλαίας reappear at Acts 10: 37 and may be Lucan rather than from a source. (This is disputed; a firm decision is difficult.) (g) In Acts, Luke does not simply record accusations against Stephen, Paul and Silas, and others, but places them in the mouth of their accusers, as in Luke 23. (Cf. Acts 6: 11, 13; 16: 20; 21: 28; 24: 5–6.) The accusations against 'Jason and some of the brethren' (Acts 17: 6–7) provide a direct parallel with Luke 23: 2 and are listed in the same order.

	Luke 23: 2	Acts 17: 6–7
(i) disturbance	διαστρέφοντα τὸ ἔθνος ἡμῶν	οἱ τὴν οἰκουμένην ἀναστατώσαντες...
(ii) Caesar	κωλύοντα φόρους Καίσαρι διδόναι	οὗτοι πάντες ἀπέναντι τῶν δογμάτων Καίσαρος πράσσουσιν
(iii) another king	λέγοντα ἑαυτὸν Χριστὸν βασιλέα εἶναι	βασιλέα ἕτερον λέγοντες εἶναι Ἰησοῦν

46

traditions and his indirect characterisation are, as will be shown in chapter 5, precisely the methods of character portrayal found in the well-educated writers of Luke's day.

There is a very much more firmly drawn portrait of Jesus in Luke's passion narrative, but Luke has not redrawn the Marcan portrait of Jesus from a new 'biographical' perspective, replacing the stark tragedy of Mark with an account of a martyrdom which emphasises the high human qualities of the character of Jesus. Luke's distinctive portrait of Jesus arises partly from his use of non-Marcan material which has its own particular features. But even more important is the way in which Luke shapes stylistically both the Marcan and non-Marcan traditions he weaves together: Luke's distinctive contribution, over against his sources, is literary, even dramatic, rather than theological.

II LUKE AS BIOGRAPHER

Luke has frequently been singled out as the biographer among the evangelists. Luke is said to part company with Mark and with the earlier independent gospel traditions and understand and present traditions about Jesus from a biographical rather than from a kerygmatic standpoint.

Luke's account of the twelve-year-old Jesus in the temple is often cited as the clearest evidence of his intention to write an edifying biography of Jesus. Luke 2: 40–52 has long been a favourite passage with biographers of Jesus; it has provoked many conjectures about the 'hidden years' of Jesus, his education, the sights he saw from the hill behind Nazareth and life in the carpenter's shop! R. Bultmann claims that these verses are the only exception to the rule that the gospel traditions contain no interest in the βίος of Jesus in a purely historical sense.[1]

Considerable biographical interest in the birth and youth of Jesus can be found in many second century (and later) writings, but does Luke intend to satisfy biographical curiosity

---

[1] *Synoptic Tradition*, pp. 306f. See also, M. Kähler, *The So-Called Historical Jesus and the Historic Biblical Christ* (Philadelphia, 1964), p. 50; H. Sahlin, *Der Messias und das Gottesvolk: Studien zur protolukanischen Theologie* (Uppsala, 1945), p. 310; Dibelius, *Tradition*, pp. 106ff.

with at least some information about the youth of Jesus?[1] What is the main point of the narrative in its present setting?[2] It is often taken to be the amazing wisdom of Jesus. But Jesus is not depicted here as a child prodigy. Luke tells us nothing about the matters under discussion; Jesus is not a διδάσκαλος. Those who heard Jesus were amazed at his σύνεσις (verse 47), but the σύνεσις of Jesus is not his intellectual powers, his intelligence, for it refers back to the listening and questioning of the previous verse. It was not unusual for a boy to ask questions in this manner. If Luke had wished to depict Jesus as a child prodigy, he would have made Jesus dominate the scene, as in the long tradition in Christian art.

In the frequently cited parallels the person concerned is depicted much more clearly as a prodigy or genius than is Jesus in Luke.[3] This is underlined by a comparison with the account of this incident in the *Infancy Gospel of Thomas*,[4] a parallel which has, surprisingly, been almost totally neglected

[1] See the material assembled and discussed by W. Bauer, *Das Leben Jesu im Zeitalter der neutestamentlichen Apokryphen* (Tübingen, 1909). O. Cullmann notes that, unlike the New Testament infancy traditions, narrative interests became predominant in the later apocryphal material: *New Testament Apocrypha*, ed. E. Hennecke, 1 (E.T. London, 1963), 366.

[2] The traditio-historical question is particularly complicated. On the one hand there is a high percentage of typically Lucan words and expressions (see B. van Iersel, 'The Finding of Jesus in the Temple', *NovT* **4** (1960), 166ff. for details). On the other hand, the paratactic structure is striking – this would be consistent with Lucan redaction of a Semitic source. (See E. Schweizer, 'Eine hebraisierende Sonderquelle des Lukas?', *TZ* **6** (1950), 161ff.; Schweizer notes that καί is used in the Semitic paratactic style 8 times more frequently in the *Sonderquelle* than in the latter half of Acts.)

[3] See R. Bultmann, *Synoptic Tradition*, pp. 300f.; W. Grundmann, comm. *ad loc.*; R. Laurentin, *Jésus au Temple* (Paris, 1966), pp. 154ff.

[4] The Greek text referred to is Tischendorf's text, as quoted in *Synopsis Quattuor Evangeliorum*, ed. K. Aland (Stuttgart, 1964), p. 18. See also the reconstruction of the Greek 'Vorlage' by A. de Santos Otero, *Das kirchenslavische Evangelium des Thomas* (Berlin, 1967), pp. 167f. There are some differences between the texts, but they do not affect the points made below. A. de Santos Otero claims that the original text included a number of gnostic motifs hidden or lost in Tischendorf's 'textus receptus' (pp. 172ff.). The Jesus of the *Infancy Gospel* is thus seen not as a performer of remarkable miracles, but as the pre-existent Logos who knows all the secrets of the world, to whom the key of truth is entrusted. But this is not entirely convincing, for typical gnostic themes are almost entirely absent from the

by New Testament scholars.[1] The apocryphal account follows Luke's pericope closely until verse 47, where the Lucan emphasis is altered considerably.[2] 'προσεῖχον δὲ πάντες καὶ ἐθαύμαζον πῶς παιδίον ὑπάρχων ἀποστομίζει τοὺς πρεσβυτέρους καὶ διδασκάλους τοῦ λαοῦ, ἐπιλύων τὰ κεφάλαια τοῦ νόμου καὶ τὰς παραβολὰς τῶν προφητῶν.' Although Luke's ἐξίσταντο is certainly a strong expression of amazement, the two verbs in the apocryphal account strengthen the astonishment of the listeners; Jesus 'stops the mouth of the elders and teachers'. Here the topics involved are mentioned specifically; the child prodigy has become the focus of the pericope. Although the Lucan saying of Jesus is retained, this is no longer the key pronouncement. The *Infancy Gospel* drops completely the contrast between Mary's word, 'ἰδοὺ ὁ πατήρ σου κἀγὼ...' and the reply of Jesus 'ἐν τοῖς τοῦ πατρός μου...', which lies at the very heart of Luke's pericope. The words of the scribes and Pharisees to Mary, which follow the saying of Jesus, become the focal point of the whole story: μακαρία σὺ εἶ ἐν γυναιξίν, ὅτι ηὐλόγησεν ὁ θεὸς τὸν καρπὸν τῆς κοιλίας σου. τοιαύτην γὰρ δόξαν καὶ τοιαύτην ἀρετὴν καὶ σοφίαν οὔτε ἴδομεν οὔτε ἠκούσαμέν ποτε. Mary receives praise and honour for the excellence and wisdom of Jesus.

In Luke 2: 51 Mary hides πάντα τὰ ῥήματα in her heart, the words of Jesus in 2: 49; this logion is the whole point of Luke's account. But in the *Infancy Gospel* Mary does not hide the words of Jesus in her heart, but πάντα τὰ γενόμενα. Mary ponders the extraordinary events, the silencing of the teachers and the teaching of Jesus on κεφάλαια τοῦ νόμου καὶ τὰς παραβολὰς τῶν προφητῶν; the words of Jesus in 2: 49 have faded into the background.

Infancy Gospel. So also S. Gero, 'The Infancy Gospel of Thomas', *Nov T* **13** (1971), 74ff.

Dating the *Infancy Gospel* is extremely difficult. Although it undoubtedly rests on earlier traditions, it may not have been written down (in its earliest versions) before the fifth century. See Gero, 'Infancy Gospel', p. 56 n. 1.

[1] R. Laurentin does not consider the alterations to the Lucan pericope in his monograph on Luke 2: 48–50, *Jésus au Temple*.

[2] However, in comparison with the earlier chapters of the *Infancy Gospel*, which do not follow any biblical material, its rewriting of Luke's pericope is very restrained! Compare *Infancy Gospel* 16 (the child Jesus heals a viper bite) and Acts 28: 3ff. (Paul's viper bite).

If Luke had intended to tell a story about a child prodigy, the *Infancy Gospel* shows how he might have done it. In Luke the σύνεσις is only a minor theme mentioned almost in passing in a narrative which reaches its climax at 2: 49. But in the *Infancy Gospel* the logion of Jesus plays only a minor role; many other words of Jesus have already been recorded.

Luke's account can be regarded as a 'paradigm' or 'apophthegm' as the narrative before the logion in 2: 49 is purely preparatory. This logion echoes many of Luke's theological themes and is paralleled in meaning, if not wording, elsewhere in the gospel traditions.[1] The 'δεῖ' motif, the 'temple' and 'Jerusalem' motifs, Jesus' Sonship, and his relationship with Mary, are all major Lucan emphases. The latter theme is particularly important – it is Mary who speaks in verse 48 and is mentioned again in the concluding comment, possibly Lucan, in verse 51.[2] Luke 2: 33ff. and 8: 19–21 are especially relevant. At Luke 8: 21 Luke revises the Marcan narrative: those who hear and act on the word of God – which Luke understands as the Christian message – are 'related' to Jesus, rather than those who stand in any sort of a physical relationship to him. Once the logion in 2: 49 is taken as the point of the pericope, however it is interpreted in detail, the preceding narrative is seen not as purely biographical, but as leading up to the main point.[3] If, as in the *Infancy Gospel*, Jesus'

---

[1] See Laurentin, *Jésus au Temple*. Laurentin's case, however, is overstated, for he tends to make the logion foreshadow the whole of Lucan theology, from divine Sonship to the passion, resurrection and ascension! His discussion of parallels in Johannine thought is instructive: pp. 111ff.

[2] Grundmann notes that there is a double conclusion, one concerning Jesus and one Mary; but both conclusions revolve around the relationship between Jesus and Mary: comm. *ad loc.*

[3] B. van Iersel, 'Finding', *NovT* **4**, 161ff., argues convincingly that this pericope is a good example of a paradigm which is neither legendary nor novellistic. However, his hypothesis that verses 44 and 47 are Lucan interpolations is less convincing. He argues that grammatically the subject of ἰδόντες in verse 48 should be πάντες οἱ ἀκούοντες αὐτοῦ, not οἱ γονεῖς αὐτοῦ. But the earlier part of the narrative leaves no doubt about the subject of ἰδόντες; it is simply understood to be οἱ γονεῖς αὐτοῦ. The vocabulary of verse 44 does not necessarily point to a Lucan interpolation. While frequent usage of καί instead of δέ suggests a Semitic background, use of δέ can hardly be used to support isolation of Luke's own hand.

amazing wisdom is the main point of the pericope, the earlier narrative serves a biographical rather than a 'theological' purpose.

It is not possible to contrast biographical and kerygmatic interest in this pericope and claim that these verses are quite unlike other gospel traditions.[1] Luke's primary intention is neither to edify, nor to show psychological insight into the personality of the youthful Jesus, nor to provide hints about the hidden years, but to proclaim Jesus by means of a story which reveals his unique relationship to his parents and to his Father. Only in the *Infancy Gospel*'s version does the narrative intend to satisfy biographical curiosity, to tell a story about the extraordinary wisdom of a child prodigy.

There is no doubt that many aspects of the character of Jesus are found more clearly and extensively in Luke than elsewhere, but it is not easy to discern whether this arises from his own emphases or from the sources at his disposal. Luke certainly did not write the L traditions himself, and while he made them his own by using them, they do not necessarily reflect distinctive features of Luke's approach to the life of Jesus.

A large proportion of the traits usually noted as Luke's special interests or emphases are not unique, but are represented in other gospel strata.[2] Some traits often taken as indications of Luke's concern to sketch out the biography of Jesus, to emphasise his high human qualities or his piety, turn out, on closer inspection, to be much more intimately linked to Luke's theological emphases.[3] In order to clarify Luke's methods, one

[1] Luke 2: 40 and 52 might be taken as a biographical note, but in fact this is a traditional way of speaking of a prophet's childhood; John the Baptist is spoken of in a similar way (cf. 1: 80 and 1: 66).

[2] E.g., Jesus' concern for the socially ostracised and his attitude towards women. V. Taylor sketches out the portrait of Jesus in Proto-Luke, but admits that it has much in common with the Marcan delineation: *Behind the Third Gospel* (Oxford, 1926), p. 264.

[3] Take, for example, the more numerous references in Luke to Jesus at prayer. Dibelius links this to Luke's biographical presentation of Jesus as a pious man: *Gospel Criticism*, p. 54. But references to Jesus at prayer are to be connected with Luke's understanding of the Spirit. See G. W. H. Lampe, 'The Holy Spirit in the Writings of St Luke' in *Studies in the Gospels*, ed. D. E. Nineham (Oxford, 1955), pp. 169f.; also H. Greeven, art.

cannot merely concentrate on traditions found only in Luke's Gospel; the way such traditions are used by Luke is of much greater significance and this can be traced easily only where Luke's redaction of Marcan or Q material is visible. While the L traditions give a very different appearance to Luke's Gospel, there is little evidence from these traditions alone which suggests that they were used and understood before Luke or by Luke himself in a fundamentally different way to other strata of the synoptic traditions: they present a rich but not an essentially new portrait of Jesus; they are not significantly more biographical and less kerygmatic than other gospel traditions.

Luke's methods and intentions emerge particularly clearly in Acts; for in writing Acts Luke was much less hampered by his traditions than he was in the Gospel, for we know from his use of Mark that he was reluctant to revise the teaching of Jesus in the traditions he used. An examination of Luke's presentation of Paul, who is plainly his hero, sheds light both on his abilities as a biographer and on their limits. There is no doubt that Luke has succeeded in portraying Paul vividly. When Luke was interested in a person, as he was in Paul, he was able to indicate clearly the character of the person concerned. Paul is portrayed through an account of his actions, his speeches, and through the comments and reactions of others. Even in setting out the character of his hero, Luke did not go beyond such simple methods; he does not supply a character sketch of Paul in his own words. Character development is found only in the broad general sense of change from 'bad' to 'good' known in the ancient world. However, the 'external' progress of Paul is traced with skill and attention to detail. Acts underlines Luke's stylistic and literary abilities, but confirms that simple and unsophisticated methods of characterisation could be used to sketch out a clear and rich portrait of a person.

But Luke's considerable literary skills were not utilised in order to set out the life of Paul in either the ancient or the

'εὔχομαι', *TWNT*, II, 801, and W. Ott, *Gebet und Heil: die Bedeutung der Gebetsparänese in der lukanischen Theologie* (Munich, 1965). Luke's avoidance or toning down of some of the Marcan passages which seem to ascribe harshness or sternness to Jesus is shared by Matthew.

modern sense. Luke was either unable to do this, or uninterested in such a project. The narrative stops once the 'theological', not the 'biographical', goal is reached. If a life of Paul lay beyond Luke's abilities or intentions, even though the narrative of the latter half of Acts stems much more directly from his own hand than does his Gospel, a firm question mark must be placed against any suggestion that he has reshaped the gospel traditions into a life of Jesus.

This suggestion finds some support from the hints in Acts which indicate that although Luke's style and vocabulary is nearly always visible, he was reluctant to go beyond his sources even where his narrative might have been enhanced had he done so. His presentation of Peter and Paul is completely different: in spite of the often observed apparent parallelisms between the actions of Peter and Paul, Peter is not portrayed with the clarity and richness found in Luke's treatment of Paul. Since Peter plays such a prominent role in the first part of Acts, and since Luke exhibits no anti-Petrine bias, one might have expected Luke to have characterised Peter more clearly at many points.[1] The absence of chronological, geographical and other incidental details in this part of Acts is also in clear contrast to the latter half of the book. The sketchy account of Herod's persecution of the church and of the martyrdom of James is a good example of Luke's refusal to go beyond his sources (Acts 12: 1–2).[2] These are no more than hints, but they do suggest that Luke's intention was not to provide edifying biographical narrative. Where he was able to embellish his narrative with incidental detail, he did so, but he did not alter his traditions about Peter in this direction, in spite of all the literary and dramatic skill he was able to utilise.

The evidence of Acts suggests that while Luke was able to present a vivid character portrait with considerable literary

[1] There is some evidence which suggests that the D text was conscious of this deficiency and sought to rectify it. See J. Crehan, 'Peter According to the D Text of Acts', *Theological Studies* **18** (1957), 596ff.; also E. J. Epp, *The Theological Tendency of Codex Bezae Cantabrigiensis in Acts* (Cambridge, 1966), pp. 154ff. It is possible to show from Luke's use of Mark that he has neither enhanced nor made less significant the role of Peter in the Gospel.

[2] As A. Harnack noted wryly, Clement of Alexandria knew more about the Herodian persecution than Luke!

skill, he is unlikely to have been interested in a biography or to have reshaped traditions to this end. This is precisely what we find in the Gospel: there is a vivid character portrait of Jesus, but not a biography; there is considerable evidence of editorial, literary and stylistic activity, but not an embellishment and expansion of traditions in order to provide a biographical narrative.

The 'traditional' view of Luke's Gospel as the biography among the four Gospels looks primarily to the additional material found in Luke's Gospel: the infancy narratives, passages such as Luke 3: 1ff., and the L traditions with their rich character portrait of Jesus. If the term 'biography' is defined with sufficient care, it may still be legitimate to describe Luke as the biographer among the evangelists, but there are many reasons for hesitation. Luke's additional material does not in itself suggest that he evaluated the gospel traditions from a new perspective and intended them to be biographical and to record the life of a hero-martyr. At Luke 2: 40–52 the apparently biographical preliminary narrative serves only to lead up to and to introduce a logion of Jesus in a way not strikingly different from a large number of other gospel pericopae. As if to confirm that he does not intend to write a biography of Jesus, but, like Mark, to set out traditions about the life and character of Jesus in order to proclaim him, Luke's narrative is even less chronologically precise than Mark's.[1]

---

[1] Earlier writers and commentators usually took it for granted that Luke carried out his intention to write his Gospel καθεξῆς, which was understood as chronological order. Where chronological links between pericopae were missing, the traditions were assumed nevertheless to stand in chronological order.

But Marcan chronological expressions often become less precise in Luke (cf., e.g., Luke 9: 28 and Mark 9: 2; Luke 8: 22 and Mark 4: 35); Luke's chronology often seems to be deliberately vague (e.g. Luke regularly avoids the frequent Marcan εὐθύς; Luke's favourite link word ἐγένετο is quite rare by comparison in Mark). Nor is there a more precise chronology in the non-Marcan sections of the Gospel; in the so-called travel narrative, arranged by Luke himself, there are few chronological, or even geographical references.

As a good example of Luke's method, cf. Mark 3: 1 with Matt. 12: 9 and Luke 6: 6. Mark is ambiguous; it is possible to assume that the pericope concerning the man with the withered hand took place on the

III LUKE AS THEOLOGIAN OF THE LIFE OF JESUS

In recent studies of Luke–Acts, Luke's distinctive theological perspective is often held to carry as a corollary the production of the first life of Jesus. Luke is still the biographer *par excellence* among the evangelists, but attention has shifted from his sources and his unique material to his theological interpretation of the traditions he uses. Luke is again the innovator who understands the life and character of Jesus in a new and distinctive way.

This more recent interpretation of Luke is especially associated with H. Conzelmann's important monograph, *Die Mitte der Zeit*.[1] Luke, Conzelmann insists, looks back to the life of Jesus as the central epoch of *Heilsgeschichte*; the life of Jesus is the period of the manifestation of salvation, a period in which Satan was far away, a period strictly defined as to its beginning and end. Luke's new interpretation leads to greater elaboration in the description of the ministry which he sets out in three stages. Thus the distinctive features of Luke's presentation of Jesus are linked to his theological perspective.

For Luke, unlike Mark, the narrative is not a broad unfolding of the kerygma, but the historical foundation which is added as a secondary factor to the kerygma, a knowledge of which is taken for granted. The acts and words of Jesus during his lifetime become 'normative' and exercise their influence in the present; the church can endure in the world because it possesses an account of Jesus which can never be lost. In particular, in the life of Jesus – the time of salvation *par excellence* – a picture is given of the future time of salvation, a picture that is now the ground of the church's hope.

Does Luke's new perspective imply that whereas traditions about the life and character of Jesus had been understood and used earlier as proclamation of the Risen and Present Lord, they were intended by Luke to refer to Jesus of Nazareth,

same day as the preceding pericope on the plucking of grain on the sabbath. Matthew makes it clear that both incidents *did* happen on the same sabbath. Luke's introduction is deliberately vague – ἐν ἑτέρῳ σαββάτῳ; he has carefully avoided imposing a chronological framework on the traditions.　　　　　[1] E.T. *The Theology of St Luke*.

a figure of past history? This is the basic point at issue. Serious criticisms can be levelled against Conzelmann's interpretation of Luke's distinctive approach to the life of Jesus.

Jesus and John the Baptist

H. Conzelmann insists that Luke's view of the life of Jesus is determined by its role as the central epoch of a distinct and special period of salvation history which is strictly defined as to its beginning and end. Neither the beginning nor the end of the central epoch is as clearly delineated as Conzelmann contends. Conzelmann claims that Luke has redacted the John the Baptist traditions in order to separate Jesus from the Baptist. John belongs to the epoch of the law and prophets; only after John was the Kingdom of God preached. Luke carefully avoids portraying John as the 'forerunner', as the one whose appearance marked the beginning of the new eschatological age.

This interpretation of Luke's presentation of John the Baptist has been severely and effectively criticised by W. C. Robinson[1] and W. Wink[2]; their work is largely independent and, taken together, indicates clearly that Conzelmann has grossly exaggerated Lucan *Tendenz* and that many of the alleged Lucan peculiarities are shared by Mark, Matthew or Q. The detailed exegetical criticisms need not be repeated here.[3] While both writers agree that Luke is much less 'Lucan' and much more 'synoptic' than Conzelmann allows, their own interpretations of the features of Luke's narrative, to which Conzelmann appeals, differ. W. C. Robinson alleges

[1] W. C. Robinson, 'The Way of the Lord' (typescript, Basel, 1962); translated as *Der Weg des Herrn, Studien zur Geschichte und Eschatologie im Lukas-Evangelium* (Hamburg, 1964).

[2] W. Wink, *John the Baptist in the Gospel Tradition* (Cambridge, 1968). See also P. S. Minear, 'Luke's Use of the Birth Stories', *Studies in Luke-Acts* (Festschrift P. Schubert), eds. L. E. Keck and J. L. Martyn (London, 1966), pp. 121ff.; S. G. Wilson, 'Lukan Eschatology', *NTS* **15** (1970), 330–47.

[3] Both W. C. Robinson and W. Wink are especially critical of Conzelmann's view that Luke separates Jesus and John geographically ('The Way', pp. 5ff.; *John the Baptist*, pp. 49ff.), and of his interpretation of Luke 16: 16 ('The Way', pp. 13ff.; *John the Baptist*, pp. 51f.).

'Christological anti-Baptist apologetic', while W. Wink revises Conzelmann's analysis of the sub-epochs of *Heilsgeschichte*.[1] Each writer's monograph criticises effectively the explanation of Luke's presentation of John offered by the other: W. Wink shows convincingly that it is an over-simplification to claim that Luke is engaged in anti-Baptist polemic;[2] W. C. Robinson shows that Conzelmann's division of the ministry of Jesus into three sub-epochs (extended by W. Wink to four sub-epochs)[3] is untenable.[4] Hence the proposed alternatives to H. Conzelmann's interpretation largely cancel each other out. If Luke has re-interpreted his traditions neither 'theologically' (W. C. Robinson), nor 'schematically' (W. Wink), is there another possibility?

Some of the phenomena of Luke's narrative to which Conzelmann has called attention can be accounted for in terms of Luke's superior stylistic abilities. Conzelmann supports his hypothesis largely by pointing to details of Luke's narrative in chapter 3 which are alleged to tie in with his interpretation of Luke 16: 16. But the 'pre-Lucan' meaning of this logion and Luke's understanding of it need much more thorough investigation than Conzelmann has offered.[5] An interpretation completely contrary to H. Conzelmann's is more plausible: μέχρι 'Ιωάννου may well exclude John from the time of the law and the prophets. Luke 16: 16 cannot be used as the key to the interpretation of chapter 3.

When Luke's overall presentation of the opening of the ministry of Jesus is examined, the orderliness of his narrative in chapters 3, 4 and 5 is striking. A stylistic and 'dramatic' construction similar to that found in other parts of Luke–Acts is evident. Luke has separated his 'Jesus' and 'John the Baptist' material neither as part of his division of salvation history into closely defined periods, nor in the interests of anti-Baptist polemic, but for purely stylistic reasons: he wishes to sketch

---

[1] 'The Way', p. 23 *et al.*; *John the Baptist*, p. 55.

[2] *John the Baptist*, pp. 82ff.   [3] *John the Baptist*, p. 56.

[4] 'The Way', pp. 24ff.

[5] See now, W. G. Kümmel, 'Das Gesetz und die Propheten gehen bis Johannes – Lukas 16, 16 im Zusammenhang der heilsgeschichtlichen Theologie der Lukasschriften', *Verborum Veritas* (Festschrift G. Stählin), eds. O. Böcher and K. Haacker (Wuppertal, 1970), pp. 89–102.

out the roles of John and Jesus separately, focussing attention on one person at a time.

This apparently naïve explanation is supported by our earlier observation that in the passion narratives Luke has deliberately revised Marcan and other material, in order to separate Jesus from those around him and so allow him to dominate the scene. And, in addition, we may note that Luke is consistent and skilful in the order in which he places the names of men in his narratives.[1]

In chapters 4 and 5 Luke takes pains to focus attention on Jesus, allowing other named persons (the disciples) to enter the scene only gradually. Jesus dominates the opening scenes of the ministry; there is no room for Simon, Andrew, James and John as in the Marcan traditions on which Luke drew. The disciples are carefully excluded from the beginning of Luke's narrative and are introduced only after the very important account of Jesus' initial teaching in the synagogue at Nazareth (Luke 4: 16–30), in which Luke gives the reader a summary of the character of Jesus' ministry. If Luke 4: 16 is partly dependent on Mark 6: 1f., the disciples have been deliberately excluded. In Mark 1: 21 Simon, Andrew, James and John go into Capernaum with Jesus; in Luke's account (4: 31) Jesus is alone. The verbal similarities between Mark 1:

---

[1] Two examples may be given: (*a*) At Luke 8: 51 Luke lists 'Peter and John and James', deliberately revising the Marcan order 'Peter and James and John' (Mark 5: 37). Similarly at Luke 9: 28 = Mark 9: 2. Both passages reflect the pattern of the early chapters of Acts where Peter and John appear together a number of times. But Luke retains the Marcan order, 'James and John', whenever Peter is not involved, as at Luke 5: 10; 6: 14 (Peter is linked with his brother Andrew to form a pair); and 9: 54. Whenever Peter is in view, the order is 'Peter and John' (cf. Luke 22: 8 and Acts 1: 13, 3: 1 *et al.*), and only then is James mentioned, if at all. (*b*) In the first references to Barnabas and Saul, Barnabas always precedes Saul (Acts 11: 30; 12: 25; 13: 1, 2, 7). At 13: 9 Luke first uses the name Paul, noting that Paul was filled with the Holy Spirit; henceforth Paul becomes the dominant partner and precedes Barnabas (cf. 13: 43, 46, 50; 14: 20 etc.). Luke has taken pains to show how Paul emerged gradually as a leader, carefully mentioning that he was filled with the Spirit just as he begins to 'surpass' Barnabas. The exceptions prove the rule. At 14: 12, 14 Barnabas precedes Paul; as senior partner Barnabas was named Zeus, the father of Hermes. At 15: 12, 25 Barnabas' seniority is again recognised.

29–31 and Luke 4: 38–9 are so marked that there is no doubt that Luke has used and revised Mark. The singular verb in 4: 38 (εἰσῆλθεν) is no mere accident; Simon is introduced, as it were, only in passing – Luke does not even mention that he was present in the house. At the end of the chapter Luke deliberately omits Mark's reference to Simon and the other disciples who followed Jesus to the place where he prayed (cf. Luke 4: 42 with Mark 1: 36).

Luke 5: 1–11 is of special importance in this overall pattern. This pericope is not a striking example of Luke's theological *Tendenz*, but of his method of presenting Jesus and the disciples. Advocates of the former view have drawn attention to Luke's concentration on Peter and his exclusion of James and John from the foreground (until verse 10 their presence is only hinted at) and to the complete disappearance of Andrew from Luke's pericope (although he appears with Simon in Mark 1: 16). In verse 11 James and John, as well as Simon, leave everything and follow Jesus, yet in the preceding verse Jesus has spoken only to Simon.[1]

But in this pericope Luke has carefully and deliberately focussed attention on Jesus and Simon Peter as part of his overall 'dramatic' method in the opening narratives of the ministry of Jesus. As is often the case, Luke has used some Marcan material in the introduction (Mark 4: 1–2) and conclusion (Mark 1: 16ff.); the non-Marcan 'core' has been strongly revised by Luke himself. Hence the distinctive features of the pericope cannot be attributed to the traditions Luke has used. Simon is the only disciple named at first, not because of any Lucan intention to enhance his position, but as part of Luke's presentation of Jesus. Simon's reference to himself as ἁμαρτωλός, even though he has yet to show that he is sinful, serves to characterise Jesus indirectly; it is not an indication that the pericope was originally a post-resurrection

---

[1] K. Zillesen claims that Luke has retrojected his view of the history of the primitive church into this pericope. Luke intends to indicate that authentic proclamation is found only in Peter's church; the companions in the other ship, whose assistance is required, become the Pauline mission! According to Luke, Paul is only an assistant, even though he is especially chosen and successful. 'Das Schiff des Petrus und die Gefährten vom andern Schiff: zur Exegese von Luc 5: 1–11', *ZNW* **57** (1966), 137ff.

incident. Jesus dominates the whole pericope and initiates all the action. Andrew disappears from Luke's account and only emerges with the rest of the disciples at 6: 14 because he will play a much less important role in Luke–Acts than James and John. James and John are left in the background neither through an oversight nor because of some special Lucan *Tendenz*, but because Luke wishes to concentrate attention on Jesus and Simon in the first pericope in which disciples are found.

These features of Luke 5: 1–11 and Luke's earlier omission of Mark's references to Simon, Andrew, James and John, are linked to his rearrangement of Mark's account of the opening of the ministry and the prominence given to Jesus' appearance in the synagogue at Nazareth. Luke 5: 1–11 has been introduced into a block of Marcan material; this is not Luke's usual method. The pericope could conceivably have been introduced into Mark's narrative at an earlier point.[1] Only after Jesus has dominated the opening of the ministry without any 'distraction' from the disciples are Simon Peter and, later, James and John, allowed to appear.[2]

Hence Luke 3 must be seen as part of Luke's overall presentation of the beginning of the ministry of Jesus. His summary account of John the Baptist's imprisonment is included at this point simply because he wishes to round off the story of John before beginning his carefully constructed account of the beginning of Jesus' ministry. The preceding verses have summed up the ministry and message of John in some detail. Once the ministry of Jesus has begun and his disciples have been introduced gradually, there will be no room for an account of John the Baptist's imprisonment and death; Luke probably saw the Marcan pericope as an irrelevant and unnecessary interlude in the story of Jesus.

The omission of reference to the name of John in the account of the baptism of Jesus is not completely surprising: Luke's

---

[1] Luke carefully introduces οἱ ὄχλοι into 4: 42 (cf. Mark 1: 36) in order to prepare for 5: 1.

[2] Cf. K. L. Schmidt's observation that Luke has reversed the order of Mark 3: 7–12 and 13–19, and so set out Jesus' *audience* in an orderly fashion *a minori ad maius*: (*a*) the 12 apostles, (*b*) the wider circle of disciples, (*c*) the crowds: *Der Rahmen der Geschichte Jesu* (Berlin, 1919), p. 113. Schmidt notes a similar intentional development in the places mentioned by Luke: Nazareth, Capernaum, Galilee: *Rahmen*, pp. 38ff.

main interest is in the descent of the Spirit (cf. Luke 3: 16, 22; 4: 1, 14, 18). There is a parallel in Acts to Luke's presentation of Jesus and John: as soon as Luke notes that Paul is filled with the Spirit, Barnabas fades into the background.[1] In a similar way, Luke intends to concentrate attention on Jesus here and so omits reference to John in 3: 21; in addition explicit reference to John might have been considered inconsistent with 3: 20. However, Luke probably intends to indicate that Jesus was baptised by John. Certainly the narrative implies that 'all the people' were baptised by John (3: 21); the preceding narrative has already prepared for this (3: 15, 16). If Luke had intended to exclude the mediation of John from the baptism of Jesus (3: 21b), the reference to 'all the people' in the preceding clause (3: 21a) would have been omitted.[2]

Luke does not always succeed in removing inconsistencies, especially where Mark's order has been rearranged.[3] The narrative of Jesus' baptism involves neither a 'de-emphasis' of John,[4] nor is John excluded deliberately from the period of the ministry of Jesus.[5] Luke wishes to round off the story of John the Baptist before beginning his account of the ministry and teaching of Jesus for 'dramatic' reasons;[6] his theological

[1] See p. 58 n. 1 above.

[2] W. Wink suggests that βαπτισθέντος is intended to be taken as 'baptised himself'; no one else is there to baptise Jesus! *John the Baptist*, p. 83 n. 1. Conzelmann admits that Luke has not entirely eliminated overlapping of the activity of Jesus and John, and notes that according to 3: 21f., Jesus is baptised as one of the people, like everyone else: *Theology of St Luke*, p. 21.

[3] Cf. Luke 4: 23 – reference to Jesus' previous ministry at Capernaum, even though Nazareth is the opening scene of the ministry; cf. also Luke 4: 44.   [4] *Contra* W. C. Robinson, 'The Way', p. 8.

[5] *Contra* Wink, *John the Baptist*, p. 55; Conzelmann, *Theology of St Luke*, passim.

[6] S. G. Wilson ('Lukan Eschatology', *NTS* **15** (1970), 332) rejects G. B. Caird's similar explanation on two grounds: (*a*) If Luke had only wanted to separate the ministries of the two men he could have related John's imprisonment between Luke 3: 22 and 23. But this would have interrupted Luke's account of the opening of the ministry of Jesus, with its emphasis on the descent of the Spirit. (*b*) At several points Luke seems concerned to interweave the chronology and significance of John and Jesus. This is certainly true, but the case argued here is not affected: Luke separates Jesus and John in order to focus attention on Jesus – he does not thereby imply that they have nothing to do with each other.

purpose in chapter 3 is much more closely linked to the role of the Spirit than to polemic against John, or to a scheme of *Heilsgeschichte* which involves a new way of looking at the life and character of Jesus.

Luke 3: 16 provides a further example of Luke's redaction of an earlier tradition which is stylistically rather than theologically motivated. H. Conzelmann notes that Luke omits ὀπίσω μου in 3: 16 as part of his rejection of the 'precursor' motif: John is the last of the prophets.[1] W. C. Robinson rejects this interpretation, explaining the omission as anti-Baptist apologetic; Luke wanted to avoid any suggestion that Jesus was the Baptist's disciple.[2] But we have noted that as part of his more vivid presentation of Jesus in the passion narratives, Luke makes others follow behind Jesus. For example, in 23: 26 he adds ὄπισθεν τοῦ 'Ιησοῦ to Mark 15: 21 in order to indicate that Simon of Cyrene did not walk in front of Jesus. Luke constantly avoids focussing attention on someone other than Jesus. Hence, although Luke can say that Jesus came after John *in time* (Acts 10: 37; 13: 25; 19: 4), he is reluctant to suggest that Jesus 'followed behind' John. Luke's stylistic redaction does not necessarily carry as a corollary an attempt to minimise the role of the other person; his primary concern is to make his presentation of Jesus more vivid by refusing to allow anyone else to dominate the scene.

When these considerations are added to W. C. Robinson's and W. Wink's convincing and detailed criticisms of H. Conzelmann's discussion of the relationship between Jesus and John, it is clear that Luke has not carefully separated Jesus and John in order to mark the beginning of the ministry as the central epoch of *Heilsgeschichte*. As in the infancy narratives, so in later chapters of Luke–Acts, the coming of both Jesus and John marks the beginning of the time of fulfilment. Nor is the close of H. Conzelmann's 'central epoch' clearly defined by Luke. W. C. Robinson notes that Conzelmann himself refers to no fewer than seven possible divisions between the epoch of Jesus and that of the church![3] Hence it is difficult to agree that Luke has

---

[1] *Theology of St Luke*, pp. 24f.

[2] 'The Way', pp. 22ff. Similarly, Wink, *John the Baptist*, p. 55.

[3] 'The Way', p. 29. Robinson notes that Conzelmann warns against 'pressing the structure indices too hard'. (Cf. *Theology of St Luke*, p. 76

set out the ministry as a special period of time, and in so doing, views the life and character of Jesus from a new perspective.

Stages of psychological development in the life of Jesus

H. Conzelmann links together Luke's view of the ministry of Jesus as a distinct epoch and his intention to set out the life of Jesus with three distinct stages of Jesus' 'internal' development and psychological understanding of himself.[1] But this ingenious interpretation is less than convincing. As will be shown in a later chapter, the whole notion of character or psychological development was foreign to the ancient world. Conzelmann's interpretation of the three 'sub-epochs' in the life of Jesus seems to have been influenced unduly by modern biographical method, although he would certainly deny that Luke's work is biographical in the modern sense.

Conzelmann is somewhat inconsistent as to the three divisions: in particular, it is difficult to locate the beginning and the end of the third sub-epoch.[2] Conzelmann claims that the beginning of each sub-epoch is marked by an epiphany and a rejection. In the epiphany scenes Jesus becomes conscious of his mission: at the Baptism he becomes aware of Messiahship, at the Transfiguration he realises that it is to be a suffering Messiahship; but both the triumphal entry and the Mount of Olives are suggested as the third epiphany. Luke's alterations of Mark are not linked to an attempt to set out the ministry of Jesus in three stages of development; at many points too much significance has been pressed out of the differences between the two evangelists.[3]

Scant attention is paid to the infancy narratives.[4] When account is taken of this important part of the Gospel, which

n. 1.) But Conzelmann also claims that the period of the ministry of Jesus is *strictly* defined as to its beginning and end (p. 195). He is rather more cautious in his recent essay, 'History and Theology in the Passion Narratives of the Synoptic Gospels', *Interpretation* **24** (1970), 196.

[1] *Theology of St Luke*, *passim*, esp. pp. 17 and 193ff.

[2] See W. C. Robinson's discussion, 'The Way', pp. 24ff.

[3] Robinson, 'The Way', pp. 33ff., discusses the exegetical points in some detail.

[4] See P. S. Minear, 'Luke's Use of the Birth Stories' in *Studies in Luke-Acts*, pp. 120ff.

is permeated with Lucan theology, it is even more difficult to accept that Luke intends to portray Jesus' development during the course of his life. In the infancy narratives, the last stage of the ministry is already anticipated at the beginning, for the true nature of Jesus and his ministry is revealed to the 'participants' in the opening chapters. The concept of a suffering Messiahship first appears, not following the Transfiguration,[1] but in Simeon's words to Mary (2: 35). One might even speak of a 'rejection' at this point. If 'epiphany' is understood as a heavenly revelation of the nature of Jesus and his ministry, this is already disclosed to the reader in the infancy narratives (1: 30ff.; 2: 10ff.). It might just be possible to distinguish between Luke's presentation of Jesus for the reader of the Gospel and his presentation of the stages of Jesus' own understanding of himself, but this is not a distinction Conzelmann makes.[2] Nor does Acts suggest that Luke intended to portray 'psychological' development in the life of Jesus, for this is conspicuously absent from his otherwise detailed presentation of Paul, and cannot be traced, even in summary form, in the speeches in Acts 10 and 13.[3]

Conzelmann's insistence that Luke presents the ministry of Jesus as a unique time of salvation when Satan was far away is equally unconvincing. Conzelmann links Luke 4: 13 with 22: 3 and 35–6. While Luke's addition of ἄχρι καιροῦ at 4: 13 is striking, the phrase is almost certainly no more than his way of 'rounding off' the temptation narratives; in the only other example of this phrase in the New Testament, Acts 13: 11, the meaning is simply 'for a while'. Luke 22: 3 is closely paralleled by John 13: 2, 27 and probably comes from non-Marcan tradition rather than from Luke's own hand.

But 22: 28 is even more difficult for Conzelmann's hypothesis. He claims that this verse refers only to the period since the passion, but one may well ask what are the πειρασμοί envisaged between Luke 22: 3 and 28;[4] the Mount of Olives scene is

---

[1] Conzelmann, *Theology of St Luke*, pp. 17 and 57ff.
[2] Cf. *Theology of St Luke*, pp. 193f.   [3] *Contra* Wink, *John the Baptist*, p. 56.
[4] W. Ott, *Gebet und Heil*, pp. 85ff., claims that the perfect tense in 22: 28, διαμεμενηκότες, refers not to any sort of past events which have been reported, but to the present – to the disciples who have not fled.

yet to come – *then* Jesus says to the disciples, 'Pray that you may not enter into temptation' (22: 40). Nor can the force of 22: 28 be evaded by admitting that Luke's own view and that of his traditions clash at this point.[1] While Luke has not always succeeded in removing inconsistencies from his narrative, if the ministry of Jesus was considered to be a distinct period free from temptation and Satan, such a blatant contradiction would not have been allowed to stand, especially in a group of logia which owe their present arrangement to Luke's own hand. As P. S. Minear notes, Conzelmann places tremendous weight upon an uncertain interpretation of the very difficult 22: 36 and especially the phrase ἀλλὰ νῦν.[2] Is 22: 36 really intended by Luke to mark the end of the epoch of Jesus and the beginning of a new period under the sway of Satan? Satan appears in Acts only twice as tempter (Acts 5: 3; 13: 10); in both passages the power of the gospel over him, rather than his threat to the church, is stressed.[3]

While Luke has emphasised that salvation is associated with the coming of Jesus (Luke 4: 16ff., especially 4: 21), he does not restrict salvation to the special period of the ministry. In Acts 13: 26 Paul announces to those gathered in the synagogue in Pisidian Antioch ὑμῖν ὁ λόγος τῆς σωτηρίας ταύτης ἐξαπεστάλη. Luke uses ὁ λόγος to refer to Christian proclamation: 'the word of salvation' does not belong to the past preaching of Jesus nor to the period of his ministry; it is also associated with the proclamation of the word in the church.

H. Conzelmann's *Die Mitte der Zeit* will long stand as a landmark in the history of New Testament scholarship. His main contention is firmly established: Luke's contribution as a *theologian* of *Heilsgeschichte* is extremely significant in the history of primitive Christianity. But Luke's theological perspective

But it is one thing to admit that the perfect tense also refers to present time, quite another to dismiss all past reference!

[1] Cf. Conzelmann, *Theology of St Luke*, p. 80 n. 4 and K. G. Kuhn, 'New Light on Temptation, Sin, and Flesh in the NT', *The Scrolls and the NT*, ed. K. Stendhal (London, 1958), pp. 269f.

[2] 'A Note on Luke 22: 36', *NovT* **7** (1964), 128ff.

[3] E. E. Ellis, *The Gospel of Luke* (London, 1966), at Luke 22: 3. Ellis also notes that in the pre-resurrection mission demonic activity is the activity of Satan, referring to Luke 13: 11 and 16; 10: 18; 11: 14–28; Eph. 6: 12.

is neither as new, nor as unique, nor as rigidly and carefully formulated, as Conzelmann claims. Luke's theological alterations of his sources have been pressed too vigorously: he has not forced the life and character of Jesus into a new mould, a pattern of epochs and sub-epochs which show that he is looking back to the past of Jesus in a new way. Insufficient attention has been paid to Luke's stylistic and dramatic abilities: frequently his concern for an 'orderly' narrative has been misunderstood and interpreted as part of a 'theological' pattern. While his stylistic ability most certainly cannot be used to explain away every alleged Lucan theological redaction of the gospel traditions, it is a neglected factor, which, taken with others,[1] helps to redress the balance and allow his interpretation of the life and character of Jesus to be seen as less 'Lucan' and more 'synoptic'. Luke's narrative of the ministry of Jesus is not a new development. He looks back to the past of Jesus not because it was an idyllic period of salvation, but because the story of Jesus of Nazareth is the story of the fulfilment of God's promises, a story which began with the coming of Jesus and John, and which, through the Spirit, continues.

The earlier estimate of Luke as the biographer among the evangelists can also be misleading. For it is difficult to find clear-cut evidence which confirms that he has 'bent' the synoptic traditions in a biographical direction. It is by no means self-evident that he has intended either to make Jesus into a hero-martyr, or to give prominence to particular character traits and so, in a new way, make the biography of Jesus a central aspect of the Christian message. There is a subtle temptation to make Luke into the precursor of the nineteenth-century biographers of Jesus and damn or praise him accordingly.

Luke undoubtedly does have a richer and more carefully drawn character portrait of Jesus than the other evangelists. This arises not so much from his new theological perspective as from his superior stylistic abilities and his considerable powers of characterisation.

[1] See T. Schramm's claim that recent redaction critical studies have paid insufficient attention to careful source criticism: *Der Markus-Stoff bei Lukas: eine literarkritische und redaktionsgeschichtliche Untersuchung* (Cambridge, 1971). Cf. G. N. Stanton's review in *Theology* **76** (1973), 36f.

CHAPTER 3

PRE-LUCAN TRADITIONS
ABOUT JESUS IN THE SPEECHES
IN ACTS

Luke envisages that outside Jerusalem, where knowledge of Jesus could not simply be assumed, a sketch of the life and character of Jesus was an integral part of missionary preaching. Is Luke, far from reproducing examples of primitive preaching, showing his readers that this is how the gospel is preached and ought to be preached in his own day?[1] C. H. Dodd's view that the speeches in Acts could be taken with some confidence to represent, 'not indeed what Peter said upon this or that occasion, but the kerygma of the early church at Jerusalem at an early period',[2] has been vigorously challenged. In this chapter the origin of the speeches in Acts 1–13 is reconsidered; particular attention is given to Peter's speech to Cornelius at Caesarea (Acts 10: 34–43). This speech contains the only extended summary of the ministry of Jesus; but a lengthy account of the life and character of Jesus is unnecessary: Luke has set out the story of Jesus in full in his Gospel and there is thus no need for extensive repetition.

There are a number of Lucan expressions in this speech; Luke's stylistic and theological imprint can be traced with some confidence. But this need not necessarily lead to the conclusion that Luke has composed this speech himself and that its references to the ministry are a summary of his own Gospel. For we know from his Gospel that Luke places his own stamp upon the earlier traditions he uses. Conversely, we cannot isolate a few traces of pre-Lucan tradition and then claim that the whole speech is an example, from a very early period, of the preaching of the church. Traditional material and Lucan redaction must be distinguished as carefully as possible.

It is relatively easy to find traces of Luke's own hand in this speech. At least 52 chapters in the New Testament come

---

[1] Cf. Dibelius, *Studies*, p. 165. [2] *Apostolic Preaching*, p. 37.

from Luke's pen,[1] and his treatment of Mark allows his style, vocabulary, and theological *Tendenz* to be established with some certainty. But as we have no direct examples of early evangelistic preaching outside Acts with which to test the speeches,[2] it is far from easy to isolate traditional material from Luke's redaction of it.

An underlying Aramaic source in Acts 1–13 was one of the pillars of C. H. Dodd's view. Dodd rejected the possibility that Semitisms were of the kind which result from an imitation of the translation-Greek of the Septuagint; he quoted Acts 10: 36ff. after C. C. Torrey's restored Aramaic and noted that in this speech evidence for an Aramaic original was at its strongest.[3]

But Torrey's hypothesis is generally considered to have been undermined by more recent work, especially by the frequently quoted article by H. F. D. Sparks.[4] The alleged Semitisms in the speeches are taken as 'Septuagintisms' by Haenchen and Wilckens and are dismissed merely by reference to Sparks' article.[5] But does an appeal to Luke's deliberate policy of writing in a 'Biblical' and archaic way in the first half of Acts account for all the evidence? The vocabulary, tone, style and even the theology of the first chapters of Acts all differ so markedly from the later chapters that if all the material stems

---

[1] Even more, if Luke had a hand in the composition of the Pastoral epistles (so, C. F. D. Moule, *BJRL* **47** (1965), 430ff.), of Ephesians (so, R. P. Martin, *ExT* **79** (1968), 297ff.), and if he also translated Hebrews (as some in the time of Eusebius of Caesarea believed, Eus., *Hist.* III, 38)!

[2] Such kerygmatic material as can be distilled from the epistles and even from the gospels is not without relevance, but it is never cast in the form of a direct report or statement of the content of evangelistic proclamation. I Cor. 15: 3ff. is a partial exception, but it is a confessional formula rather than a summary of evangelistic preaching.

[3] *Apostolic Preaching*, pp. 34f. Dodd refers to C. C. Torrey, *The Composition and Date of Acts* (Cambridge, Mass., 1916) as support for his views. Similarly F. F. Bruce, *The Speeches in the Acts of the Apostles* (London, 1942), pp. 8f. In addition to the literature referred to below, see D. F. Payne, 'Semitisms in the Book of Acts' in *Apostolic History and the Gospel* (Festschrift F. F. Bruce), ed. W. W. Gasque and R. P. Martin (Exeter, 1970), pp. 55–67.

[4] 'The Semitisms of Acts', *JTS* **I** (1950), 16ff.

[5] E. Haenchen, *Die Apostelgeschichte*, p. 66 (E.T. *Acts*, p. 74); U. Wilckens, *Missionsreden*, p. 11.

from Luke's pen, he must have been one of the most brilliant authors and stylists of the first centuries of the Roman Empire.

M. Wilcox has rejected the conclusions of both Torrey and Sparks, arguing that although Luke's hand can be seen throughout Acts, including the speeches, there are indications of the use of traditional material, and that insofar as an appeal to Aramaic may be suggested anywhere, it would seem to be most reasonable in the speeches in Acts 1–15.[1] Wilcox suggests that the difficult verse 10: 36 does not require a hypothesis of an Aramaic original, as argued by Torrey and Dodd,[2] but that in Peter's speech to Cornelius a Semitic tradition underlies to some extent the text as we now have it.[3]

The whole question has been approached from a completely different angle by R. A. Martin who, from study of the frequencies of three syntactical features in the Septuagint, non-Biblical writers, Acts, and the rest of the New Testament, shows that markedly different statistics occur whenever 'translation Greek' is analysed.[4] Not only are there substantial differences in the frequency of 'translation Greek' phenomena in Acts 1–15 in comparison with the rest of Acts, but as 'translation Greek' frequencies are found only in certain sub-sections, it is very unlikely that these frequencies are due either to the natural style of Luke or to deliberate imitation of the Septuagint by him. Martin concludes that Aramaic sources can be detected as lying behind those sub-sections of Acts 1–15 which have

---

[1] *The Semitisms of Acts* (Oxford, 1965), pp. 154, 183f. But see also J. A. Emerton's discussion of Wilcox's book in *JSS* **13** (1968), 282–92.

[2] *Semitisms*, pp. 152f.

[3] Neither of the two possible traces of Semitic tradition is particularly strong. (a) At 10: 38 the most difficult reading is Dc ὃν ἔχρισεν αὐτὸν ὁ θεός, a Semitic reading which reflects an original similar to that of the Syriac versions; a corrector of D may possibly have preserved an unrevised element of primitive tradition (p. 118). But the other explanations suggested by Wilcox himself are more probable – the reading is either an assimilation to Syriac versions or is due to the activity of a Semitic-thinking scribe. (b) 10: 39b, together with 5: 30, alludes to Deut. 21: 22, but the wording differs slightly from the LXX, possibly pointing to a non-Septuagintal text of some sort (pp. 34f.).

[4] 'Statistical Evidence of Aramaic Sources in Acts 1–15', *NTS* **11** (1964–5), 38ff. Martin discusses the use of καί (copula) and δέ, the use of certain prepositions and the separation of the article from its substantive.

the greatest preponderance of 'translation Greek' frequencies for the syntactical phenomena chosen.

Acts 10: 26–43 is listed as a possible example of a sub-section where features of 'translation Greek' are so prominent that Luke seems either to be translating Semitic sources himself, or to be using with little modification Greek sources which are themselves translations of Semitic material.[1] As some of the sub-sections used by Martin are as short as, or shorter than, Peter's speech to Cornelius, this part of Acts 10: 26–43 (Martin's sub-section) was examined, using Martin's methods and criteria. In one case – the proportion of καί copula to δέ – the speech gives even stronger evidence of 'translation Greek' than does the whole sub-section, which already has a higher proportion than usual.[2] But this is no more than a straw in the wind.

The work of Wilcox and Martin indicates that the phenomena of Acts 1–15 do not point to Luke's use of a Septuagintal style in his composition of all the material, and that there is probably sufficient evidence to confirm that some Semitic material lies behind parts of Acts 1–15. Peter's speech contains neither striking evidence nor lack of evidence of a possible Semitic source in comparison with the rest of Acts 1–15. More clear-cut evidence of pre-Lucan tradition in Acts 10 needs to be found before confident conclusions can be drawn.

This speech contains clear allusions to four Old Testament passages; the use of the Old Testament provides some important clues as to its origin. The opening of the speech proper (verse 36) is largely a linking of two passages – Ps. 107: 20 (Ps. 106 LXX) and Isa. 52: 7:[3]

---

[1] Martin stresses that as 'translation Greek' frequencies do not invariably appear in translated books of the Old Testament (LXX), sub-sections which do not have 'translation Greek' frequencies may nevertheless also be dependent on Semitic sources (p. 52).

[2] The speech does not contain any uses of δέ – this is unusual even in sections as short as Peter's speech. There is no δέ in only four of Martin's fifty sub-sections of Acts 1–15; δέ occurs in all thirty-three sub-sections of Acts 16–28, while in not one of these sub-sections is there a proportion of καί to δέ similar to that in 'translation Greek'.

[3] T. Holtz, *Untersuchungen über die alttestamentlichen Zitate bei Lukas* (Berlin, 1968), concentrates on explicit Old Testament citations and does

Ps. 107: 20 LXX ἀπέστειλεν τὸν λόγον αὐτοῦ καὶ ἰάσατο
αὐτούς...

Isa. 52: 7 LXX...πόδες εὐαγγελιζομένου ἀκοὴν εἰρήνης...

Acts 10: 36 τὸν λόγον ὃν ἀπέστειλεν τοῖς υἱοῖς Ἰσραηλ
εὐαγγελιζόμενος εἰρήνην...

The beginning of Peter's speech provides a number of problems for the exegete. C. C. Torrey accepted the more difficult reading τὸν λόγον ὅν (10: 36a) and suggested an Aramaic reconstruction.[1] However, it is much more likely that the reading of AB et al., which omits the relative ὅν, is to be preferred. The ὅν might be explained either as a dittography of the last two letters of λόγον,[2] as an attempt at amelioration,[3] or as a combination of dittography of λόγον and omission of αὐτοῦ. The transition from verse 35 to verse 36 is grammatically abrupt, and to a certain extent there is a break in thought. In verse 35 Peter speaks of God's acceptance of those in every nation who fear him and do what is right, but verse 36 speaks of the word sent to Israel.

These difficulties are lessened if verses 19 and 20 of Ps. 107, or parts of them, were originally part of an Old Testament citation at the beginning of Peter's speech. The citation may have read thus: καθὼς γέγραπται, ἐκέκραξαν πρὸς κύριον ἐν τῷ θλίβεσθαι αὐτούς, καὶ ἐκ τῶν ἀναγκῶν αὐτῶν ἔσωσεν αὐτούς, ἀπέστειλεν τὸν λόγον αὐτοῦ καὶ ἰάσατο αὐτούς καὶ ἐρρύσατο αὐτοὺς ἐκ τῶν διαφθορῶν αὐτῶν.[4]

There is now an explicit subject for the verb ἀπέστειλεν – κύριος. The citation is particularly appropriate to the occasion. The theme of the Psalm is the response of God in his redemptive acts to the needs of men. God's redemptive acts are marks of his chesed; four times in the Psalm God replies to the plea of men: 'Then they cried to the Lord in their trouble and he

not discuss the allusions in Acts 10: 36ff. M. Rese includes allusions in his examination of the use of the Old Testament in Luke–Acts; he discusses possible allusions to Isa. 61: 1, Gen. 39: 21 and Deut. 21: 22 in Acts 10: 36ff., but he does not mention Ps. 107: 20 and Isa. 52: 7: Alttestamentliche Motive in der Christologie des Lukas (Gütersloh, 1969).

[1] Composition, p. 35. [2] Wilcox, Semitisms, p. 152.
[3] J. H. Ropes in The Beginnings of Christianity, eds. F. J. F. Jackson and K. Lake (London, 1920ff.), III, 98.
[4] This follows the Septuagint; the Massoretic text is not significantly different.

delivered them out of their distress' (vv. 6, 13, 19, 28). The particular redemptive act of God which is selected in Acts 10: 36 is the one which is most appropriate to the ministry of Jesus: God sends forth his word to those in distress and heals them.

There are a number of further factors which support the hypothesis that there was a more extensive citation of this Psalm at an earlier stage in the history of the tradition, in spite of the caution necessary in arguing from silence. The longer kerygmatic speeches in chapters 2, 3 and 13 make much more extensive and explicit use of the Old Testament. All have Old Testament citations immediately after the speaker's opening words of address to his audience, and in each case the citation is much longer than in chapter 10. As will be shown later, the brief reference to the ministry of Jesus in Acts 2: 22 is an exposition of part of the preceding Old Testament citation. The same process is seen in chapter 10. As if to make this possibility more likely, the speech ends with a reference to Jesus as the one to whom the prophets bore witness (10: 43). This expression, as Dodd notes, may be extended by implication beyond its immediate application to cover all allusions to the Old Testament in the context.[1]

Peter's references to the ministry of Jesus in 10: 36–9 allude to parts of Ps. 107: 20 beyond the actual words quoted. Only the first phrase, 'he sent his word', is quoted (10: 36), but the remaining three phrases are picked up or echoed later in Peter's sketch of the ministry of Jesus.

Ps. 107: 20   καὶ ἰάσατο αὐτοὺς καὶ ἐρρύσατο αὐτοὺς ἐκ τῶν διαφθορῶν αὐτῶν

Acts 10: 38c   καὶ ἰώμενος πάντας τοὺς καταδυναστευομένους ὑπὸ τοῦ διαβόλου

In a further way Acts 10: 36–9 may be understood partly as an expansion or exposition of this part of the Psalm. In Ps. 107: 21 the recipients of God's redemptive acts are τοῖς υἱοῖς τῶν ἀνθρώπων; this expression may well account for the phrase τοῖς υἱοῖς Ἰσραηλ at 10: 36.

A similar use of Ps. 107: 20 lies behind Acts 13: 26, Paul's speech in the synagogue at Pisidian Antioch. At 13: 26b the

[1] *According to the Scriptures* (London, 1952), p. 52.

coming of Jesus is summed up as ὑμῖν ὁ λόγος τῆς σωτηρίας ταύτης ἐξαπεστάλη. The parallel with 10: 36 is clear – both are allusions to Ps. 107: 20. The preceding verse of the Psalm makes the allusion at 13: 26b even more explicit: ἔσωσεν αὐτούς is echoed in τῆς σωτηρίας. Again there is an allusion to this part of the Psalm beyond the words echoed. Ps. 107: 20 is quoted inexactly in order to make the reference to the ministry of Jesus stand out in stronger relief. As in 10: 36, the emphasis falls on ὁ λόγος; in both passages in Acts this word is deliberately placed first – through Jesus Christ, God has spoken and acted.

Two scholars have suggested independently that longer Old Testament citations were cut, probably by Luke himself, in other speeches in Acts. J. Bowker notes that James' speech in Acts 15: 14–21 may be a fragment of a longer discourse which included more Old Testament material, and a citation from Nahum 1: 15 may have been eliminated when Peter's speech in Acts 3: 12ff. was incorporated into Acts because it appeared to be irrelevant.[1]

More extensive evidence is supplied by J. Dupont who lists a number of examples from the speeches (but not Ps. 107: 20), and shows that while Luke tends to abridge Old Testament citations and to neglect Old Testament allusions found in the sources of his Gospel, examples of the reverse process are rare.[2]

Peter's speech originally included a longer citation from Ps. 107; the first section of the speech, which refers to the ministry of Jesus, seems to be an exposition of Ps. 107: 20 and its immediate context. The use of Ps. 107 in both Acts

[1] J. W. Bowker, 'Speeches in Acts: A Study in Proem and Yelammedenu Form', *NTS* **14** (1967–8), 106ff.

[2] 'L'Utilisation Apologétique de l'Ancien Testament', *ETL* **29** (1953), 289–387; now reprinted in *Études sur les Actes des Apôtres* (Paris, 1967), pp. 245ff. See esp. pp. 271ff. and n. 52. Dupont assumes that Luke used Mark and Matt., but his results do not depend on this presupposition. He notes that Lucan abbreviation of Old Testament citations was first observed by F. H. Woods in his article 'Quotations' in *Hastings' Dictionary of the Bible*. Woods does not refer to Acts 10. R. Harris argued that the speeches at the beginning of Acts have been abbreviated and that Ezek. 34: 23 originally stood at the beginning of Acts 2: 32: 'A Lacuna in the Text of the Acts of the Apostles', *ExT* **36** (1924–5), 173ff.

10: 36f. and Acts 13: 26 conforms remarkably closely to the pattern of Biblical exegesis in the early church which C. H. Dodd elucidated and which has been confirmed in more recent studies.[1] Dodd showed that when an Old Testament verse is cited or alluded to, the original *context* of the verse is frequently in view and is sometimes the basis of the argument.[2] The context of Ps. 107: 20 is relevant to the point being made in both Acts 10 and 13, for its message is, in essence, *Heilsgeschichte*, the very theme of the speeches.

The allusion to Isa. 52: 7 noted above also conforms to the pattern established by Dodd, for it both illustrates and elucidates the meaning of the main reference to the Old Testament, Ps. 107: 20. εὐαγγελιζόμενος εἰρήνην, from Isa. 52: 7, expands and explains the nature of τὸν λόγον, from Ps. 107: 20. Although Ps. 107: 20 is not as well attested as the passages discussed by Dodd, there is a strong case for regarding it as a further example of an Old Testament passage which was used by the earliest Christians in their efforts to understand and commend the contents of the kerygma. There is no evidence to suggest that either Ps. 107: 20 or Isa. 52: 7 may have been Old Testament passages to which Luke himself looked for illustration of the significance of the ministry of Jesus.[3]

---

[1] *According to the Scriptures*, p. 126. J. de Waard, *A Comparative Study of the OT Text in the Dead Sea Scrolls and in the NT* (Leiden, 1966), pp. 83f., notes that Dodd is undoubtedly right when, adhering to the possibility of existing *testimonia*, he speaks of 'an original coherent and flexible method of biblical exegesis'; there is an excellent prototype of this in the midrash pesher from Qumran. Cf. also J. A. Fitzmyer, 'The Use of Explicit OT Quotations in Qumran Literature and in the NT', *NTS* **7** (1960–1), 298.

Ps. 107 is not discussed by Dodd, although it is alluded to in the New Testament outside Acts 10 and 13. B. Lindars suggests that Ps. 107: 26 has been utilised by Paul in Rom. 10: 6, and that Ps. 107: 10 may lie behind the use of Isa. 8: 23ff. in Matt. 4: 15f.: *New Testament Apologetic* (London, 1961), pp. 239ff. and 197f. D. R. Jones notes allusions in Luke 1: 53 and 1: 79: 'The Background and Character of the Lukan Psalms', *JTS* **19** (1968), 43. Cf. also Matt. 8: 11 = Luke 13: 29. This logion, especially in its Lucan form, probably alludes to Ps. 107: 3.

[2] This conclusion has been challenged frequently. While Dodd may have exaggerated his case, it would be impossible to maintain that the original context is never in view; each passage must be investigated individually.

[3] The account of the healing of the centurion's servant in Luke 7: 1–10 (Q) is often taken as a parallel to Acts 10 – a parallel which Luke

Ps. 107: 20 seems to have been a *testimonium* used in the early church to point to the significance of the ministry of Jesus.[1] Peter's speech to Cornelius contains another such *testimonium* which is much more widely referred to in the New Testament – Isa. 61: 1–2. This passage is quoted in Luke 4: 18–19, alluded to in Q (Matt. 11: 5 = Luke 7: 22) and Matt. 5: 4, as well as in Acts 10: 38.[2] The occurrence of a more easily recognised *testimonium* in this speech makes our suggestions about the use of Ps. 107: 20 much more plausible.

The words of Isa. 61: 1 found in Acts 10: 38 are a conflation or summary of the Old Testament verse. Bearing in mind that a New Testament reference to an Old Testament verse is very often intended to evoke the whole passage from which it has been selected,[3] it becomes clear that Isa. 61: 1 ties together the main thrust of both Ps. 107: 20 and Isa. 52: 7:

Ps. 107: 20 ἀπέστειλεν τὸν λόγον αὐτοῦ καὶ ἰάσατο αὐτοὺς
καὶ ἐρρύσατο αὐτοὺς ἐκ τῶν διαφθορῶν αὐτῶν.

Isa. 52: 7 ὡς πόδες εὐαγγελιζομένου ἀκοὴν εἰρήνης...

Isa. 61: 1 πνεῦμα κυρίου ἐπ' ἐμέ, οὗ εἵνεκεν ἔχρισέν με.
εὐαγγελίσασθαι πτωχοῖς ἀπέσταλκέν με, ἰάσασθαι
τοὺς συντετριμμένους...

The link between Ps. 107: 20 and Isa. 52: 7 was noted above; Isa. 61: 1 must now be added for it picks up the idea of 'sending' and 'healing the distressed' from Ps. 107: 20 and 'proclaiming good news' from Isa. 52: 7. Such a linkage of

himself enhances. It may be significant that Matthew's version of the Q narrative (Matt. 8: 5–13) includes a logion found elsewhere in Luke (13: 28–9) which is probably an allusion to Ps. 107: 3 (cf. also Isa. 49: 12). If Luke had been familiar with the Psalm, one might have expected his account of the Gentile centurion to have alluded to this passage, especially as the allusion to Ps. 107 is a little clearer in Luke 13: 29 than in Matt. 8: 11.

[1] Ps. 107, together with Psalms 31 and 51, was a favourite with the author of 1QH. J. de Waard, *Comparative Study*, p. 62.

[2] On the use of Isa. 61: 1–2 (and Isa. 52: 7) in Q and in Luke 4: 18–19, see G. N. Stanton, 'On the Christology of Q', *Christ and the Spirit in the New Testament* (Festschrift C. F. D. Moule), eds. B. Lindars and S. S. Smalley (Cambridge, 1973), pp. 25–40.

[3] Cf. B. Lindars, *NT Apologetic*, p. 14, summarising Dodd's view.

verses is common in rabbinic exegesis and in the exegesis of the early church.[1]

The fourth Old Testament passage alluded to in Peter's speech was also almost certainly a primitive *testimonium*; the words κρεμάσαντες ἐπὶ ξύλου in 10: 39 derive from Deut. 21: 22.[2] Paul, in Gal. 3: 13, and Luke, in Acts 10: 39, use different parts of the passage to stress different aspects of the death of Jesus.[3] This is precisely the pattern found elsewhere in the early church's use of *testimonia*. Once again there is no indication that use of this Old Testament passage originated with Luke himself; it is not found at all in the Lucan passion narratives to refer to the death of Jesus – the one occurrence of the verb in the Gospel refers to one of the thieves, not to Jesus (Luke 23: 39)![4]

Peter's speech originally contained a longer citation from Ps. 107: 20; certainly this part of the Psalm lies at the base of Peter's sketch of the ministry of Jesus. Luke may have dropped an originally longer citation, partly because of his own tendency to abbreviate Old Testament citations, and partly because he considered that a longer citation was inappropriate in a narrative which recorded the conversion of a Gentile, even if he was a devout man who feared God. In doing so, he has partially obscured the way in which the references to the Old Testament in the first part of the speech interlock. The majority of the aspects of the ministry of Jesus which are mentioned are closely related either to the Old Testament words actually used or to their immediate context. These include God's sending of Jesus, his message of good news through Jesus, the anointing of Jesus with the Spirit, Jesus' healing of those in dire difficulties, and the death of Jesus on the cross. The first three passages alluded to (Ps.

---

[1] J. W. Doeve, *Jewish Hermeneutics in the Synoptic Gospels and Acts* (Assen, 1954), p. 89 *et al.*

[2] This passage is cited, with an introductory formula, in Gal. 3: 13, and the same phrase is found at Acts 5: 30.

[3] Luke uses the passage to show the guilt of those responsible for the death of Jesus; this is clearer in Acts 5: 30 than in 10: 39.

[4] Cf. Lindars' discussion of the use of Deut. 21: 22 in the early church: *NT Apologetic*, pp. 232–7. 'Luke is not averse to using biblical material taken from current apologetic...', p. 234.

107: 20, Isa. 52: 7 and Isa. 61: 1) are not random choices, but seem to have been woven together to provide a scriptural summary of the nature and significance of the ministry of Jesus. In Acts 10: 36–9 we have the 'fossils' of three passages which may have been linked together at a very early period to answer the question, 'What did Jesus do before his crucifixion?', or, 'How was his earthly life significant?'. The first part of Peter's speech, at least, is better understood as an exposition of Ps. 107: 20, with reference to Isa. 52: 7 and Isa. 61: 1, than as Luke's summary of his own Gospel. Some of the alleged Lucan vocabulary in this speech (εὐαγγελιζόμενος, εἰρήνη, ἰώμενος) arises from the use made here of the Old Testament. It is not surprising that U. Wilckens, who argues that Peter's speech is Luke's summary of his own Gospel, pays scant attention to the role of Old Testament allusions in these verses.

A pattern of scriptural exegesis found in many places in the New Testament, and stemming from an early period, is reflected in Peter's speech to Cornelius. It is difficult to estimate the precise origin of these verses – the brief allusions are no more closely related to the Septuagint than to the Massoretic text and hence offer no evidence of their period of origin in the primitive church.[1]

The way in which these passages are woven together discounts the possibility that Luke is merely summarising his own Gospel or freely composing these verses. Nor, if the above hypothesis is plausible, can one imagine why Luke would have cut his own originally longer speech. The use of the Old Testament in this speech, even though it is less rich and explicit than in the other speeches, underlines its links with them. It is surely significant that almost all references to the Old Testament in Acts are in the speeches, particularly those in Acts 1–15. Recent work on the other speeches points to Luke's use of primitive exegetical traditions.[2] The key to a

---

[1] Note de Waard's comment on the primitive material in the speeches, which he refers to as *pesharim* and *midrashim*: 'The usual reasoning from the LXX character of the texts urgently needs revision in the new light of the Septuagintal tendency of the proto-Masoretic Qumran texts'; *Comparative Study*, pp. 8of. and see especially the references on p. 81, n. 1.

[2] J. W. Doeve, *Jewish Hermeneutics*, p. 182; J. W. Bowker, 'Speeches', *NTS* 14, 96ff.; D. Goldsmith, 'Acts 13: 33–37; a Pesher on II Samuel 7',

more precise estimate of the their origin lies in further examination of their use of the Old Testament; a consensus of
opinion quite different from U. Wilckens' conclusions is likely
to emerge.

Wider questions, such as the role of speeches in ancient
historiography,[1] are not irrelevant, but lie beyond the scope
of this investigation. Nor is the question of pre-Lucan traditions
in the other speeches in Acts 1–13 irrelevant, as, on any
reckoning, the speeches are very closely related to each other;
in particular, the christological expressions in the other
speeches confirm that Luke has drawn on earlier traditions.[2]

Other features of this speech which differ from Luke's own
emphases, and which may be taken as marks of pre-Lucan
tradition, may be mentioned briefly. (*a*) εἰρήνην διὰ Ἰησοῦ
Χριστοῦ (verse 36) is more Pauline (cf. Rom. 5: 1) than
Lucan. (*b*) If it is true that later stages of Christian tradition,
and Luke in particular, played down the role of John the
Baptist, then the prominence of the reference to John in 10:
37 (and also in Acts 13: 24), in such a brief summary, may
well point to primitive tradition.

(*c*) These verses emphasise God's proclamation of good news
through Jesus and Jesus' healings (10: 38). Jesus is portrayed
as a miracle worker and, as it were, a prophet, rather than
as a teacher. But Luke's Gospel adds very few miracle stories
to the Marcan material: Luke emphasises the teaching of
Jesus. If Peter's speech, as U. Wilckens urges, is a summary
of Luke's Gospel, it is surprising, especially in view of Acts 1: 1,
that Jesus the teacher is not more prominent.

(*d*) H. Conzelmann notes that in Luke's Gospel Satan's
activity is described more from the psychological angle than

JBL **87** (1968), 321ff.; E. E. Ellis, 'Midrashic Features in the Speeches in
Acts', *Mélanges Bibliques* (Festschrift B. Rigaux), eds. A. Descamps and
A. de Halleux (Gembloux, 1970), pp. 303–12. An expanded version,
'Midraschartige Züge', has been published in *ZNW* **62** (1971), 94–104.

[1] See A. W. Mosley, 'Historical Reporting in the Ancient World', *NTS*
12 (1965–6), 10–26; C. F. Evans, '"Speeches" in Acts', *Mélanges Bibliques*
(Festschrift B. Rigaux), pp. 287–302.

[2] U. Wilckens' denial has by no means closed the discussion. See
I. H. Marshall, 'The Resurrection in the Acts of the Apostles' in *Apostolic
History and the Gospel* (Festschrift F. F. Bruce), eds. W. W. Gasque and
R. P. Martin (Exeter, 1970), pp. 92–107.

in Acts 10: 38 where he is the oppressor, the traditional conception.[1] Even if this expression does not echo Ps. 107: 19–20,
as suggested above, it is Mark's Gospel, rather than Luke's,
which is paralleled here.[2]

(e) Acts 10: 42, as E. Schweizer notes, does not contain
the thought of Acts 1: 8, so important for Luke, that the
Risen Lord gave a commandment about the mission to the
heathen.[3] (f) κριτὴς ζώντων καὶ νεκρῶν (10: 42d) is certainly
not Lucan. Together with Acts 3: 20f. it brings an eschatological
note not prominent in the speeches in Acts.[4]

Taken cumulatively, these observations strongly support the
conclusions drawn from the use of the Old Testament in this
speech. And, in addition, many of the traces of Luke's hand
or of a 'summary' of Luke's Gospel listed by Wilckens are
less than convincing. Three points closely linked with the
references to the ministry of Jesus in this speech may be noted
briefly.

Wilckens claims that the temporal separation of Jesus and
John the Baptist is a Lucan conception.[5] Even if this is so in
the Gospel,[6] the motif is not prominent in Acts 10, for the
speech merely tells us that Jesus began his ministry in Galilee
after the baptism which John preached, and this might well
be taken as a summary of Mark 1: 1–14.[7] Would the brief
reference to John the Baptist have been understood as anything but a summary of Mark, if we did not possess Luke's
Gospel?

Wilckens suggests that the verbs in 10: 38, διῆλθεν, εὐεργετῶν,
ἰώμενος correspond to Luke's view that the time of salvation
has begun with the person of Jesus. ἰᾶσθαι is a favourite Lucan
word.[8] But, as noted above, ἰώμενος is to be linked to the

---

[1] Theology of St Luke, p. 157.   [2] Cf. E. Haenchen, comm. ad loc.
[3] 'Discipleship and Belief in Jesus', NTS **2** (1955–6), 92.
[4] U. Wilckens takes this phrase as an exception to the otherwise completely Lucan pattern in this speech: 'Kerygma und Evangelium', ZNW
49 (1958), 235. The phrase is found in 1 Peter 4: 5; 2 Tim. 4: 1; Barnabas
7: 2; 2 Clement 1: 1; Polycarp, Phil. 2: 1; Justin, Dial. 118: 1. (Cf.
Beginnings of Christianity IV, 122.) See also E. G. Selwyn, The First Epistle of
St Peter (London, 1946), pp. 33–6.
[5] 'Kerygma und Evangelium', ZNW **49**, 231.
[6] See above, pp. 56ff.   [7] Cf. Acts 10: 37 and Mark 1: 4, 14.
[8] 'Kerygma und Evangelium', ZNW **49**, 233.

allusion to Ps. 107: 20. διῆλθεν and εὐεργετῶν are so vague that they could be said to echo any of the Gospels.

Wilckens argues that Luke's geographical references in Peter's speech reflect the inaccurate geographical scheme found also in the Gospel, where Judaea and Galilee are thought of as two adjoining regions.[1] But καθ᾽ ὅλης τῆς 'Ιουδαίας (10: 37) and ἐν τῇ χώρᾳ τῶν 'Ιουδαίων (10: 39) are simply loose ways of referring to Judaea and Galilee together, which are not specifically Lucan but reflect the usage of the time.[2] In Acts 10: 39, and in Luke 23: 5, Galilee is denoted as the original area of the ministry of Jesus within the land of the Jews. Ισραηλ (10: 36) is used with Old Testament texts to denote the area where 'Ιουδαῖοι live – both terms are virtually synonymous with 'Ιουδαία in this passage.[3] 'Ιουδαία is used of the whole of Palestine, especially, as in Luke 23: 5, as a non-Jew is being addressed. To this virtual equation the two references to ὁ λαός (10: 41, 42) may be added.

There are good reasons for concluding that Peter's speech shows traces of pre-Lucan tradition and that Luke's own

[1] *Ibid.*, 230; cf. Conzelmann, *Theology of St Luke*, p. 70, and the criticisms of W. C. Robinson, 'The Way', pp. 43–56.

[2] 'Ιουδαῖοι not Ισραηλ is used by the Jews themselves in diplomatic communications with non-Jewish states (so, W. Gutbrod, art. 'Ισραηλ', *TWNT* III, 362) and is an appropriate term to use when speaking to a Roman, Cornelius. There is nothing unusual in the separate reference to Jerusalem in verse 39. See the comments and references in A. Neubauer, *La Géographie du Talmud* (Paris, 1868), p. 1. Conzelmann seems unaware of this usage (*Theology of St Luke*, p. 70 and cf. p. 43 n. 3.).
In the synoptics 'Ιουδαία usually refers only to Judaea, but Matt. 19: 1 is an example of the wider usage, referring to the whole of Palestine, especially by foreigners who do not distinguish between the various parts. Other examples are Luke 1: 5, 4: 44; 7: 17; 23: 5; Acts 2: 9; 11: 1, 29; 1 Thess. 2: 14. F.-M. Abel gives a large number of references, ranging from Clearchus of Soli 320 B.C. to Eusebius. Josephus sometimes referred to Judaea in this broader sense. See, especially, *Antiq.* xii: 4, 11 and Dio Cassius xxvii: 16, 5: F.-M. Abel, *Géographie de la Palestine* I (Paris, 1933), 312–13. W. Bauer also supports the wider usage in his lexicon, *sub* 'Ιουδαία. Conzelmann seems unaware of the extent of the references supporting this broader usage of 'Ιουδαία: *Theology of St Luke*, p. 70.

[3] Ισραηλ (Acts 10: 36) corresponds to the expression most frequently used in the rabbinic literature to refer to Palestine: Judaea, Galilee, Samaria and Peraea is 'land of Israel'. A. Neubauer, *Géographie*, p. 1.

stylistic and theological emphases are not all-pervading. But while one may distinguish Lucan and pre-Lucan material somewhat more confidently than in the case of, say, Mark's Gospel, the method has definite limitations. Paul, for example, uses pre-Pauline material simply because he does agree with it, and the most appropriate criterion for distinguishing it is its 'formula' content and form.[1] Thus it is not necessary to prove that every single phrase in this speech runs directly counter to Lucan emphases. There is also the possibility, admittedly difficult to prove, that if Peter's speech did come to Luke from an earlier source, he might have been influenced by it considerably: this may account for some of the 'Lucan' theological expressions in his Gospel!

Pre-Lucan material lies at the heart of Peter's speech, though it would be rash to attempt to locate its origin more precisely on the internal evidence of the speech alone. Good reasons have been adduced for concluding that Luke's own influence was less marked than some writers have maintained.[2] Reference to the ministry of Jesus cannot be a later addition to the speech; it is closely woven into the argument, just as it is in the speeches in chapters 2 and 3, even though they are all only summaries.

Peter's speech to Cornelius has been examined in some detail, as these verses contain much more detailed reference to the ministry of Jesus than do the other speeches. But such references to Jesus as there are in the other speeches do not seem to stem from Luke's own hand. In the Joel citation in Acts 2: 17ff. three words have been added in verse 19 to the Septuagint: ἄνω...σημεῖα...κάτω.[3] The word σημεῖα was introduced in order to focuss less attention on αἷμα καὶ πῦρ καὶ ἀτμίδα καπνοῦ on the earth, and to place emphasis on σημεῖα ἐπὶ τῆς γῆς κάτω.[4] This brings out more clearly the

---

[1] Vocabulary statistics are usually a less satisfactory criterion, at least for isolating pre-Pauline material.

[2] So also F. Bovon, 'Tradition et Rédaction en Actes 10, 1 – 11, 18', *TZ* **26** (1970), 39ff.

[3] Surprisingly, recent writers seem not to have considered the reasons for the additions.

[4] The western text is a further example of less emphasis being placed on a difficult part of the original text: in this textual tradition the blood, fire and smoke were omitted. H. J. Cadbury and K. Lake suggest that

parallel between τέρατα...καὶ σημεῖα (Acts 2: 19), τέρασι καὶ σημείοις (Acts 2: 22, of Jesus) and τέρατα καὶ σημεῖα (Acts 2: 43, of the apostles). In only two other places in Acts (6: 8 and 7: 36) does τέρατα precede σημεῖα; in 2: 22 and 2: 43 the usual Septuagint and New Testament order is reversed in order to keep in line with the Joel citation and to make the fulfilment of prophecy more explicit.

As Acts 2: 43 appears to be part of a Lucan summary, these examples of the order τέρατα...σημεῖα might well be taken as an indication of Luke's own hand. But Luke could very well have written 2: 43 as a summary to extend the Joel–Jesus pattern to the apostles.[1] Acts follows the usual Septuagint and New Testament order four times (4: 30; 5: 12; 14: 3; 15: 12).[2] The order found in chapter two occurs only in Acts 6: 8, referring to Stephen, and in Acts 7: 36, Stephen's speech; both verses are in passages where many scholars are prepared to see evidence of the use of sources. Hence the order found in chapters 2, 6 and 7 may indicate pre-Lucan tradition; the additional words added to the Joel citation probably reflect *pesher* exegesis.[3] The addition of σημεῖα and its use in 2: 22 with reference to the ministry of Jesus, and in 2: 43 with reference to the apostles, show that the σημεῖα of Jesus and the apostles are fulfilment of scripture.[4]

Paul's address to the synagogue at Pisidian Antioch makes

the western text may possibly be original, but the evidence they themselves cite against this hypothesis is surely decisive: *Beginnings of Christianity*, eds. F. J. F. Jackson and K. Lake (London, 1920ff.), IV, *ad loc.*

[1] If one allows that Luke 21: 25–6 is a Lucan redaction of Mark 13: 24–5, it may just be significant that Luke speaks of σημεῖα ἐν ἡλίῳ καὶ σελήνῃ καὶ ἄστροις. In Acts 2: 19 σημεῖα are ἐπὶ τῆς γῆς κάτω but in Luke 21: 25 ἐπὶ τῆς γῆς there is συνοχὴ ἐθνῶν ἐν ἀπορίᾳ ἤχους θαλάσσης καὶ σάλου....

[2] Although σημεῖα καὶ τέρατα is very frequent in the LXX, from Hatch and Redpath, *Concordance to the Septuagint* (Oxford, 1897–1906), Wisdom 10: 16 seems to be the only example of the reverse order which is found in Acts 2.

[3] Cf. E. Ellis, 'Midrashic Features' in *Mélanges Bibliques* (Festschrift B. Rigaux), p. 307.

[4] For a different view, see R. F. Zehnle, *Peter's Pentecost Discourse* (Nashville, 1971), pp. 33f. Zehnle notes that the Joel citation forms an integral part of the whole discourse and suggests that Luke himself may possibly have adapted the citation.

a number of points about Jesus. There are more details about John the Baptist and about the accusations made against Jesus than in Acts 10, but there is no mention of Jesus' healing ministry. As with Peter's speech to Cornelius, there is a strong difference of opinion about the origin of the speech. U. Wilckens detects Lucan emphases in the references to John the Baptist and the ministry of Jesus.¹ Other writers have found impressive evidence of Luke's use of primitive exegetical traditions.²

As was noted earlier, there is a striking allusion to Ps. 107: 20 in the references to the coming of Jesus in Acts 10: 36 and 13: 26b. The allusion at 13: 26b is even more explicit: τῆς σωτηρίας echoes ἔσωσεν αὐτούς in the preceding verse of the Psalm. Once again there is an allusion to the Psalm beyond the words used.³

U. Wilckens suggests that in the curious reference to the coming of Jesus in verse 24, πρὸ προσώπου τῆς εἰσόδου αὐτοῦ, Luke is probably echoing phraseology used of the arrival of a missionary.⁴ But this phrase is quite without a close parallel in the New Testament. The phrase seems to be an unexpected allusion to Mal. 3: 1: ἰδοὺ ἐγὼ ἐξαποστέλλω τὸν ἄγγελόν μου, καὶ ἐπιβλέψεται ὁδὸν πρὸ προσώπου μου... καὶ τίς ὑπομενεῖ ἡμέραν εἰσόδου αὐτου; If so, this may be another hint of pre-Lucan tradition. For Luke himself could hardly have alluded consciously to Mal. 3: 1: with reference to Jesus, as at Luke 7: 27 he uses the Q tradition which links Mal. 3: 1 with Ex. 23: 20 with reference to John the Baptist!⁵

At first sight 13: 25b ἀλλ' ἰδοὺ ἔρχεται μετ' ἐμὲ οὗ οὐκ εἰμὶ ἄξιος τὸ ὑπόδημα τῶν ποδῶν λῦσαι looks like Luke's summary of his own Gospel.⁶ But the wording differs sig-

¹ *Missionsreden*, pp. 102ff. and 134ff.

² See above, p. 77 n. 2. In addition, see J. de Waard, *Comparative Study*, pp. 18f.; E. Lövestam, *Son and Saviour: a Study of Acts 13: 32–37* (Lund and Copenhagen, 1961); O. Glombitza, 'Akta 13: 15–41: Analyse einer lukanischen Predigt vor Juden', *NTS* **5** (1958–9), 306ff.

³ See above, pp. 72f.

⁴ *Missionsreden*, p. 102 n. 1. The parallels cited by Wilckens (Acts 1: 21; 1 Thess. 1: 9 and 2: 1) are not close.

⁵ Wilckens does note as possible an allusion to Mal. 3: 1, and refers to H. J. Cadbury in *Beginnings of Christianity* IV, 152; but neither writer discusses the implications of this allusion.

⁶ So, Wilckens, *Missionsreden*, p. 103.

nificantly from Luke 3: 16, and there are parallels with Johannine traditions in these words and in the preceding sentence. Nor is it easy to see the picture of John the Baptist in 13: 24–5 as part either of Luke's alleged separation of Jesus and John or of his portrayal of John as the last prophet of the old era.[1] For attention is focussed firmly on Jesus as the Saviour sent to Israel (13: 23) even before John is mentioned for the first time!

As in Acts 10, it is exceedingly difficult to separate traditional material and Luke's redaction of it. The references to John and the ministry of Jesus do not all stem from Luke's hand; some signs of Luke's use of earlier material can be found.

Interest in the past of Jesus is not simply Luke's prerogative. While it is impossible to date with any accuracy the material on which Luke draws, the use of the Old Testament uncovered in Acts 10 and discerned by a number of writers in the other speeches points to a very early period indeed – certainly well before the emergence of any of the gospels. Peter's speech to Cornelius shows that early communities grouped together passages of scripture to expound and defend their interpretation not only of the death, resurrection and exaltation of Jesus, but also of his earthly ministry.

For Luke a sketch of the ministry of Jesus is an integral part of evangelistic preaching. While it is not possible to prove that the traditional material on which he drew originally had this *Sitz im Leben*, this setting remains at least as likely as any other; the material would have been entirely appropriate in discussion with Jews about the significance of the earthly life of Jesus.[2]

In a number of ways Peter's summary of the ministry of Jesus in Acts 10: 36ff. reflects the pre-resurrection situation whenever this is in view.[3] Yet Peter does not proclaim Jesus

---

[1] *Contra* Wilckens, *Missionsreden*, pp. 102ff. See above, pp. 56ff.

[2] On the question of the *Sitz im Leben* of accounts of the deeds and words of the apostles, see J. Jervell, 'Zur Frage der Traditionsgrundlage der Apostelgeschichte', *ST* **16** (1963), 25ff.

[3] Peter introduces his speech by referring to God's acceptance of everyone in every nation who fears him, but the beginning of the summary of the ministry of Jesus speaks of the word sent to Israel. οὗτός ἐστιν

as a past historical figure. Jesus Christ is κύριος πάντων, he has been raised from the dead and is the one ordained by God to be judge of the living and the dead (10: 40, 42). Peter's speeches in Acts make it quite clear that the early church did not proclaim Jesus of Nazareth without at the same time proclaiming him as the Risen One, Lord and Christ; nor did it proclaim the Risen Christ and sidestep or minimise the significance of the pre-resurrection events and the character of the One who was raised from the dead.

πάντων κύριος refers most naturally to Jesus as Lord of both Jews and Gentiles, and almost seems to be a parenthesis to redress the balance after the preceding statement (cf. G. Stählin, *Die Apostelgeschichte* (Göttingen, 1962), *ad loc.*). In verse 42 Jesus' command to preach 'to the people' refers to the Jewish nation, as frequently in Luke–Acts, but the perspective is widened again in Peter's final words: everyone who believes in Jesus receives forgiveness of sins.

CHAPTER 4

JESUS IN PAUL'S PREACHING

Was Paul interested in the 'past' of Jesus? Is there any evidence which suggests that for Paul, as for Luke, this interest formed part of his missionary preaching? The extent to which Paul's preaching referred to the life and character of Jesus of Nazareth is a very elusive and vexed part of the whole question of the relationship between Paul and Jesus. Surprisingly few discussions have arisen out of recent interest in the continuity or discontinuity of the primitive kerygma and the historical Jesus. For many scholars it has become an axiom that Paul was satisfied with the mere fact of the historical existence of Jesus; the case is regarded as closed once it is recognised that Paul disregarded the ministry of Jesus, and, apart from a few sayings, his teaching. If this is so, one is forced to conclude that there is a considerable gap between the Pauline literature and the gospel traditions. This is accepted by many and explained in terms of the development of primitive Christianity, whose message, it is alleged, began to be concerned with the 'past' of Jesus only in the post-Pauline period.

Many attempts have been made to prove that Paul was well acquainted with some of the gospel traditions, and to account for their absence from the epistles. The 'traditional' view that Paul's missionary preaching must have included reference to the life and character of Jesus has been defended frequently.[1]

---

[1] The 'traditional' view has been defended by J. Schniewind, G. Kittel, and W. G. Kümmel, among many others. (For details, see V. Furnish, 'The Jesus–Paul Debate: From Baur to Bultmann', *BJRL* **47** (1965), 367 and 375.) See especially A. Oepke, *Die Missionspredigt des Apostels Paulus* (Leipzig, 1920), and 'Irrwege der neueren Paulusforschung', *ThLZ* **77** (1952), 453f. (both missed, apparently, by V. Furnish).

For more recent discussions of the 'traditional' view, see B. C. Lategan, *Die aardse Jesus in die Predikung van Paulus volgens sy briewe* (Rotterdam, 1967) (this book is not available to me; there is an English summary in *NT Abstracts* **12** (1968), 263); C. F. D. Moule, 'Jesus in New Testament Kerygma', *Verborum Veritas* (Festschrift G. Stählin), eds. O. Böcher and K. Haacker (Wuppertal, 1970), pp. 15–26; J. Blank argues that Luke is

It is especially associated with J. Weiss, who claimed that without such reference Paul's demand for faith in Jesus would have been preposterous.[1] Weiss's comments are often appealed to by scholars attempting to counter the view that Paul was uninterested in the ministry of Jesus.

How strong is this case? Is one compelled to admit that Paul's initial proclamation of Jesus Christ by-passed any consideration of the life and character of Jesus of Nazareth? As the content of Paul's missionary preaching is rarely mentioned explicitly in the epistles, and as an answer based solely on silence is vulnerable, wider issues must be considered. Since the 'traditional' view supports the understanding of the nature and purpose of the gospel traditions which is advocated in later chapters of this book, the full weight of the opposite position must be allowed to fall against it.

R. Bultmann's consistent advocacy of the 'negative' case[2] has been sharpened and extended by several recent writers.[3] This approach emphasises that even if one could prove that Paul must have learned a good deal about Jesus of Nazareth from his contacts with primitive Christianity, both before and

in fact the originator of the 'traditional' view: *Paulus und Jesus: eine theologische Grundlegung* (Munich, 1968), p. 65.

[1] See, for example, *The History of Primitive Christianity* I (E.T. London, 1937), 225ff., and *Paul and Jesus* (E.T. London and New York, 1909), pp. 17ff. J. Weiss's view is discussed by E. Güttgemanns, *Der leidende Apostel und sein Herr* (Göttingen, 1966), pp. 351ff.

[2] In addition to his comments in his *Theology of the New Testament* I (E.T. London, 1952), 188f., Bultmann has devoted three major essays to this question. 'Die Bedeutung des geschichtlichen Jesus für die Theologie des Paulus' in *Glauben und Verstehen* I (Tübingen, 1933), 188–213 [E.T. in *Faith and Understanding* I (London, 1969)]; 'Jesus und Paulus' in *Jesus Christus im Zeugnis der Heiligen Schrift und der Kirche* (Munich, 1936), pp. 68–90 [E.T. in *Existence and Faith* (London, 1961)]; 'Das Verhältnis der urchristlichen Christusbotschaft zum historischen Jesus', *Sitzungsberichte v. d. Heidelberg. Akad. Wiss., Phil.-hist. Klasse* (1960) [E.T. in *The Historical Jesus and the Kerygmatic Christ*, eds. C. E. Braaten and R. A. Harrisville (Nashville, 1964)]. See also R. Bultmann's most recent comments, 'Antwort an E. Käsemann' in *Glauben und Verstehen* IV (Tübingen, 1965), 196.

[3] See, for example, W. Schmithals, 'Paulus und der historische Jesus', *ZNW* **53** (1962), 145–60; E. Haenchen, 'Die frühe Christologie', *ZTK* **63** (1966), 145–59; S. Schulz, 'Markus und das Urchristentum', *Studia Evangelica* II (1964), 141f.

after his conversion, his silence on almost all aspects of Jesus' ministry is surprising. Paul either knew nothing about the life of Jesus or he deliberately dismissed the relevance of what he did know – 2 Cor. 5: 16 is frequently understood to support the latter view. References to the teaching of Jesus are few; some, at least, must be attributed to the Risen Lord. If Paul knew a good deal of the teaching of Jesus, why did he not refer more frequently to his authoritative words to settle disputed questions? Even if there are many allusions to the teaching of Jesus, the paucity of explicit citations and the lack of allusions to the deeds of Jesus must still be explained. References to the character and example of Jesus are to be understood, it is alleged, as references to the pre-existent Jesus, not to the historical Jesus. Such conclusions carry important implications not only for Paul's preaching, for Christology and for the whole wider Jesus–Paul question, but also for our understanding of the development of primitive Christianity in the first decades.

The 'negative' case has been argued so persuasively that its force cannot be brushed aside by proposing novel solutions. The history of scholarly discussion also offers a warning against facile assertions; most of the issues, including the question of Paul's missionary preaching and his knowledge of the gospel traditions, were thoroughly debated between 1900 and 1920.[1] Those who uphold the 'traditional' view still tend to lean on contributions to the earlier debate; with the notable exception of W. G. Kümmel, few fresh observations have been added.[2] Some of the central pillars of the 'negative' argument are discussed in the first section of this chapter.

Although a thorough examination of Paul's understanding of the significance of Jesus of Nazareth lies beyond the scope of this investigation, some aspects are considered in the second section. Such evidence is certainly relevant to the question of Paul's missionary preaching, but it is not in itself decisive,

[1] See the following surveys: V. Furnish, 'Debate', *BJRL* **47** (1965), 342ff.; E. Güttgemanns, *Der leidende Apostel*, pp. 329–412; E. Jüngel, *Paulus und Jesus* (Tübingen, 3rd ed. 1967), pp. 5–16; D. L. Dungan, *The Sayings of Jesus in the Churches of Paul* (Oxford, 1971), pp. xvii–xxix.

[2] W. G. Kümmel, 'Jesus und Paulus', *Theologische Blätter* **19** (1940), 211ff.; 'Jesus und Paulus', *NTS* **10** (1963–4), 163ff. (Both essays are now reprinted in W. G. Kümmel, *Heilsgeschehen und Geschichte*.)

for the epistles do not set out Paul's initial proclamation. Paul's missionary preaching and his preaching to converts were not necessary identical.

One important factor must be noted at the outset: both the 'traditional' and the 'negative' viewpoints have tended to equate Paul's interest in Jesus of Nazareth with the *form* such interest takes in the gospel traditions. But it is at least possible that even in his missionary preaching, Paul's interest in Jesus took a quite different *form*.[1] Merely to prove that knowledge of the gospel traditions is not even echoed in the epistles by no means limits one to the conclusion that Paul was uninterested in the life Jesus. The evidence, slight though it may be, must be weighed without such a presupposition.

I WAS PAUL UNINTERESTED IN JESUS?

2 Cor. 5: 16[2] is often taken as an exclusion of any interest in Jesus of Nazareth.[3] R. Bultmann has always supported his position by referring to Paul's rejection of Χριστὸς κατὰ σάρκα in 2 Cor. 5: 16:[4] 'For Paul, Christ has lost his identity as an

[1] So, E. Güttgemanns, *Der leidende Apostel*, p. 34.

[2] The literature on this verse is vast. See the following lists: V. Furnish, 'Debate', *BJRL* **47** (1965), 355 n. 3; J. Dupont, *Gnosis, La Connaissance Religieuse dans les Épîtres de Saint Paul* (Louvain and Paris, 2nd ed. 1960), p. 181 n. 2; E.-B. Allo, *Seconde Épître aux Corinthiens* (Paris, 1956), pp. 179ff. See also, J. Blank, *Paulus and Jesus*, pp. 304–26; J. L. Martyn, 'Epistemology at the Turn of the Ages' in *Christian History and Interpretation* (Festschrift J. Knox), eds. W. R. Farmer, C. F. D. Moule, R. R. Niebuhr (Cambridge, 1967), pp. 269–87; J. W. Fraser, 'Paul's Knowledge of Jesus: II Corinthians 5: 16 Once More', *NTS* **17** (1971), 293–313. This verse is prominent in several recent discussions of Paul's opponents in 2 Corinthians.

[3] J. Weiss (*Paul and Jesus*, pp. 41ff.) and others have argued that 2 Cor. 5: 16 proves that at one stage Paul knew the earthly Jesus. This view is not now taken very seriously, though W. C. van Unnik rather rashly suggests that Acts 22: 3 supports it: *Tarsus or Jerusalem* (E.T. London, 1962), p. 54. I Cor. 9: 1 surely proves that Paul cannot have seen the earthly Jesus. H. Lietzmann (*An die Korinther 1, 2* (1949)), among others, suggests that if Paul had seen Jesus briefly, he would not have used ἐγνώκαμεν in this verse.

[4] Even though Bultmann first linked κατὰ σάρκα to Χριστόν, and later to ἐγνώκαμεν, he has always (not only since 1947, as J. L. Martyn implies in 'Epistemology' in *Christian History*, p. 271) insisted that the choice is unimportant. See, for example, 'Kirche und Lehre im NT' in *Glauben*

89

individual person'.[1] H. Conzelmann claims that 2 Cor. 5: 16 is a 'definite theological programme'.[2]

A number of objections must be raised against this interpretation. (a) As will be shown below, it is not confirmed by other evidence from the epistles. (b) If Paul is implying that he is not interested in Jesus of Nazareth κατὰ σάρκα as opposed to κατὰ πνεῦμα, he is separating Jesus of Nazareth from the Risen Christ, and placing himself on the side of those whom he opposed in 1 Cor. 12: 3.[3] (c) Even if κατὰ σάρκα is taken with Χριστόν, the phrase does not have negative undertones elsewhere in Paul, as Rom. 9: 4f. makes clear.[4] (d) Bultmann maintains that his interpretation of the verse is valid even if κατὰ σάρκα is taken with ἐγνώκαμεν, 'for a "Christ regarded in the manner of the flesh" is just what a "Christ after the flesh" is'.[5] But to equate the two grammatical possibilities is an over-simplification.[6] There are many good reasons for linking κατὰ σάρκα with the verbs.[7] Once the phrase is separated from Χριστόν, it becomes clear that 2 Cor.

und Verstehen 1 (1933), 185 (E.T. in Faith and Understanding, p. 217) and 'Das Verhältnis' (E.T. in Historical Jesus, eds. C. E. Braaten and R. A. Harrisville, p. 20).

[1] Primitive Christianity in its Contemporary Setting (E.T. London, 1956), p. 197.

[2] 'Jesus von Nazareth und der Glaube an den Auferstandenen', in Der historische Jesus und der kerygmatische Christus, ed. H. Ristow and K. Matthiae (Berlin, 1962), p. 189. J. M. Robinson notes that this view of 2 Cor. 5: 16 has become so common that in current discussion the expression κατὰ σάρκα is used for the technical meaning of 'historical Jesus': 'Kerygma and History in the New Testament' in The Bible in Modern Scholarship, ed. J. P. Hyatt (Nashville and New York, 1966), p. 165 n. 24.

[3] J. M. Robinson virtually equates 1 Cor. 12: 3 and 2 Cor. 5: 16, suggesting a Pauline volte-face in 2 Cor.: Paul now agrees with his opponents in 1 Cor. But Paul is unlikely to have contradicted himself within such a short space of time. 'Kerygma', pp. 142ff.

[4] E. Schweizer, art. 'σάρξ', TWNT VII, 130 n. 259.

[5] Theology of the NT I, 239.

[6] J. L. Martyn ('Epistemology' in Christian History, p. 283), correctly stresses the importance of a decision on this point. Cf. also A. Oepke, 'Irrwege', ThLZ 77 (1952), 454.

[7] See G. Friedrich, 'Die Gegner des Paulus im 2. Korintherbrief' in Abraham Unser Vater (Festschrift O. Michel), eds. O. Betz, M. Hengel, P. Schmidt (Leiden, 1963), p. 190; E.-B. Allo, comm. ad loc.; E. Schweizer, art. 'σάρξ', TWNT VII, 130f.

5: 16 does not mean that Jesus of Nazareth no longer interests Paul. (*e*) If verse 16b means that Paul is not interested in Jesus of Nazareth, 16a must imply that he is not interested in people in general, which, from his epistles, is manifestly not the case.[1]

W. Schmithals and E. Güttgemanns have also criticised Bultmann's interpretation of 2 Cor. 5: 16, but their own solution is scarcely more convincing.[2] Schmithals claims that as this verse suits neither the immediate context nor the whole thrust of Paul's theology, it must be a gnostic gloss. Güttgemanns finds himself forced, almost against his better judgement, to agree with Schmithals.[3] Such a desperate proposal only underlines the futility of assuming that the verse intends to say anything about the interest of either Paul, or of his opponents, in Jesus of Nazareth.

This verse does not intend to give any information about the significance Paul attached to the ministry of Jesus.[4] Paul is not contrasting two kinds of 'Christ', a Χριστὸς κατὰ σάρκα and some implied alternative, but in this verse and in his whole argument from 2: 14 to 6: 10 he is emphasising the new situation brought about by Christ's death and resurrection.[5] From 5: 11 onwards Paul has his opponents in mind; this is made clear in verse 12, where their pride in outward appearances is criticised. The key to the immediate context is verse 14: ἄρα οἱ πάντες ἀπέθανον; the ἡμεῖς and the subjects of the verbs in verse 16 are to be interpreted with this clause, as is verse 17. The death and resurrection of Jesus have brought a new order for all Christians. Two consequences are mentioned – a negative one in verse 16 and a positive one in verse 17.

Verse 16b must not be interpreted in isolation from 16a. In verse 16a Paul stresses that under the new order Christians, including himself, no longer consider anyone from the old pre-Christian perspective (κατὰ σάρκα), merely on outward

[1] J. Dupont, *Gnosis*, p. 185.
[2] W. Schmithals, *Die Gnosis in Korinth* (Göttingen, 2nd ed. 1965), pp. 286ff.; Güttgemanns, *Der leidende Apostel*, pp. 290ff.
[3] *Der leidende Apostel*, p. 298, esp. n. 97a. For a critical discussion of Schmithals' hypothesis, see G. Friedrich, 'Die Gegner' in *Abraham Unser Vater*, pp. 193f.
[4] So also, W. G. Kümmel's *Anhang* to H. Lietzmann's comm. (4th ed. Tübingen, 1949), p. 205.
[5] Cf. J. L. Martyn, 'Epistemology' in *Christian History*, p. 271.

appearances (verse 12); relationships with others are no longer established according to purely selfish criteria.[1] The precise nature of knowledge from the new perspective is not clarified in verse 16a, but Paul has already indicated in verses 14 and 15 what he considers to be the opposite of knowledge κατὰ σάρκα: there he refers to the constraint of the love of Christ and living no longer for oneself but for Christ. Verse 16b underlines the main point of 16a: οὐδένα must include Christ. The implication is that Paul's opponents have failed to grasp the significance of the new situation because they insist on considering Christ from the old perspective.[2]

This general interpretation of 2 Cor. 5: 16 has been criticised in recent discussion: if κατὰ σάρκα is construed with the verb, why does Paul use a conditional sentence?[3] But, as often in the epistles, Paul's choice of expression is far from precise.[4] Perhaps the εἰ καί clause is deliberately ambiguous:[5] some of those whom Paul includes with ἡμεῖς have assessed Christ from the old pre-resurrection perspective, others are included hypothetically.

W. Schmithals agrees that 16a and 16b must be taken together, but argues that Paul cannot mean that he is unwilling to know anybody as an ordinary human being, for Paul is certainly not a gnostic![6] But ἐγνώκαμεν κατὰ σάρκα does not have to be interpreted as rigidly as this.[7] Paul is not concerned to

[1] Cf. A. Oepke, *Die Missionspredigt*, p. 133 n. 2 and J. Blank, *Paulus und Jesus*, p. 318.

[2] J. L. Martyn attempts to show how Paul's two groups of opponents, the gnostics and the 'super-apostles', would have understood the phrase: 'Epistemology' in *Christian History*, pp. 275ff.

[3] D. Georgi, *Die Gegner des Paulus im 2. Korintherbrief* (Neukirchen-Vluyn, 1964), p. 291; W. Schmithals, *Die Gnosis in Korinth*, p. 294; cf. also D. W. Oostendorp, *Another Jesus: a gospel of Jewish Christian Superiority in 2 Corinthians* (Kampen, 1967), p. 53.

[4] Recognition of this also meets the objection that in such circumstances Paul would not have used Χριστός.

[5] There is a long-standing debate over the interpretation of the clause; arguments supporting a real and an unreal condition have been marshalled. See E. Haenchen, 'Christologie', *ZTK* **63** (1966), 153 n. 17 and J. W. Fraser, 'Paul's Knowledge of Jesus', *NTS* **17** (1971), 300.

[6] *Die Gnosis*, p. 294.

[7] Cf. J. Dupont: 'Nos relations avec les hommes ne sont plus fondées sur la chair, mais sur une base toute différente', *Gnosis*, p. 185.

spell out the precise meaning of the phrase, for all the emphasis is on the fact of the change brought about by the death and resurrection of Jesus.[1]

2 Cor. 5: 16 cannot be used as an interpretative key to solve the question of Paul's understanding of the significance of Jesus of Nazareth, for that is not the question Paul is discussing here. The main point of 2 Cor. 5: 16 is clear: as a consequence of the death and resurrection of Jesus, Christians have a new perspective on all things and all people and no longer 'know' κατὰ σάρκα. Any attempt to evaluate others, even Christ, as though the death and resurrection of Jesus had not brought about a totally new situation is to be rejected most firmly.

Scholars who attempt to draw out the continuity between Paul and Jesus insist that Paul must have known something about the person whose disciples he persecuted; after his conversion Paul was always in close touch with those who had known Jesus, especially with Peter and James.[2] G. D. Kilpatrick's translation of Gal. 1: 18 as 'to get information [about Jesus] from Cephas' is often utilised,[3] and C. H. Dodd's quip that Peter did not spend a fortnight in Jerusalem talking about the weather is repeated frequently.[4]

In his *Tarsus or Jerusalem*, W. C. van Unnik argues that although Paul was born in Tarsus, he was brought up and educated for the rabbinate in Jerusalem; if this is correct, it further underlines the probability that Paul gained more information about the ministry and character of Jesus of Nazareth than he chooses to refer to in his epistles.

Arguments along these lines have an impressive cumulative force. But even if it were possible to establish each of these

[1] Cf. W. G. Kümmel's *Anhang* to H. Lietzmann's comm., p. 205.

[2] E.g. F. Prat, *The Theology of Saint Paul* II (London, 1927), 23f.; Oepke asks whether Paul could have hermetically sealed himself off against all the material about Jesus which his fellow workers such as Barnabas, Silas and John Mark could and certainly did give him: *Die Missionspredigt*, pp. 135f.

[3] G. D. Kilpatrick, 'Galatians 1: 18 "ΙΣΤΟΡΗΣΑΙ ΚΗΦΑΝ"', in *New Testament Essays* (T. W. Manson Memorial volume), ed. A. J. B. Higgins (Manchester, 1959), pp. 144ff. See W. D. Davies' discussion, *The Setting of the Sermon on the Mount* (Cambridge, 1964), pp. 453ff.

[4] *Apostolic Preaching*, p. 26.

points, this sort of approach can only show that Paul *could* have been interested in the pre-crucifixion events. However, they show how very unlikely are hypotheses which claim that Paul tells us very little about Jesus of Nazareth because he himself knew next to nothing.[1]

If Paul's contacts with the first Christians, especially Peter and James, make it certain that he could have gained information about the life and character of Jesus, the question of his attitude to the primitive tradition is immediately raised. Did Paul deliberately disparage the relevance of information about the ministry of Jesus?

K. Wegenast has sought to prove that for Paul, only his revealed gospel, Christ as Son and Lord, is the norm of his preaching and the norm over all tradition.[2] Any information Paul received about Jesus was given a very subordinate place and had nothing to do with his gospel. But this view can be maintained only by unnecessarily contrasting tradition and revelation. Could not Paul have held the two in tension in such a way that in some circumstances in his letters he places the emphasis in one direction, in other circumstances in another? Wegenast takes as his starting point Gal. 1 and 2, and 1 Thess. 2: 13, and has little difficulty in proving that the gospel as something revealed always takes priority over tradition.[3] But one can justifiably ask whether the gospel does not nevertheless include tradition. Why, on this view, did Paul visit Peter?

Wegenast's examination of pieces of tradition such as 1 Cor. 15: 1ff., Rom. 1: 3f. and Phil. 2: 5ff. is unsatisfactory, for while Paul does not simply equate 'tradition' and 'gospel', Wegenast does not clarify the meaning of the tradition of an event, such as the death of Jesus, for Paul's proclamation. If tradition plays only a secondary role in comparison with revelation, it is very difficult to account for the frequency with which Paul cites or alludes to it; the significance of 1 Cor. 15:

---

[1] W. Schmithals argues that, in general, primitive Christianity knew very little about the life of Jesus. The Jerusalem church may have been almost as ignorant of the historical Jesus as was Paul: 'Paulus', *ZNW* **53** (1962), 151 and *Paul and James* (E.T. London, 1965), p. 103 n. 2. Cf. also U. Wilckens, 'Tradition', *RHPR* **47** (1967), 20.

[2] *Das Verständnis der Tradition bei Paulus und in Deuteropaulinen* (Neukirchen, 1962). See W. G. Kümmel's review in *ThLZ*, **89** (1964), 754.

[3] *Das Verständnis*, p. 50.

3ff. and 1 Cor. 11: 23ff.[1] cannot be nullified simply by pointing to the alterations and additions Paul makes to the tradition.

Gal. 1 and 2 cannot be placed over against 1 Cor. 15, or *vice versa*.[2] Both passages refer to Paul's gospel, as the wording of 1 Cor. 15: 1 and Gal. 1: 11 is strikingly similar. Paul's emphasis in Gal. 1: 11ff. on the divine origin of the gospel and its independence of human agencies does not carry as a corollary a denigration of facts or tradition about Jesus.[3] 1 Cor. 15: 3ff. stresses the form and content of the gospel Paul preached, while Gal. 1: 11ff. underlines its essential dynamic character; both passages include at least an echo of the main thrust of the other.[4]

For Paul, tradition is neither purely dynamic and kerygmatic nor purely historical, for both are held together;[5] Paul's gospel is closely related to the primitive tradition. One cannot appeal to an alleged secondary and insignificant role played by tradition in order to show that Paul was unconcerned with Jesus of Nazareth, and looked instead to the exalted Christ. Similarly, Paul's own emphasis in Galatians on the importance of his conversion does not exclude the possibility that he was

[1] L. Goppelt insists that 1 Cor. 11: 23ff. assumes familiarity with a narrative of the passion and that the small number of citations of the gospel traditions does not mean that they are not at the very basis of Pauline theology; 'Tradition nach Paulus', *KD* **4** (1958), 223. E. Haenchen argues that as the historical Jesus did not have the authority for Paul which is claimed here, these verses contain an echo of a Christology which belonged to non-Pauline circles which laid greater emphasis on memories of the historical Jesus! 'Christologie', *ZTK* **63** (1966), 155.

[2] Cf. W. Baird, 'What is the Kerygma?', *JBL* **76** (1957), 181ff. B. Gerhardsson's attempt to separate rigidly these two passages is unconvincing. He argues that τὸ εὐαγγέλιον in Gal. 1: 11ff. comes directly from the Risen Lord and is to be distinguished from 1 Cor. 15: 1ff.; the latter verses contain ὁ λόγος τοῦ θεοῦ (*didache*), traditions which emanate from Jerusalem, the doctrinal centre of primitive Christianity. An unwarranted interpretation of τίνι λόγῳ (1 Cor. 15: 2) is used to draw the distinction between the two passages; *Memory*, pp. 273 and 296ff.

[3] Cf. D. L. Dungan, *The Sayings of Jesus*, p. xxv, referring to Heitmüller.

[4] W. Baird, 'Kerygma', *JBL* **76** (1957), 190f. L. Goppelt argues that in Gal. 1: 9 and 1 Thess. 2: 13 παραλαμβάνω is used in a similar way to its use in 1 Cor. 15: 1ff.: 'Tradition', *KD* **4** (1958), 218. Cf. K. Wegenast, *Tradition*, pp. 44ff.

[5] So, Goppelt, 'Tradition', *KD* **4** (1958), 221, with reference to the rejection of the former in 1 Cor., and the latter in 2 Cor.

influenced to a considerable extent by such information about Jesus as he had gained prior to his conversion.

Was Paul uninterested in the teaching of Jesus? While many scholars maintain that Paul allows the teaching of Jesus to colour his thought to a considerable extent,[1] others claim that Paul (and primitive Christianity generally) made little use of it either because Paul had no interest in it, or, as is argued frequently by recent writers, because he was almost completely ignorant of the teaching of Jesus.[2]

Scholars who make the latter claim insist that many of the words of Jesus which Paul does cite are to be ascribed to the exalted Lord speaking in the post-Easter church, rather than to Jesus of Nazareth.[3] This is certainly the case at 2 Cor. 12: 9, but here the context leaves no doubt that the words which Paul quotes are given directly to Paul in a vision by the exalted Lord, and are in no way related to the teaching of Jesus of Nazareth.

In other passages the context gives no such indication.[4] I Cor. 11: 23–5 clearly envisages a pre-Easter situation, even though κύριος is used.[5] The tense of διέταξεν in 1 Cor. 9: 14 indicates that Paul was consciously alluding to a 'past' origin in the teaching of Jesus, again in spite of his use of κύριος. The fact that 1 Thess. 4: 15ff. does not correspond verbally with extant logia of Jesus does not mean that Paul is referring to words which he received as a direct revelation from the Risen Lord.

---

[1] See, for example, C. H. Dodd, 'The Ethics of the Pauline Epistles' in *The Evolution of Ethics*, ed. E. H. Sneath (New Haven and London, 1927), pp. 301ff.; 'Matthew and Paul' in *New Testament Studies* (Manchester, 1953), pp. 53ff. See also J. P. Brown, 'Synoptic Parallels in the Epistles and Form-History', *NTS* **10** (1963–4), 48. [2] See above, p. 87 n. 3.

[3] W. Schmithals, 'Paulus', *ZNW* **53** (1962), 157. Cf. Wilckens, 'Tradition', *RHPR* **47** (1967), 2ff.

[4] *Contra* Schmithals, who acknowledges that 2 Cor. 12: 9 originates with the Risen Lord and suggests that this may also be the case with other logia: 'Paulus', *ZNW* **53** (1962), 147. E. Haenchen assigns 1 Thess. 4: 15, as well as 2 Cor. 12: 8f., to the Risen Lord, but states that 1 Cor. 7: 10 is more difficult! 'Christologie', *ZTK* **63** (1966), 154.

[5] See Goppelt, 'Tradition', *KD* **4** (1958), 223. O. Cullmann correctly discounts the possibility that the words were given to Paul in a vision: 'The Tradition' in *The Early Church*, ed. A. J. B. Higgins (E.T. London, 1956), pp. 6of.

Further confirmation that Paul was not uninterested in the teaching of Jesus is provided by 1 Cor. 7. In verse 10 Paul appeals to the teaching of Jesus as authoritative;[1] in verses 12 and 25 he regrets that he is forced to indicate his own opinion, as he is unable to appeal to words of Jesus.

The extent of Paul's knowledge of the teachings of Jesus must remain as an open question. But even from his explicit citations we can see that his knowledge must have been quite extensive. 1 Cor. 7: 25 suggests that the *paradosis* contained sayings dealing with the most detailed aspects of conduct.[2] However, if Paul had access to an extensive collection of logia, it is difficult to understand why he did not cite logia of Jesus more frequently in dealing with disputed questions.

Nor do the many allusions to synoptic logia take us much further.[3] C. H. Dodd's conclusion that 1 Thess. 5 and Rom. 12 indicate that Paul had given careful study to the tradition of the teaching of Jesus and that he based his own ethic on a profound understanding of it, may not be an exaggeration.[4]

---

[1] The force of 1 Cor. 7: 10 cannot be avoided by suggesting, as Wilckens does, that although some words of Jesus passed into the tradition of the Hellenistic churches and were regarded as authoritative words of Jesus, this was not Paul's own attitude! 'Tradition', *RHPR* **47** (1967), 5. Cf. E. Haenchen's similar comments with reference to 1 Cor. 11: 23ff., p. 95 n. 1 above.

On the whole question of Paul's instructions on marriage and the sayings on divorce in the synoptic gospels, see D. L. Dungan, *Sayings of Jesus*, pp. 83–131.

[2] Cf. also Rom. 14: 14; ἐν κυρίῳ 'Ιησοῦ probably means 'on the authority of the Lord Jesus', as in the footnote to the 2nd ed. of the New English Bible. See O. Cullmann, 'Tradition' in *The Early Church*, p. 65.

[3] For recent attempts to discern Paul's use of the teaching of Jesus, see R. Schippers, 'The Pre-Synoptic Tradition in 1 Thess. 2: 13–16', *NovT* **8** (1966), 223–34; P. Nepper-Christensen, 'Das verborgene Herrnwort, Eine Untersuchung über 1 Thess. 4: 13–18', *ST* **19** (1965), 136–54. See also C. F. D. Moule, 'The Use of Parables and Sayings as Illustrative Material in Early Christian Catechesis', *JTS* **3** (1952), 75–9.

In *The Sayings of Jesus* D. L. Dungan argues that Paul is alluding to the workman/food saying of Jesus all through the context of 1 Cor. 9: 4–14; even when Paul comes to the actual reference to the Lord's command he does not stop alluding to this saying. Dungan reaches similar conclusions in his examination of 1 Cor. 6: 15f. and 7: 12–16.

[4] *The Epistle of Paul to the Romans* (London, 1932), p. 208.

Yet since Pauline ethical injunctions were certainly not drawn solely from traditions of Jesus' teaching, one is faced with the difficulty that Paul does not distinguish between dominical and other material, nor is it likely that his readers were able to do so. Lists of allusions and parallels to the synoptic logia underline their influential role in the primitive church, but they do not reveal Paul's own interest in Jesus of Nazareth. As V. Furnish observes, the whole Jesus–Paul debate has never been significantly advanced – in spite of many notable attempts – nor will a solution ever be finally achieved, by cataloguing parallel passages in Paul and the Gospels.[1]

In spite of the problems which surround Paul's knowledge and use of the teaching of Jesus, there is no doubt that he was not indifferent to it. There are a number of hints that he distinguished between his own teaching and that of Jesus, and that he was aware of the difference between words of Jesus of Nazareth and words of the exalted Lord given directly in a vision. This suggests, as does Paul's attitude to tradition, that he was aware of the difference between the 'past' and 'present' of Jesus Christ, yet underlined the identity of Jesus of Nazareth and the exalted Lord by introducing words of whose pre-Easter origin he was well aware, as words of ὁ κύριος.

The view that Paul was not interested in the life and character of Jesus of Nazareth is built on a series of unjustifiable assertions. It is true that Paul refers to no more than a handful of 'facts' about Jesus of Nazareth, but this needs to be balanced against the paucity of references to some cardinal aspects of Pauline theology, such as the eucharist. There is no reason to suppose that Paul knew very little about Jesus or that he ignored what he did know. There are no *a priori* reasons why reference to the life and character of Jesus should not have played an important role in his missionary preaching. Before this specific

---

[1] 'Debate', *BJRL* **47** (1956), 374. W. G. Kümmel notes that words of Jesus are particularly extensive in the paraenetic material in Romans, a letter sent to a community not founded by Paul himself, and suggests that this may be taken as an indication that the words of Jesus played a much greater role in Paul's missionary preaching than the epistles lead us to suppose; 'Jesus und Paulus', *Theologische Blätter* **19** (1940), 212 (now in *Heilsgeschehen*, p. 84).

question is discussed, some passages which indicate that Paul was interested in the character of Jesus are considered.

II PAUL AND THE CHARACTER OF JESUS

The richness and depth of Paul's presentation of the character of Jesus Christ is frequently appealed to by those who claim that Paul's preaching and teaching, including his missionary preaching, took account of the life and character of Jesus of Nazareth, as well as of his death and resurrection, however central and dominant the latter were.[1] Others have dismissed these 'character traits' as references to the pre-existent Christ rather than to Jesus of Nazareth.[2] Since Paul did not make rigid distinctions between the pre-existent Christ and Jesus of Nazareth, wider issues, such as the influence of some sort of 'gnostic-Saviour' myth on Paul's Christology, or his knowledge of gospel traditions, tend to influence exegesis.

Phil. 2: 6–11 may be taken as a convenient test case, for many of the same issues are involved in the other passages in question.[3] Does Paul intend to stress the character of Jesus of Nazareth? Or are these verses concerned with 'actions' in a mythical drama which says little more about Jesus than that he existed as a human and died? Although most recent investigations have taken the literary form of the hymn as the starting point, I shall concentrate on Paul's interpretation and use of these verses rather than on their original meaning and purpose, if a sharp distinction can, in fact, be drawn.[4] Interesting and important though the literary form is, it can

[1] E.g. C. H. Dodd, *History and the Gospel* (London, 1938), p. 65.

[2] E.g. R. Bultmann in *Glauben und Verstehen* I, 206; also W. Schmithals, 'Paulus', *ZNW* **53** (1962), 147.

[3] See R. P. Martin, *Carmen Christi, Phil. 2: 5–11 in recent interpretation and in the setting of early Christian worship* (Cambridge, 1967). Literature up to 1962 is discussed; a summary of the literature between 1963 and 1966 is included on pp. 313–19. Some of the more recent literature is noted below.

[4] Cf. E. Käsemann's discussion of the passage. Verse 5 and the use Paul makes of the hymn are taken up only after the exegesis of the hymn has been established: 'Kritische Analyse von Phil. 2: 5–11' in *Exegetische Versuche und Besinnungen* I (Göttingen, 1960), 90ff. [E.T. 'A Critical Analysis of Philippians 2: 5–11' in *Journal for Theology and the Church* **5** (1968), 45–68].

all too easily predetermine the exegesis of the passage.[1] Comparatively little is known about primitive Christian worship, and even less about the earliest forms of hymns. Precise stylistic criteria must be at least partly conjectural; the variety of suggested literary forms indicates that caution is necessary and that the form of the hymn is not a sufficiently firm foundation for the exegesis of the text.[2]

A more appropriate starting point is the immediate context in Phil. 2, though this raises the question of the validity of the so-called 'ethical interpretation'. Until recently it was generally agreed that in this passage Paul, who has deplored the pride, self-interest and disunity of the Philippians (1: 27 – 2: 4), wishes to remind his readers of the example of Jesus Christ. This view, which regards Phil. 2: 6–11 less as a formal discussion of Christology than as a 'piece of popular theology',[3] is usually believed to be supported by 2: 5.

E. Käsemann,[4] and, following him, R. P. Martin,[5] have vigorously attacked the ethical interpretation. Paul, they claim, rarely uses the example of Jesus Christ to enforce an exhortation. But even if this is accepted – and it has been strongly denied[6] – there is no reason why these verses should not be unique. The 'occasional' character of the epistles means that not all aspects of Pauline theology are found in every epistle; some are found very infrequently. Rom. 15: 1–7 provides a striking parallel to Phil. 2 – both in the circumstances of those addressed and in the appeal to Christ who did not please himself.

The hymn is said to be a soteriological drama which traces the steps through which Christ passed from pre-existence to

[1] Cf. R. P. Martin's criticism of an interpretation on the grounds of the structure of the hymn, *Carmen Christi*, p. 64 n. 1.

[2] Attempts to establish the structure of the hymn continue. See, for example, C. H. Talbert, 'The Problem of Pre-Existence in Phil. 2: 6–11', *JBL* **86** (1967), 141–53; C.-H. Hunzinger, 'Zur Struktur der Christus-Hymnen in Phil. 2 and 1 Petr. 3' in *Der Ruf Jesu und die Antwort der Gemeinde* (Festschrift J. Jeremias), ed. E. Lohse (Göttingen, 1970), pp. 142–56.

[3] R. P. Martin, *Carmen Christi*, p. 69, quoting A. T. Robertson.

[4] E. Käsemann, 'Analyse', *Exegetische Versuche* I, 90ff. (E.T. pp. 83ff.).

[5] *Carmen Christi*, pp. 71ff. and 84ff.

[6] So, E. Larsson, *Christus als Vorbild* (Uppsala, 1962); W. P. de Boer, *The Imitation of Paul* (Kampen, 1962); E. J. Tinsley, *The Imitation of God in Christ* (London, 1960), pp. 134ff.

5 | 994

exaltation: it is more concerned with what Christ did than with who he was.[1] Even if this is the case, there is no reason why such a hymn could not have been given a new setting in the context of the epistle. R. Deichgräber has recently argued convincingly that primitive hymns about Christ have come down to us only because they were used in a secondary way, especially in paraenesis.[2]

At first sight Käsemann's interpretation of Phil. 2: 5 seems to be a weightier objection to the ethical interpretation. According to Käsemann, 2: 5 introduces a hymn with the apostolic preface that the Philippians are to act to one another as is fitting for those who are in the sphere of Christ's rule as his people.[3] The absence of a verb in 2: 5b is difficult. Many exegetes take φρονεῖτε or φρονεῖν δεῖ as understood, and ἐν Χριστῷ 'Ιησοῦ as 'in the company of Christ's people'.[4] But if φρονεῖτε is taken as understood, as it is by Käsemann, it would be tautologous and the καί superfluous. But the καί is not superfluous, it brings out the parallel between ἐν ὑμῖν and ἐν Χριστῷ; it is found in other passages where exhortation is made with a reference to Christ.[5] C. F. D. Moule translates the opening of the hymn: 'Adopt towards one another the same attitude which (was) also (found) in Christ Jesus...'.[6] No verb need be supplied; such a translation gives the καί its full force.[7]

[1] See Martin's summary of E. Käsemann's interpretation: *Carmen Christi*, pp. 90ff.

[2] R. Deichgräber, *Gotteshymnus und Christushymnus in der frühen Christenheit* (Göttingen, 1967), p. 190.

[3] 'Analyse', *Exegetische Versuche* I, 57 (E.T. p. 84). Cf. Martin, *Carmen Christi*, pp. 84ff.

[4] See Martin, *Carmen Christi*, pp. 70ff. for details.

[5] R. Deichgräber refers to Rom. 15: 7 (cf. also Rom. 15: 3); Ign. *Eph.* 21: 2; *Phld.* 7: 2, 11: 1; and Mark 10: 45, *Gotteshymnus*, p. 192. Cf. A. Schulz, who compares Phil. 2: 5 to the καὶ γάρ of Rom. 15: 3 and the γάρ of 2 Cor. 5: 14; 8: 9; *Nachfolgen und Nachahmen* (Munich, 1962), p. 288.

[6] 'Further Reflexions on Philippians 2: 5–11' in *Apostolic History and the Gospel* (Festschrift F. F. Bruce), eds. W. W. Gasque and R. P. Martin (Exeter, 1970), p. 264. Cf. R. Deichgräber, *Gotteshymnus*, p. 193.

[7] E. Larsson criticises Käsemann's interpretation of 2: 5 along similar lines: *Vorbild*, pp. 232ff. I. H. Marshall notes that the ethical interpretation does not stand or fall with any particular interpretation of 2: 5. 'The Christ Hymn in Phil. 2: 5–11', *TB* **19** (1968), 118.

Martin considers that Käsemann's strongest point is his insistence that on any ethical interpretation verses 9–11 must be regarded as an appendix, with no relevance to the exhortation.[1] But the humiliation–exaltation pattern, which lies at the heart of Phil. 2: 6–11, is frequently used as a motif in exhortation,[2] and there would seem to be no reason why this should not be the case here. ὑψοῦν is not found in Phil. 2: 1–5, but many aspects of the epistle as a whole make a promise of 'exaltation' relevant.[3] In this epistle Paul emphasises his own circumstances: he is imprisoned and is suffering, yet he is confident that his present adverse circumstances will turn out to be an advantage (1: 12ff.). He is so confident of ultimate vindication/exaltation (1: 21b; 3: 11) that he accepts his present lot for the sake of the Philippians, even though he is aware of the possibility of a violent death (2: 17).

The circumstances of the Philippians, especially their suffering (1: 30), are at least partially parallel to Paul's. They are to imitate Paul (3: 17) – this may include suffering the loss of all things in order to gain Christ (3: 8) and complete vindication, εἰς τὴν ἐξανάστασιν τὴν ἐκ νεκρῶν (3: 11). Certainly the reversal of both Paul's and the Philippians' circumstances is expected confidently in 3: 20–1, verses which have striking verbal and conceptual affinities with Phil. 2: 6–11.[4] Paul insists that he and his readers should rejoice (2: 18); eager expectation of the day of Jesus Christ and confidence in ultimate vindication (1: 19) characterise the whole letter.

The humiliation–exaltation motif is appropriate for both Paul's and the Philippians' circumstances. The hymn lies at the heart of the epistle. Not only Christ's humility, but also his exaltation is relevant, for the fact that Christ was exalted is an indication that God is at work in the midst of the

---

[1] *Carmen Christi*, p. 85. Martin criticises both W. P. de Boer and E. Larsson for failing to account satisfactorily for 2: 9–11.

[2] Cf. Luke 18: 14 and 14: 11; Matt. 23: 12 and 18: 4; Jas. 4: 10 and 1 Peter 5: 6. R. Deichgräber also refers to 1 Sam. 2: 7; Job 5: 11; T. Benj. 5: 5; 4 Esr. 8: 48ff.; Luke 1: 52; *Gotteshymnus*, pp. 193f.

[3] See W. G. Kümmel, *Introduction to the New Testament* (E.T. London, 1966), pp. 235ff. and T. E. Pollard, 'The Integrity of Philippians', *NTS* **13** (1966–7), pp. 57–66, for defences of the unity of Philippians.

[4] Cf. N. Flanagan, 'A Note on Philippians iii. 20, 21', *CBQ* **18** (1956), 8f.

Philippians and that τὸ σῶμα τῆς ταπεινώσεως ἡμῶν will be exalted (3: 21). The parallels between the hymn and the rest of the epistle must not be pressed, but the hymn as a whole provides the basis for a good deal of Paul's teaching in the epistle.

Martin rejects the argument that the exaltation of Christ is understood as prototypical for Christians, even though the paraenetic consequences of Christ's exaltation are not expressly stated, by insisting that this is an unwarranted inference from the text.[1] But as soon as one admits that Paul may be using the hymn as an ethical exhortation, the second part of the hymn, just as much as the first part, is seen as relevant to the epistle as a whole. Paul and his readers were well aware of the uniqueness of Jesus Christ; although he could not be imitated in all respects, aspects of his character and the fact of his exaltation provided the supreme example.

Whatever its original *Sitz im Leben* and meaning may have been, Paul uses the hymn as an exhortation to the Philippian Christians, setting before them the character of Jesus Christ.[2] The διὸ καὶ ὁ θεός (2: 9) is the turning point in the hymn, breaking it into two halves,[3] the second of which is concerned with God's exaltation of Jesus[4] and is less relevant to the present study. To what extent is the first part of the hymn concerned with the character of Jesus of Nazareth rather than with actions in a mythical drama? The discussion which follows moves from verse 8 back to verse 6, from the clauses which are most clearly setting out the character of Jesus to those which are more difficult to interpret.

[1] *Carmen Christi*, p. 88.

[2] R. P. Martin insists that the text of the hymn must be taken on its own, irrespective of the application which is made in the neighbouring verses; once this is done, it becomes increasingly difficult to follow the ethical interpretation: *Carmen Christi*, p. 215. But the original meaning cannot wholly determine the meaning of the hymn in its present context; the context in Philippians makes it clear that the hymn was understood to be appropriate for ethical exhortation.

[3] E. Lohmeyer's analysis brings this out, though it is partially obscured in Jeremias' and Martin's analyses. Martin, *Carmen Christi*, pp. 32ff.

[4] Note the emphatic position given to ὁ θεός at the beginning and end of this part of the hymn.

Verse 8 undoubtedly speaks of the humility and obedience of Jesus Christ.[1] O. Michel observes that humility and obedience are frequently brought together by Jewish pietists, who realised that although the righteous man must inevitably suffer in a world like this, his suffering, humiliation and shame would be followed by his vindication.[2]

If the validity of the preceding defence of the ethical interpretation and emphasis on Paul's own understanding and use of the hymn be granted, there are good reasons for accepting parts of verses 6 and 7 as references to the character of Jesus of Nazareth. σχήματι εὑρεθεὶς ὡς ἄνθρωπος is an allusion to the Danielic Son of Man,[3] providing a link with the words which follow in verse 8. Supernatural-apocalyptic features are not characteristic of the Son of Man in Daniel: the Son of Man is the elect, obedient, faithful and therefore suffering one who will be vindicated in the future.[4] The relevance of a reference to the Son of Man to the epistle as a whole is not difficult to see: Paul is already being persecuted, his very life is threatened, and as the Philippians are in similar circumstances (1: 30), Paul points to Jesus, the Son of Man who was humble and obedient, who suffered and was persecuted, whom God exalted and vindicated.

The preceding words, ἐν ὁμοιώματι ἀνθρώπων γενόμενος, are even closer to the text of Dan. 7: 13, as M. Black notes.[5] If the variant ἀνθρώπου (P⁴⁶ et al.) is accepted, the reference to the Danielic ke barnash, 'one like a man', is difficult to dispute.[6]

---

[1] E. Käsemann is forced to admit that it is here that the attempt at an ethical interpretation finds its strongest support. 'Analyse', Exegetische Versuche i, 79 (E.T. p. 70).

[2] O. Michel, 'Zur Exegese von Phil. 2: 5–11', Theologie als Glaubenswagnis (Festschrift K. Heim) (Hamburg, 1954), p. 86. Martin's reasons for rejecting this interpretation are not convincing, Carmen Christi, pp. 223ff.

[3] So E. Lohmeyer et al. See Martin, Carmen Christi, pp. 207ff. See also C. F. D. Moule, 'From Defendant to Judge – and Deliverer', now in The Phenomenon of the New Testament (London, 1967), p. 93.

[4] M. D. Hooker, The Son of Man in Mark (London, 1967), p. 190. This interpretation of 'Son of Man' is discussed in some detail below, pp. 156ff.

[5] 'The Son of Man Problem in Recent Research and Debate', BJRL 45 (1963), 315. This important suggestion seems to have been missed by Martin.

[6] M. Black compares Rev. 14: 14, ὅμοιον υἱόν (υἱῷ v.l.) ἀνθρώπου: 'The Son of Man Problem', BJRL 45 (1963), 315.

ἀλλὰ ἑαυτὸν ἐκένωσεν μορφὴν δούλου λαβών is probably not to be restricted to Isa. 53, nor is Jesus called 'servant' because he placed himself in bondage to the demonic powers of the Hellenistic world, but δοῦλος as well as ὑπήκοος point to the portrait of the obedient righteous man of Judaism of which Isa. 53 is the supreme example.[1]

Verses 7 and 8 contain a series of expressions which sum up the character of Jesus of Nazareth in terms of the humble, obedient and suffering figure of the Old Testament and late Judaism. This part of the passage is less concerned with a logical series of actions of self-abasement than with the sort of person Jesus was.

Do the opening words of the hymn in verse 6 also refer to the character of Jesus? ἀλλά marks not so much a new stage in a 'time-series' or a new 'form' of development, but is a link which brings out a contrast. Since the second part of the contrast refers so clearly to the character of Jesus, the possibility that this is the intention of verse 6 is worth considering. If this is so, the older, now almost forgotten, interpretation of ἁρπαγμόν may be correct: neither *res rapta, res rapienda*, nor *res retinenda*, but *raptus*. C. F. D. Moule defends *raptus* and paraphrases the opening of the hymn thus: 'Adopt towards one another the same attitude which (was) also (found) in Christ Jesus ,who, although in the form of God (and therefore, by worldly reckoning, one who might have been expected to help himself to whatever he wanted), did not reckon that equality with God consisted in snatching, but instead, emptied himself and took the form of a slave...'.[2]

To ask where the hymn moves from pre-existence to the

[1] So, both E. Schweizer, *Erniedrigung*, pp. 97ff. (cf. also p. 31), and Martin, *Carmen Christi*, pp. 191ff. Martin correctly notes that the objections of G. Bornkamm and others largely fall to the ground once one accepts that a strictly 'chronological' and logical progression of thought is not to be expected. Scholars who stress the link with Isa. 53 emphasise that ἑαυτὸν ἐκένωσεν is a literal rendering of Isa. 53: 12c. See especially J. Jeremias, 'Zu Phil ii: 7: EAYTON EKENΩΣEN', *NovT* **6** (1963), 182ff.

[2] 'Further Reflexions on Philippians 2: 5–11' in *Apostolic History*, pp. 264ff. This interpretation answers the main objection which Martin and others have brought against the active meaning: what exactly was it our Lord refused to plunder? *Carmen Christi*, pp. 135ff.

incarnation may, then, be the wrong question.[1] Paul seems to have 'fused' the character of Jesus of Nazareth and the pre-existent Christ together and to have had neither *simpliciter* in mind. Verse 6 may not, as is usually held, indicate a choice the pre-existent Christ made, but may provide a rich character portrait, which is underlined in the following clauses which clearly include Jesus of Nazareth within their perspective.[2] This view is supported by the prominence of the humiliation–exaltation motif in this passage, and its relevance to the epistle as a whole.

Important conclusions have emerged. Paul is concerned about the Philippians' selfishness and is anxious to encourage them in the midst of adverse circumstances and suffering; the first part of the hymn is appropriate to these twin themes of the epistle, the second part more especially to the latter. Paul intends to tell his readers far more about Jesus of Nazareth than the fact that he existed as a human being; he reminds them of the character of Jesus of Nazareth in terms of the suffering Son of Man and the obedient righteous man of Judaism. If verse 6 refers specifically to the pre-existent Son, then, on almost any interpretation of this verse, the sort of person depicted corresponds with the character portrait of Jesus of Nazareth which emerges so clearly in verses 7–8. Paul was interested in Jesus of Nazareth and saw the significance of his character not only for ethical exhortation, but also for Christology, for in Phil. 2: 6–11 both are woven inextricably together.[3]

2 Cor. 8: 9 also utilises a Christological statement in ethical exhortation and includes the character of Jesus of Nazareth within its perspective. If taken as a paradoxical incarnational formula, in isolation from its context, verse 9a might be

[1] Cf. U. Luck, 'Der "historische Jesus" als Problem des Urchristentums', *WD* **7** (1963), 66.

[2] If this approach is valid, the hymn contains a two-stage rather than a three-stage Christology.

[3] Contrast Martin's summary: 'The stress falls more on what He accomplished than upon who He was. It is the record of His acts, more than of His character and traits of personality, that occupies the centre of interest.' *Carmen Christi*, p. 295.

interpreted as contrasting the glory of the pre-existent Christ and the earthly ministry, which is assessed in negative terms as a time of 'poverty'. But in its present context, as the ἵνα clause in 9b makes clear, Paul sees the ministry in a positive light, as part of Jesus Christ's selfless giving for the benefit of others.[1]

Although Paul is not appealing to the literal poverty of Jesus of Nazareth (for that would carry the most unlikely implication that Jesus was literally wealthy),[2] the ministry of Jesus is not by-passed. Paul's starting point is the pre-existent Christ. But why did he speak of the pre-existent Christ in such deeply personal terms? The answer surely lies in Paul's understanding of the character of Jesus of Nazareth, for Jews had believed only in the pre-existence of a personification.[3]

Rom. 15: 3 and 8 confirm that Paul was well aware of the sort of person Jesus was; these verses cannot be taken as references to the pre-existent Christ.[4] Rom. 15: 3 appeals to the character of Christ to support the preceding exhortation to show concern for others and not to think of one's own interests. Paul notes that Christ did not please himself[5] – otherwise he might have avoided the reproaches heaped upon him. Paul appeals to Ps. 69: 9 to support his summary of the character of Christ.[6] This Psalm was widely understood in

[1] In 2 Cor. 8: 1ff. Paul is reawakening the Corinthians' zeal for 'the relief of the saints' by appealing to the example of the churches in Macedonia, and, to clinch the argument, to the example of Jesus Christ. Note the use of χάρις in 2 Cor. 8: 6, 7 to refer to the enterprise of selfless giving for others.

[2] G. W. Buchanan suggests that πλούσιος here may well mean literally wealthy: 'Jesus and the Upper Class', *NovT* 7 (1964), 195ff. C. H. Dodd notes that the point of 2 Cor. 8: 9 is sharper if the readers are assumed to know the tradition that Jesus did embrace poverty and had nowhere to lay his head: *Apostolic History*, p. 96 n. 2.

[3] So, G. B. Caird, 'The Development of the Doctrine of Christ in the New Testament', in *Christ for Us Today*, ed. N. Pittenger (London, 1968), pp. 79f. Caird notes that neither the Fourth Gospel nor Hebrews ever speaks of the eternal Word or Wisdom of God in terms which compel us to regard it as a person.

[4] *Contra* H. D. Betz, *Nachfolge*, p. 162, who interprets Rom. 15: 3 in terms of his understanding of Phil. 2: 6ff.

[5] Cf. C. K. Barrett, 'The verb sums up the work and character of Christ throughout his life', *Commentary on the Epistle to the Romans* (London, 1957). [6] Cf. O. Michel, *ad loc.*

the early church as referring to the reproaches Jesus endured as the righteous one *par excellence*.[1] From its use elsewhere in the New Testament and from its use in this context, it is clear that Paul's citation is not used merely of the crucifixion but also to summarise the nature of Jesus Christ's whole ministry. Rom. 15: 3, as well as Acts 10: 36f., shows that the primitive church looked to the Old Testament to support its interpretation not only of the significance of Christ's death and resurrection, but also of the sort of person he showed himself to be in his life.

Similarly, Rom. 15: 8 sums up the character of Jesus: he became διάκονος περιτομῆς.[2] Since Christ's example is being appealed to, the choice of διάκονος is striking, especially in view of Mark 10: 45 and the gospel traditions generally.[3] The whole context of Rom. 15: 1–13, as well as verse 7 and the λέγω γάρ of 8a, confirm that Paul is referring to the character of Jesus of Nazareth. As O. Michel notes, Rom. 15: 1–6 and 7–13 have a similar form: both end with a prayer, both refer to the historical Jesus and include reference to the Old Testament, both refer to glorifying God.[4] In each passage the example of Jesus of Nazareth is central, in different ways both refer to essentially the same aspect of the character of Jesus.

2 Cor. 10: 1 and Gal. 2: 20 are perhaps the most striking of other passages where Paul refers to the character of Jesus. The former can hardly be a reference to the pre-existent Christ.[5] In Gal. 2: 20 the choice of ἀγαπήσαντος alongside the more frequent παραδόντος, and the deeply personal note are significant. Since 1 Cor. 11: 23ff. indicates that Paul was familiar with the events surrounding the crucifixion and uses

---

[1] The New Testament passages are listed by M. J. Lagrange, *Saint Paul, Épître aux Romains* (Paris, 1916), W. Sanday and A. C. Headlam, *The Epistle to the Romans* (Edinburgh, 5th ed. 1902), *ad loc.* Cf. also E. E. Ellis, *Paul's Use of the Old Testament* (Edinburgh and London, 1957), p. 97 n. 4.

[2] I take the more difficult perfect tense as the original reading.

[3] C. K. Barrett emphasises the significance of περιτομῆς: in ministering to 'the most awkward and irritating of scrupulous persons', Jesus provided an example for all strong Christians; comm. *ad loc.*

[4] Comm. *ad loc.*

[5] *Contra* R. Leivestad, 'The Meekness and Gentleness of Christ', 2 Cor. 10: 1', *NTS* **12** (1966), 156–64.

the verb παρεδίδετο, how did Paul come to interpret the death of Christ in this way? Could he have used these words if he had not known that they were appropriate to the character of Jesus? As the history of Pauline scholarship shows,[1] it is all too easy to read references to the character of Jesus and to the gospel traditions generally into Paul's writings, but the context as well as exegetical details of a number of passages leave little doubt that he intended to refer to the character of Jesus of Nazareth.

Paul's references to the character of Jesus cannot be interpreted merely as references to the pre-existent Christ. Where does this rich portrait come from? As it cannot be attributed simply to traditional Jewish beliefs or to Christological reflection of a dogmatic kind, it must have been deeply influenced by Paul's knowledge of the earthly Jesus.[2] Support for this conclusion is provided by 1 Cor. 11: 1 and 1 Thess. 1: 6, in which Paul links his own example to that of Christ. Although Paul frequently appeals to his own conduct as an example for his readers who have known him personally, these are the only two passages where he refers explicitly to the example of Christ.[3] Since his own example is not presented merely in general terms of the pre-existent Christ, Paul must intend to refer to the character of Jesus of Nazareth.[4]

Paul's interest in Jesus was not confined to the value of his example in ethical exhortation. The passages considered are used in this way – but this is not surprising in view of the purpose of the epistles. These passages are also Christological; Paul does not merely list character traits of Jesus for imitation, but he uses christological teaching to underline his ethical instruction.

---

[1] Cf. E. Güttgemanns, *Der leidende Apostel*, pp. 359ff. F. Prat, among others, takes Rom. 1: 4 as a reference to Jesus' earthly life of holiness: *Theology* II, 155. W. D. Davies follows the suggestions of P. Feine, J. Weiss and others, and notes that the name 'Jesus' could easily be substituted for the term 'love' to supply a description of his character: *Invitation to the New Testament* (London, 1967), p. 363. Cf. H. D. Betz, *Nachfolge*, p. 156.

[2] So A. Oepke, *Missionspredigt*, pp. 136f.

[3] Paul seems to prefer to use expressions such as καθώς καί, γάρ, καί, καί γάρ, διά and κατά rather than the μιμεῖσθαι word-group to refer to the example of Christ. Cf. A. Schulz, *Nachfolgen*, pp. 288f.

[4] W. G. Kümmel, 'Jesus und Paulus', *NTS* **10** (1963–4), 176 (now in *Heilsgeschehen*, p. 451).

Paul's references to the character of Jesus provide positive support for rejection of the view that the Pauline kerygma included no more than the mere *Dass* of the historical existence of Jesus. What happened between the birth and death of Jesus and what Jesus taught were both deeply rooted in his whole theological thinking. W. G. Kümmel points to Gal. 4: 4; I Cor. 15: 20; Col. 1: 13: Paul 'looked back' and saw in the *sending*, as well as in the raising, of Jesus the eschatological *Heilszeit* breaking-in.[1] T. W. Manson argues that for Paul, 'Jesus is the one person in the history of the world of whom it can be said that he is justified ἐξ ἔργων νόμου and is therefore entitled to the reward attached to such obedience, namely, life...For the purpose of this argument, the character of the life lived by Jesus is of vital importance to Paul.'[2] The epistles show that Paul's Christology was bound up with his understanding of Jesus of Nazareth, especially, as we have seen, with the sort of person Jesus was.[3]

III PAUL'S MISSIONARY PREACHING

Did Paul include some reference to the character of Jesus in his initial preaching to unbelievers? The silence of the epistles can be, and has been, taken both to support and to deny this possibility. Hence consideration of wider issues has been necessary.

Since several examples of Paul's missionary preaching are provided in Acts, but only indirectly and very infrequently in the epistles, the evidence of Acts must not be overlooked, even though on any issue the evidence of Paul's own writings must take priority. Luke's account of Paul's speech in the synagogue in Pisidian Antioch (Acts 13: 16–41) suggests that Paul's initial preaching stressed God's action in the past and

[1] 'Jesus und Paulus', *NTS* **10** (1963-4), 172 (*Heilsgeschehen*, p. 448).
[2] Review of R. Bultmann's *Theology of the NT* I, in *JTS* **50** (1949), 206.
[3] See also B. Gärtner's perceptive discussion of references to the kingdom in the Pauline epistles. He argues that in spite of all the differences brought about by the resurrection, there is a clear line of continuity: what the kingdom stood for in the preaching of Jesus remains essential in the new teaching of the church. 'The Person of Jesus and the Kingdom of God', *Theology Today* **27** (1970), 32-43.

included reference to the ministries of John the Baptist and Jesus. The Areopagus speech (Acts 17: 22–31), and the briefer account of the preaching of Paul and Barnabas at Lystra (Acts 14: 15–17), indicate that Paul's initial preaching of the gospel was quite unlike the main theological emphases of the epistles. But can this evidence be taken at its face value?

As in the Petrine speeches in Acts, Luke's hand is undoubtedly evident: the Pauline speeches are certainly not *verbatim* accounts. There are similarities between both the form and content of the Petrine speeches and Paul's speech in Acts 13;[1] for example, as was noted in the previous chapter, Ps. 107: 20 is used in a similar way in Acts 10: 36 (Peter) and Acts 13: 26 (Paul). But there is rather more evidence than is often realised which points in the opposite direction.

It is generally agreed that Paul's speech to the Ephesian elders at Miletus (Acts 20: 18–35) shows the nearest approximation to Pauline language.[2] The parallels which have been observed are extensive and striking and cannot be dismissed by appealing to similarities between this speech and non-Pauline epistles.[3] Pauline vocabulary and distinctively Pauline theological motifs, which are not at all Lucan, are echoed in these verses.[4] The most striking is the reference in 20: 28 to the redemptive nature of Christ's death which is not Lucan, but certainly Pauline. The similarity extends to the very themes discussed in the speech, even where they are clothed in Luke's own language. The general content recalls Paul's method of encouraging and exhorting the readers of his epistles; the speech almost seems to be a Pauline epistle in miniature. It is surely significant that the Pauline speech in Acts which stands closest to Paul's epistles is the only one recorded by

[1] Cf. Dibelius, *Studies*, pp. 133 and 165ff.; E. Schweizer, 'Concerning the Speeches in Acts' in *Studies in Luke-Acts* (Festschrift P. Schubert), eds. L. E. Keck and J. L. Martyn (Nashville and New York, 1966), pp. 208ff.

[2] H. J. Cadbury, 'The Speeches in Acts', *Beginnings of Christianity* v, 412.

[3] There are some similarities. See H. J. Cadbury's list, *Beginnings of Christianity* v, 415. But the parallels are far less extensive and less impressive than those between the Petrine speeches and the non-Petrine epistles.

[4] See C. F. D. Moule, 'The Christology of Acts' in *Studies in Luke-Acts*, eds. L. E. Keck and J. L. Martyn, pp. 171ff., and H. J. Cadbury's list in *Beginnings of Christianity* v, 415.

Luke which is addressed to believing Christians to whom Paul has ministered, and who are threatened by external and internal opposition – precisely the background of many of the Pauline epistles. Luke's writings betray no close knowledge of Paul's epistles, yet Paul's method is retained here.

The preaching attributed to Paul in Acts 14: 15–17 and 17: 22–31 is delivered to Gentiles who are not familiar with the Christian message. These speeches also seem to reflect the content of Paul's preaching in such circumstances; if they are taken together, they are quite similar to Paul's own brief summary of his initial preaching to Gentiles in 1 Thess. 1: 9–10.[1]

Paul's own epistles suggest that the speeches in Acts 14, 17 and 20 may well represent the gist of Paul's preaching in the particular circumstances envisaged.[2] But no such confirmation is possible for Paul's speech to the synagogue at Pisidian Antioch – the only speech attributed to Paul which refers to the life and character of Jesus. Luke has undoubtedly used earlier traditions in the composition of the speech,[3] and there are a few hints of Pauline vocabulary and theological themes; the close of the speech may be taken as a rough summary of the Pauline doctrine of faith.[4] But this falls well short of proof that Paul referred to the ministry of Jesus in his preaching. And yet since the other speeches in Acts attributed to Paul do seem to represent the general method and content of his preaching and teaching in the circumstances depicted, it is by no means easy to accept that Acts 13 merely reflects Luke's idea of the way Paul preached to Jewish audiences.[5] A comparison of the speeches in Acts attributed to Paul and Paul's

---

[1] Cf. Acts 14: 15 and Acts 17: 24 with 1 Thess. 1: 9–10.

[2] B. Gärtner stresses that our knowledge of Paul's theology is still fairly limited and that the theology of the speech in Acts 17 does not conflict directly with that of the epistles: *The Areopagus Speech and Natural Revelation* (Lund and Copenhagen, 1955), pp. 249ff., also p. 52. For a very different assessment, see Dibelius, *Studies*, pp. 56f. and 73ff. Wilckens argues that pre-Lucan traditions lie behind the speeches in Acts 14 and 17, but not behind the earlier speeches: *Missionsreden*, pp. 86ff.

[3] See above, pp. 82ff.

[4] See C. F. D. Moule, 'The Christology of Acts' in *Studies in Luke-Acts*, p. 174; H. J. Cadbury in *Beginnings of Christianity* v, 411ff.

[5] C. H. Dodd is rather less cautious: *Apostolic Preaching*, p. 62.

own epistles strongly suggests that his initial missionary preaching and his teaching and exhortations to groups of committed Christians differed widely.

The fundamental difference between an epistle and a gospel has been blurred in much recent writing.[1] If we possessed only the Johannine epistles (and not the Fourth Gospel) and only Acts (and not Luke's Gospel), we might well conclude that neither Luke nor the Johannine community had much interest in the sort of material the Gospels contain.[2] The fact that the epistles do not intend to convey or recall initial preaching is often overlooked. The epistles are addressed to particular communities, and, at least in the case of the Pauline epistles, the writer is usually personally acquainted with the circumstances of those to whom he is writing. In several passages Paul indicates that his readers are well aware of the main themes of his proclamation; he may remind his readers of a particular point, but there is no need to repeat his initial preaching.

References to the content of the initial preaching, such as 1 Thess. 1: 9–10, and indeed, references to many central themes of Pauline theology are often incidental to the purpose of the epistles: to exhort and encourage those addressed, to deepen their faith, and to discuss difficulties and disagreements. 1 Cor. 15: 3ff. and 1 Cor. 11: 23ff. must be central in any reconstruction of Pauline theology, but neither passage is paralleled elsewhere in the Pauline corpus and both seem to have been included only because of difficulties or misunderstandings in the Corinthian church. In short, the emphases of the epistles were not those of Paul's missionary preaching.[3] Hence the possibility must be allowed that Paul laid greater emphasis on the pre-crucifixion events and the character of Jesus in his preaching than he does in his epistles.

What were the main themes of Paul's missionary preaching?

---

[1] So also, E. Güttgemanns, *Der leidende Apostel*, pp. 34ff.

[2] So also, J. Schniewind, 'A Reply to R. Bultmann', *Kerygma and Myth* 1, ed. H. W. Bartsch (E.T. London, 1953), 68 and A. Oepke, *Missionspredigt*, pp. 132ff.

[3] So also, E. Güttgemanns, *Offene Fragen zur Formgeschichte des Evangeliums* (Munich, 2nd ed. 1971), p. 112 n. 57.

There is little doubt that Christian missionary preaching in the Gentile world began with proclamation of the one God and was not simply Christological. Acts 17: 22ff. is confirmed by 1 Thess. 1: 9–10, but further explicit traces of Paul's monotheistic preaching are difficult to find;[1] this is a further indication that the epistles tell us little about the terms in which Paul preached to unbelievers. As for Paul's Christological preaching, the themes summed up in 1 Cor. 15: 3ff. were clearly central. But it is inconceivable that such a pre-Pauline confessional formula was simply repeated by rote as Paul's initial preaching; its themes must have been elaborated and expounded in many different ways.[2]

Did the pre-crucifixion events play any part in Paul's preaching? The silence of the epistles necessitates consideration of many factors in order to tip the balance of probability one way or the other. Paul was not uninterested in the life and teaching of Jesus; he knew a good deal more than is often recognised. The Pauline epistles are not alone in their virtual by-passing of material related to the life and ministry of Jesus; neither the other New Testament epistles, nor the earliest non-canonical epistles present a significantly different picture. Due recognition of the purpose of the epistles and of the hints provided by the Pauline speeches in Acts is a further factor which suggests a positive answer. The cumulative case is quite strong, but it falls short of proof.

An evaluation of the use to which the gospel traditions were put in the primitive church is an even more important factor. If the gospel traditions were used in missionary preaching and were so used over wide areas in the early church before the emergence of the gospels, there would be stronger grounds for believing that Paul used them, or their equivalent, in his initial preaching. But in order to avoid a circular argument as far as possible, conclusions drawn from the later sections

[1] R. Bultmann refers to 1 Cor. 12: 2, Gal. 4: 8 and 1 Cor. 8: 4–6. *Theology of the NT* 1, 67.

[2] Perhaps this formula included reference to the life of Jesus and Paul quoted only the part most relevant to his discussion with the Corinthians. As M. Dibelius noted, we cannot infer how the formula ended, or how it began, nor indeed what it said about the life of Jesus: *Tradition*, p. 19. Similarly, C. H. Dodd, *Apostolic Preaching*, pp. 57f. and A. Oepke, *Missionspredigt*, pp. 59f.

of this investigation must not be used to strengthen the tentative conclusions reached here.[1]

Paul's use of gospel traditions must be left as a partially open question, but his emphasis on the character of Jesus is striking and cannot be weakened by claiming that he is referring to the character of the pre-existent Christ or that it finds a place only because of its usefulness for ethical exhortation; the period between the birth and death of Jesus is not assessed solely in 'negative' terms.

Owing to the paucity of the evidence, Paul's initial preaching cannot be set out in a series of tidy statements. But one can be all but certain that whatever *form* it may have taken, reference to the life and character of Jesus was included simply because Paul's understanding of the sort of person Jesus was formed such an integral part of his Christology. Paul may well have referred to traditions of the teaching and actions of Jesus; if not, summary statements of the character of Jesus, such as are found in the epistles, may have given adequate indication of the sort of person Jesus was. Paul's understanding and proclamation of Jesus Christ did not by-pass the life and character of the One proclaimed as crucified and risen.

The pre-Lucan traditions in the speeches in Acts and Paul's epistles are complementary; neither indicates that the primitive church was uninterested in Jesus of Nazareth;[2] both suggest

---

[1] In spite of the considerations discussed, the almost complete absence of references or allusions in the epistles to gospel traditions remains puzzling. Many speculations have been offered, but there is no fully adequate explanation. Unless one is prepared to accept that Paul was uninterested in Jesus of Nazareth and that behind almost every statement of his about Jesus lurk the views of his opponents, it is difficult to be as confident as some scholars are that Paul's opponents placed more emphasis on the life of Jesus than did Paul himself. Perhaps Paul's opponents have exerted such a profound fascination in recent years that it has become too easy to accept as axiomatic that Paul and his opponents differed fundamentally on every aspect of Christology – and of theology generally!

[2] Paul's epistles have been taken as representative of the New Testament epistles as a whole, as they raise the whole question of the church's interest in Jesus of Nazareth in a more acute form than do the other epistles. R. Bultmann acknowledges that outside the synoptic gospels, Hebrews has the greatest interest in the life of Jesus (*History of the Synoptic Tradition* (E.T. Oxford, 1963), pp. 303). The specific form of that interest deserves

that primitive missionary preaching may well have referred to the life and character of Jesus. Admittedly there is not a great deal of solid evidence for the latter conclusion, but when the purpose of the Pauline epistles and the summary nature of the speeches in Acts are both borne in mind, the extent, not the paucity of the evidence is surprising. And, in addition, there is little or no evidence in the epistles and in Acts, which suggests that the early church's interest in the 'past' of Jesus is to be linked with any other *Sitz im Leben*.

Neither the speeches nor the epistles indicate that the primitive church's interest in Jesus was purely 'historical' or 'biographical'; both suggest that from a period well before the appearance of Mark, proclamation of the death and resurrection of Jesus was made more meaningful by reference to the character of the 'one who went about doing good'.

Our examination of the traditions behind the speeches and of the epistles confirms that Luke is not alone in his interest in the 'past' of Jesus of Nazareth. Not surprisingly, it has been much less easy to establish conclusively that as in Luke's day, so in earlier decades the church's initial missionary preaching referred to the life and character of Jesus, though this remains a plausible hypothesis.

careful consideration, but it lies outside the scope of this study. On Hebrews, see E. Grässer, 'Der historische Jesus im Hebräerbrief', *ZNW* **56** (1965), 63–91; U. Luck, 'Himmlisches und irdisches Geschehen im Hebräerbrief', *NovT* **6** (1963), 192–215; O. Michel in his commentary (6th ed. 1964), pp. 211ff.; M. Rissi, 'Die Menschlichkeit Jesu nach Heb 5: 7–8', *TZ* **2** (1955), 28ff.

CHAPTER 5

THE GOSPELS AND ANCIENT BIOGRAPHICAL WRITING

The Christian church has always treasured the gospels as records of the life and character of Jesus.[1] But many New Testament scholars insist that the gospels (or at least the traditions which lie behind them) are not concerned to portray the character of Jesus of Nazareth.

R. Bultmann uses his understanding of the perspective of the gospels to support his insistence that the kerygma is not concerned with more than the mere *Dass* of the existence of Jesus. He concedes that the gospels do tell us some things about Jesus of Nazareth, but this is, as it were, incidental or even contrary to their primary intention.[2]

The gospels, it is often claimed, intend to proclaim the Risen Christ and are not primarily concerned with the past of Jesus; this misunderstanding arises when they are read from a modern perspective, with its preoccupation with history and biography. The main contention of this chapter is that, on the contrary, failure to read the gospels sufficiently carefully against the background of biographical writing in the ancient world has led to confused interpretations of their nature and intention.

If one wishes to suggest that either the gospels or the gospel traditions were concerned with the past of Jesus, the tenaciously held objection that the gospels are not biographies must be met. The very word 'biography' has become to a form critic like a red rag to a bull. Almost all the standard books on the gospels state that the gospels are not biographies. Some writers repeat the received tradition, but hasten to add reservations. Others, stressing the theological perspective of the

---

[1] Part of the material in the first half of this chapter first appeared in my essay, 'The Gospel Traditions and Early Christological Reflection' in *Christ, Faith and History*, eds. S. W. Sykes and J. P. Clayton (Cambridge, 1972), pp. 191–204.

[2] 'Primitive Kerygma' in *Historical Jesus*, pp. 20ff. Cf. N. Perrin, *Rediscovering the Teaching of Jesus*, pp. 221f.

gospels, correctly note that the techniques of modern biographical writing are far removed from the approach of the
gospels, but avoid consideration of ancient biographical
writing.[1] Other scholars compare the gospels with Hellenistic
biographies and ancient memoir literature, usually concluding
that the differences show that the gospels were not written in
order to provide records about the life of Jesus.[2] R. Bultmann
denies that Hellenistic biographies provide an analogy to the
form of the gospels and then notes that 'there is no historical-
biographical interest in the gospels, and that is why they have
nothing to say about Jesus' human personality, his appearance
and character, his origin, education and development; quite
apart from the fact that they do not command the cultivated
techniques of composition necessary for grand literature, nor
let the personalities of their authors appear.'[3] This view, which
seeks to establish the perspective of the gospels partly from
a comparison with ancient biographical writing, has been
extremely influential,[4] but it is based on a quite surprisingly
inaccurate assessment of ancient biographical writing. While
there is no doubt that the gospels are comparable neither to
ancient nor to modern biographical writing,[5] the real relevance
of ancient biographical writing for the student of the gospels
has not always been appreciated.

I GREEK AND ROMAN BIOGRAPHICAL WRITING[6]

Greek and Roman biographical writing reached its zenith
shortly after the gospels were written, in the work of Tacitus,
Plutarch and Suetonius; but these writers drew, in different
ways, on traditional techniques. Of the evangelists, only Luke

[1] E.g., D. E. Nineham, *Saint Mark* (London, 1963), p. 35.
[2] W. G. Kümmel, *Introduction*, p. 32.   [3] *Synoptic Tradition*, p. 372.
[4] See, for example, W. G. Kümmel, *Introduction*, p. 32; S. Schulz, *Die
Stunde der Botschaft* (Hamburg and Zürich, 1967), pp. 37f.; W. Marxsen,
Introduction to the New Testament (E.T. Oxford, 1968), pp. 120f.; G. Bornkamm,
art. 'Evangelien, formgeschichtlich', *RGG* 3rd ed. II, col. 749f.
[5] The standard discussion is still K. L. Schmidt's 'Die Stellung der
Evangelien in der allgemeinen Literaturgeschichte' in ΕΥΧΑΡΙΣΤΗΡΙΟΝ
für H. Gunkel II, ed. H. Schmidt (Göttingen, 1923), 50–134.
[6] For a brief but perceptive recent survey see A. Momigliano, *The
Development of Greek Biography* (Cambridge, Mass., 1971). The standard

is at all likely to have been acquainted directly with the
traditional methods these writers used; but since the gospel
traditions were used, and the gospels themselves emerged in
a Hellenistic environment, consideration of the methods by
which the life of a significant person was depicted in the
Graeco-Roman world of the first and early second centuries
A.D. is not without relevance. In addition, there is increasing
evidence which indicates that the Greek language and Hellenistic
literary techniques (as well as Hellenistic culture generally)
had penetrated first-century Palestine much more deeply and
extensively than was earlier recognised.[1]

The gospels may show comparatively little interest in
chronological order when compared with modern biographical
writing, but was this a hall-mark of ancient biographical
method? Chronological order was considered formerly to have
been a feature of the Peripatetic biographers by whom Plutarch
was deeply influenced, while the other main stream of ancient
biographical writing, the Alexandrian biographers and later
Suetonius, dealt with a life *per species*, grouping together material
on topics such as conduct, business, family, attitude towards
society, friends. Whether or not Suetonius consciously adopted
the Alexandrian grammarians' biographical methods,[2] he uses

discussion is still F. Leo, *Die griechisch-römische Biographie* (Leipzig, 1901),
though a number of Leo's hypotheses have been challenged. For example,
D. R. Stuart insists that the earliest forms of Roman biographical writing
arose from *laudatio funebris* and not from Greek *encomia*: *Epochs of Greek and
Roman Biography* (Berkeley, 1928). But even if this is so, the Romans
undoubtedly used Hellenistic conventions later. So, R. E. Smith, 'Plutarch's
Biographical Sources in the Roman Lives', *Classical Quarterly* **34** (1940),
1ff., and 'The Sources of Plutarch's Life of Titus Flamininus', *Classical
Quarterly* **38** (1944), 89ff.

H. Homeyer stresses the importance of the biographical material found
in Herodotus, and his influence on later biographical writing: 'Zu den
Anfängen der griechischen Biographie', *Philologus* **106** (1962), 75ff. G.
Arrighetti provides a useful well-documented discussion of the whole
subject in his edition of *Vita Di Euripide*, *Studi Classici e Orientali* XIII (Pisa,
1964), pp. 1–34.

[1] See, for example, J. N. Sevenster, *Do You Know Greek? How much
Greek could the first Jewish Christians have known?* (Leiden, 1968); M. Hengel,
Judentum und Hellenismus (Tübingen, 1969).

[2] D. R. Stuart strenuously opposes F. Leo's view at this point: *Epochs*,
pp. 186, 226ff.; cf. also W. Steidle, *Sueton und die antike Biographie* (Munich,
1951), p. 166 *et passim*.

a chronological form rarely, and follows a chronological sequence systematically only in his biography of Julius Caesar, the first in his series of lives of the Caesars.[1]

But the discovery of fragments of Satyrus' *Life of Euripides*, the only first-hand Peripatetic biography extant, confirms that chronological order does not mark off Peripatetic biography and Plutarch from the Alexandrians and Suetonius.[2] Satyrus was one of the last Peripatetic writers, writing in the second half of the third century B.C. The extant sections of Satyrus' biography contain only one section which can in any way be called chronological,[3] yet there is a clear tendency towards an orderly grouping of material, at least under broad captions. As Satyrus stood at the end of a long line of Peripatetic biographers, there is now little doubt that this form of biographical writing was typical of the Peripatetics, who so strongly influenced Greek and Roman biographical writing of the first century A.D. and later.

Nor does Plutarch make any attempt to adopt a precise chronology; the chronological expressions he does use are nearly all vague, phrases such as 'about this time', 'some time after this', being common. Although campaigns are presented chronologically, Plutarch's basic method is *per species*. Of the three writers who represent the flower of Greek and Roman biographical writing, only Tacitus uses a chronological framework, as he marks off the different stages in Agricola's career.

Later writers present a similar picture. Arrian's *Discourses of Epictetus*, Philostratus' *Life of Apollonius of Tyana*, and the biographies of Diogenes Laertius have been suggested as possible parallels to the gospels.[4] Arrian's work is arranged

---

[1] See Suetonius' statement of his own method, *Aug.* 9.

[2] Earlier estimates of Peripatetic biography were made from scattered fragments, lists of titles, comments preserved by later writers, critical reconstruction of sources used by later writers, and from conjecture.

[3] 'During the following winter'. See D. R. Stuart, *Epochs*, p. 185.

[4] See C. Votaw, 'The Gospels and Contemporary Biographies', *AJT* **19** (1915), 45–73 and 217–49 (cf. K. L. Schmidt, 'Stellung', pp. 51ff.); H. J. Cadbury, *The Making of Luke-Acts* (New York, 1927), p. 128; G. Petzke, *Die Traditionen über Apollonius von Tyana und das Neue Testament* (Leiden, 1970), pp. 51–62. H. J. Rose discusses and rejects F. Pfister's wild theory that a life of Herakles was used as the form of the *Urevangelium*: 'Herakles and the Gospels', *HTR* **31** (1968), 113–42.

topically; the framework of Philostratus' *Life* is geographical rather than chronological, for there is no precise chronology; most of the material in Diogenes Laertius' *Lives* is collected together topically rather than chronologically.[1]

Concern for chronological order was not characteristic of ancient biographical writing.[2] As a stylistic technique, presentation of biographical material *per species* is much more common. Neither chronological references nor some indications that material has been grouped *per species* are absent from the gospels; but more significant than any such vague similarity is the fact that the gospels cannot be differentiated from ancient biographical writing because of their lack of concern for chonology.

Since chronological order was not common, it is not surprising to find that development of character was not a *sine qua non* of ancient biographical writing, although some New Testament scholars insist that this is a major difference between the gospels and Hellenistic biographies.[3] Early encomiasts, such as Isocrates and Xenophon, were not interested in development of character, for they attempted to delineate their subjects in terms of their own notions of exemplary character traits. Nor did Peripatetic biographers, and those who later inherited their techniques, trace development of character and personality, though it is an exaggeration to claim that the phenomenon of human alteration was unknown.[4] Even in Philostratus' *Life* there is no trace of development of character. The idea that a person is understood only through development is modern, and is hardly found in the ancient world.[5]

Nor can the brief character sketch, noted by W. G. Kümmel as a difference between the gospels and Hellenistic biographies, be considered as a feature of ancient biographical writing. Plutarch, for example, sometimes does include a character summary, but he makes no attempt to analyse internal

---

[1] See R. Hope, *The Book of Diogenes Laertius* (New York, 1930), pp. 145f.

[2] So also, W. Steidle, *Sueton*, p. 10. The surviving parts of Cornelius Nepos' *De Viris Illustribus*, especially *Atticus*, are an exception, though even *Atticus* concludes with material sorted into various categories.

[3] Kümmel, *Introduction*, p. 32 and see above, p. 118 n. 4.

[4] A. Dihle, *Studien zur griechischen Biographie* (Göttingen, 1956), pp. 76ff.

[5] Cf. W. Steidle, *Sueton*, pp. 10f.

development of personality. He aimed to 'paint character', but he did not always do this in his own words.[1]

Much more prominent as a method of character portrayal is the recognition that a person's actions and words sum up his character more adequately than the comments of an observer. This is a deeply-rooted tradition in ancient biographical writing. At the beginning of the *Memorabilia* Xenophon writes, 'In order to support my opinion that he benefited his companions, alike by actions that revealed his own character and by his own conversations, I will set down what I recall of these...'.[2] In *Agesilaus* 1, 6 Xenophon states that the deeds of a man best disclose the stamp of his nature. This became a conventional method which strongly influenced Plutarch.[3]

There is little doubt that direct analysis of the subject's character was rare in Peripatetic biography; the ἦθος of a person was portrayed through his πράξεις.[4] Plutarch expounded the principles on which he worked at the beginning of his life of Alexander: 'In the most illustrious deeds there is not always a manifestation of virtue and avarice, nay, a slight thing like a phrase or a jest often makes a greater revelation of character than battles where thousands fall, or the greatest armaments or sieges of cities.'[5] This method of indirect characterisation, in which the personality of the author himself remained in the background, was a widely practised technique in ancient historiography generally.[6] It is true, as R. Bultmann notes, that unlike Hellenistic biographies, the gospels do not let the personalities of their authors appear.[7] But in sketching out a person's character, ancient writers were content to let the actions and words of their subject speak for themselves; at this point the gospels do not differ markedly.

[1] N. I. Barbu, *Les Procédés de la Peinture des caractères et la Vérité historique dans les Biographies de Plutarque* (Paris, 1934), p. 86.

[2] *Mem.* I, iii, 1; cf. the similar statement in Isocrates, *Evag.* 76.

[3] Cf. A. Dihle, *Studien*, p. 64.

[4] Theophrastus' *Characters* show that it was possible to indicate character vividly merely by a few brief accounts of a person's actions and occasional words.

[5] I, 2; F. Leo collects a number of similar references, *Biographie*, pp. 184f.

[6] Cf. W. Kroll, *Studien zum Verständnis der römischen Literatur* (Stuttgart, 1924), p. 383.   [7] *Synoptic Tradition*, p. 372.

Instead of tracing character development, ancient bio-graphical writing from Plato onwards generally started and finished with the mature character of the person concerned.[1] A. Dihle emphasises that the purely psychological descriptions used in modern times to describe character development utilise concepts which do not necessarily contain moral value judge-ments. But in Greek biographical writing, psychological description is at the same time an ethical judgement, for only moral and ethical concepts were available for such descriptions.[2]

The gospels also show little interest in character develop-ment, portray Jesus from the beginning to the end of his ministry in essentially the same way, and allow his actions and words to show the sort of person he was. While it is not possible to trace ancient biographical conventions directly into the gospel traditions, their presentation of the life of Jesus is much less distinctive than has been claimed.

Attention has been drawn to the failure of the gospels to set Jesus against the wider historical background of his time (though Luke is frequently singled out as a partial exception), with the assumption that this was typical of ancient biographical writing.[3] But this feature of modern biographical writing was not known among the Greeks. Goethe was probably the first to demand that a hero should be portrayed against the back-drop of the spirit of his age.[4] Consciousness of different historical epochs was lacking in antiquity; biographical writing was never purely historical, but was always ethical in intention.[5] Biography and history were carefully held apart.[6] Even when a writer such as Suetonius writes a series of lives of the Roman emperors, he does not weave closely his historical material into his account of the life and character of the emperors concerned. Suetonius does not attempt to set the emperors against the background of their own times; the fact that historical and biographical material is found side by side arises from the general interest in everything concerned with the Caesars.

[1] Stuart, *Epochs*, p. 178.
[2] Dihle, *Studien*, p. 87. See the whole section, pp. 57–87.
[3] E.g. Kümmel, *Introduction*, p. 32.
[4] Dihle, *Studien*, p. 87.   [5] *Ibid.*
[6] Plutarch frequently differentiates biography and history; e.g. *Alex.* 1, 2f.

There is a little more justification for drawing attention to the absence from the gospels of descriptions of the personal appearance of Jesus,[1] though again this was far from being a universal feature of ancient biographical writing. Aristotle's teaching gave a great impetus to the study of human portraiture and character; Xenophon had only rarely mentioned traits of physical appearance.[2] Aristoxenus probably included the personal appearance of Socrates in his *Life*, but apart from one reference in Hieronymus of Rhodes there are no other iconistic descriptions in the extant fragments of Peripatetic biography down to the first century; the tradition, however, is defective. Both Plutarch and Diogenes Laertius have descriptions of physical appearance in some, but by no means all, of their biographies. In Roman literature, the iconistic portrait is first found in Sallust. Tacitus gives only a very brief description of the personal appearance of Agricola, while Nepos omits such a description of Atticus. From the time of Suetonius descriptions of personal appearance become a convention in Latin biography.[3]

It is not difficult to draw attention to the wide gulf between the gospels and ancient biographical writing; the gospels have nothing comparable to the many personal anecdotes, some of which were widely-used stock situations, which Plutarch and Suetonius included simply to satisfy the curiosity of their readers. The travellers' tales cast in biographical form perform a similar function in Philostratus' *Life of Apollonius*.

But many of the differences noted by some New Testament scholars are non-existent. Ancient biographical writing lacks precise chronology, lacks interest in the external and internal development of the person concerned, and makes no attempt to portray men as representatives of a past epoch, or in the context of the historical background of their age. Frequently biographical material is presented topically, hedged in by

[1] See B. Leeming's discussion of R. Eisler's theory that late descriptions of Jesus, such as in the *Letter of Lentulus*, go back to Slavonic Josephus and, originally, to a police description in Roman archives! 'Verbal Descriptions of Christ', *Irish Theological Quarterly* **22** (1955), 293–312.

[2] G. Misener, 'Iconistic Portraits', *Classical Philology* **19** (1924), 107ff.

[3] Misener, 'Iconistic Portraits', pp. 116ff. Cf. Stuart, *Epochs*, pp. 174ff.

birth and death narratives. Almost without exception there is a strong moral overtone; biography is intended to furnish an example, even where it seems merely to entertain.

The gospels must be read against the backdrop, not of modern biographical writing, but of their own times. When this is done, the gospels do not emerge as biographies of Jesus, but their presentations of the life of Jesus are seen to be less distinctive than is usually believed. Recognition of the fact that, unlike Plutarch, Suetonius and other ancient biographers, they do not draw on a long literary tradition, supports this conclusion. For if the modern preoccupation with chronological precision, historical background, personal appearance and character development is largely missing in ancient biographical writing with its strong literary tradition, the absence of these is even less surprising in the gospels, which can scarcely be described as literary productions.

A positive conclusion of some importance also emerges. Even though the Greeks and Romans did not trace character development, rarely summed up their subject's character in their own words, and described character only in ethical terms, they were interested in the character of a person and knew how to portray it.[1] Indirect rather than direct methods were preferred; character was portrayed by allowing the actions and words of a person to speak for themselves. Since this simple and rather obvious technique was widely used in 'sophisticated' ancient biographical writing, there is less reason to agree that 'unsophisticated' gospel traditions can appear to portray the character of Jesus by reporting his words and actions only if their intention is misunderstood. But even the customary comparison of the gospels to 'Kleinliteratur' rather than 'Hochliteratur' can be misleading.[2] The evangelists' abilities as theologians have recently received belated recognition; if they were able to alter, in subtle theological ways, the traditions they used, their abilities as authors concerned to present the life and character of Jesus of Nazareth ought not to be overlooked on the grounds that 'they do not command

[1] See, for example, Plato, *Symp.* 215 A and B; Theophrastus, *Characters*.
[2] K. L. Schmidt's differentiation has been very influential. 'Die Stellung' in ΕΥΧΑΡΙΣΤΗΡΙΟΝ II, ed. H. Schmidt, 68 *et al.* Cf. Bultmann, *Synoptic Tradition*, pp. 372f.

the cultivated techniques of composition necessary for grand literature'.[1]

II JEWISH BIOGRAPHICAL WRITING

Since the gospels are anchored in the Jewish world, however Hellenistic they may be, an examination of the nature and extent of Jewish material dealing with the life and character of one person may shed light on the perspective of the gospels. The portrayal of David in 1 and 2 Samuel is the only Old Testament material of any length which might be called biographical.[2] The chronological structure is usually very loose. Although David's external progress is traced, there is no analysis of his character or hint of its development. In contrast to the rest of the Old Testament, Saul's physical appearance is described briefly twice, David's three times.

Rather surprisingly, this sort of writing is conspicuous by its absence from the apocrypha and pseudepigrapha.[3] *Tobit* and *Judith* narrate only one series of events from the life of the person concerned; the *Books of Adam and Eve* contain haggadic narratives which reveal an interest in their lives – an interest which does not involve a chronological account or a psychological study of their characters. Much later Jewish writing paraphrases and elaborates Old Testament narratives, especially the Pentateuch, but the apparent biographical interest in works such as *Pseudo-Philo*, the *Genesis Apocryphon* and *Jubilees* is seen, on closer inspection, to arise from a desire to make biblical narratives relevant and intelligible in a new age.[4]

[1] Bultmann, *Synoptic Tradition*, pp. 372f.

[2] The book of Esther, for example, covers only a very brief period in her life. A. Ehrhardt suggests that the portrayal of David is a model of historical biography, unsurpassed by either Plutarch or Suetonius: 'The Construction and Purpose of Acts', *ST* **12** (1958), 46.

[3] Ehrhardt points to Jason of Cyrene's work, excerpted in 2 Macc., as a continuation of the art of historical biography found in 1 and 2 Samuel and reappearing in the writings of Luke: 'The Construction and Purpose of Acts', p. 46. But the similarities are exaggerated.

[4] Cf. G. Vermes' discussion of the motives behind the reinterpretation of the Old Testament text in *Sefer-ha-Yashar*. *Scripture and Tradition in Judaism* (Leiden, 1961), p. 95, and cf. also pp. 124ff.

Similar reasons lie behind Philo's interest in the lives of Abraham, Joseph and Moses. Although the topical arrangement of material in *De Abrahamo* recalls Greek methods, Philo's *Lives* are scarcely comparable in other respects. Philo is more concerned with his own teaching than with the character of his subjects as such, for they simply become ideal figures; he is even prepared to alter the portrait to suit the particular lessons he wishes to teach.[1] Both Josephus' *Jewish Antiquities* and the extant fragments of other Hellenistic-Jewish writings[2] present the same picture: there seems to be a strong biographical interest in the patriarchs, but the intention is to explain the biblical text to a new age rather than to furnish biographies of the great men of the past.

There has been no lack of interest in comparisons of Jesus and the Teacher of Righteousness.[3] One aspect is often overlooked; when all the material about the Teacher is assembled, one cannot but be struck by the paucity of the material available. If we could be sure that the Thanksgiving Psalms were composed by the Teacher himself, the small amount of information which can be gleaned from the non-biblical and the exegetical writings would be considerably increased. G. Jeremias has taken this question further, arguing that the Psalms are not a literary unity; those which stem from the Teacher himself reflect his personal faith and his relationship with his friends and enemies. But Jeremias is forced to conclude that even these Psalms do not extend our knowledge of his career.[4]

Although Qumran was founded and deeply influenced by a person whose teaching was respected and retained, it seems to have survived on a minimum of tradition about the founder, and to have been interested only in the teachings and the distinctive approach to biblical interpretation of the Teacher. In this respect there is a wide gap between primitive Christianity

---

[1] E.g., no praise is too high for Joseph in *De Josepho*; a very different portrait appears in the allegorical commentary.

[2] See P. Dalbert, *Die Theologie der hellenistisch-jüdischen Missionsliteratur* (Hamburg, 1954), esp. p. 138, and, for many of the texts, W. N. Stearns, *Fragments from Graeco-Jewish Writers* (Chicago, 1908).

[3] See G. Jeremias, *Der Lehrer der Gerechtigkeit* (Göttingen, 1963); also H. Braun, *Qumran und das NT* II (Tübingen, 1966), 54–74.

[4] G. Jeremias, *Der Lehrer der Gerechtigkeit*, pp. 264f.

and the Qumran community, between the gospels and the Qumran literature.[1]

The Qumran literature reminds us that in the ancient world it was by no means the normal practice to compile an account of the life of a founder of a community such as Qumran, nor even of many other types of significant figures. The nature and extent of the material relating to the life and character of the Teacher of Righteousness shows clearly that by comparison the gospels are rich in material about Jesus, however the historian may evaluate it. The reason for this must surely lie in the totally different role assigned to Jesus in primitive Christianity; the contrast with the Qumran literature provides a hint that the resurrection faith of primitive Christianity, far from overshadowing interest in the past of Jesus, may have encouraged interest in the character of the One being proclaimed.

The rabbinic literature provides even more striking evidence of the lack of almost any sort of biographical interest in Jewish writings. One might have expected that it would be possible to reconstruct an adequate biography of Yohanan Ben Zakkai, a most important and influential rabbinic teacher. But although a recent biography offers a reconstruction of his teaching and historical background, the author finds it impossible to say much about the external events in his life, even though such source material as there is has not been sifted critically.[2]

Like much of the rabbinic literature, *Pirqe Aboth*, which stands as close to the synoptic traditions as any other rabbinic document, concentrates on the teaching of particular rabbis; the synoptic 'layer of tradition', Q, comes to mind as an obvious point of comparison. When placed alongside *Pirqe Aboth*, its concentration on the teaching of one person, and the amount – admittedly small – of information about Jesus

[1] So also, J. C. G. Greig, 'Gospel Messianism and the Qumran Use of Prophecy', *Studia Evangelica* I (1959), 593ff.; H. Braun objects, claiming that the gospels provide little historical and biographical information about Jesus: *Qumran* II, 70.

[2] J. Neusner, *A Life of Rabban Yohanan Ben Zakkai* (Leiden, 2nd ed. 1970). Cf. also, J. Podro, *The Last Pharisee, the Life and Times of Rabbi Joshua Ben Hananyah* (London, 1959).

which is conveyed directly or indirectly, stand out. The *Aboth* records the teaching of a number of individual rabbis without any sort of biographical or historical interest. As W. D. Davies notes, 'to turn to the gospels is at once to recognise their "historical", "biographical" orientation. Here what Jesus *did* counts, not only what he said'.[1]

However, the gospels and the rabbinic traditions do share one important feature: in both, names of secondary characters and indications of time and place are often missing.[2] Many scholars have drawn the illegitimate observation that absence of such details confirms that the gospel traditions were intended to proclaim the message of salvation and not to preserve the Jesus tradition for posterity.

When placed alongside the rabbinic literature, the variety and richness of the material in the gospels about one person stand out,[3] for rabbinic traditions tend to refer to almost as many different rabbis as there are pericopae. There is no material in the rabbinic literature about the life and character of an individual rabbi which is comparable to the portrait of Jesus in the gospel traditions.

III THE GOSPEL OF THOMAS AND JESUS OF NAZARETH

The perspective of the gospels has been clarified by comparing and contrasting roughly similar material from the ancient world, even though similarities are only superficial. The Gospel of Thomas is closer to the canonical gospels in many respects than any of the other Nag Hammadi documents; comparison of their approaches to Jesus aids appreciation of the distinctive features of each.

The most striking difference is the almost complete absence of narrative in the Gospel of Thomas. Apart from a short

---

[1] 'Reflections on Tradition: the Aboth Revisited' in *Christian History and Interpretation* (Festschrift J. Knox), eds. W. R. Farmer, C. F. D. Moule, R. R. Niebuhr (Cambridge, 1967), pp. 158f. J. W. Doeve makes a similar point in *Jewish Hermeneutics*, pp. 178f.

[2] P. Fiebig, *Der Erzählungsstil der Evangelien* (Leipzig, 1925), p. 95 *et passim*.

[3] G. Kittel, *Die Probleme des palästinischen Spätjudentums und das Urchristentum* (Stuttgart, 1926), p. 69.

introductory sentence, it consists almost entirely of a series of sayings of Jesus introduced simply by 'Jesus said', without any indications of the circumstances or even of the audience.[1] Occasionally the disciples ask a question, but this is patently a simple literary device designed to break up the string of logia spoken by Jesus.[2] There is no trace of the opponents of Jesus,[3] nor of the very varied types of people with whom Jesus associates in the canonical gospels, nor of the deeds of Jesus. Only the disciples appear on the scene;[4] the sick, outcastes, crowds and a whole host of individuals remain unmentioned.[5]

Logion 31 provides a good example of the perspective of Thomas. 'Jesus said, No prophet is acceptable in his village, no physician heals those who know him.' Unlike the synoptic pericopae which include a similar proverbial logion, we are not told to whom Jesus is speaking, nor is there any direct indication in Thomas that Jesus himself was rejected by his own πατρίς. The context in the synoptic accounts makes it quite clear that Jesus is in his home village (Mark 6: 1–6; Matt. 13: 54–8; Luke 4: 16–30);[6] Mark and Matthew refer to the family of Jesus. The second half of logion 31, not found in the New Testament, refers to a physician, but unlike the immediate context in all four canonical gospels, there is no indication in the Gospel of Thomas that Jesus himself is a physician.[7]

Absence of any sort of a framework means that it is very difficult to say anything about the life and character of the

---

[1] Only twice are we told explicitly at the beginning of a logion that Jesus is speaking to the disciples (13 and 22). References and quotations are taken from *The Gospel according to Thomas*, ed. A. Guillaumont *et al.* (Leiden, 1959).

[2] The device is found in several other similar documents; see, for example, the *Apocryphon of John*.

[3] There are only two statements of Jesus about the scribes and Pharisees (logia 39 and 102); they do not appear in person.

[4] Mary and Salome speak in logia 21 and 61 (cf. also logia 79 and 114); in both cases the context is discipleship – the women are disciples.

[5] Logia 22 and 79 are partial exceptions.

[6] In John 4: 44 the similar logion is set within a narrative, though there is no indication of the audience.

[7] Cf. Mark 6: 5, which is, admittedly, abbreviated in Matt. 13: 58; Luke 4: 23 and 38ff.; John 4: 46ff.

Jesus of the Gospel of Thomas. A good deal can be said about the Christology of Thomas, but we are told almost nothing about Jesus beyond the bare fact that he had some disciples who included Salome, Mary, Thomas, Philip and Peter. The Jesus of the Gospel of Thomas can hardly be described as a teacher – the audience is usually missing, and the many synoptic references to Jesus as a teacher are not to be found here; Jesus is neither a teacher nor even a prophet, but a revealer.

This general observation is confirmed by a comparison of Gospel of Thomas logia which have parallels in the Q material. There is no indication that Thomas knew Q as a source, whether written or oral, for many traces of the evangelists' redaction of Q reappear in Thomas.[1] In many cases Q material is found in a slightly different form and has often, but not always, taken on new meanings in a discernibly gnostic direction.[2] We shall examine three examples.

First, Gospel of Thomas logion 89: 'Jesus said, Why do you wash the outside of the cup? Do you not understand that he who made the inside is also he who made the outside?' (Cf. Matt. 23: 25 and Luke 11: 39f.) From the whole thrust of Thomas, those addressed must be gnostics.[3] There is little doubt that at the base of Matt. 23: 25–6 and Luke 11: 37–41 lies a Q logion directed against the Pharisees; there are further such logia in the immediate context in both Matt. 23 and Luke 11. Probably both Matthew and Luke have used a Q logion in different ways: Matthew has added it to his lengthy speech, while Luke has added it to his narrative of Jesus' meal with a Pharisee. Despite significant differences in the wording and setting in Q, Matthew and Luke, the similar saying in Thomas is concerned with Jesus' relationship to *Pharisees*. The saying, even when stripped of the context given

---

[1] Cf. W. Schrage, *Das Verhältnis des Thomas-Evangeliums zur synoptischen Tradition und zu den koptischen Evangelienübersetzungen* (Berlin, 1964), p. 4.

[2] This is generally agreed, though some writers stress the Jewish Christian background. Cf. K. Grobel, 'How Gnostic is the Gospel of Thomas?', *NTS* **8** (1961–2), 367–73, and G. Quispel, *Makarius, Das Thomasevangelium und das Lied von der Perle* (Leiden, 1967), pp. 65–113. Quispel argues that there is not a single logion in Thomas which cannot be explained from encratite writings or from Jewish Christianity.

[3] W. Schrage, *Das Verhältnis*, p. 171 and E. Haenchen, *Die Botschaft des Thomas-Evangeliums* (Berlin, 1961), p. 53.

to it by Matthew and Luke, tells us, even if only indirectly, something about the ministry of Jesus and his relationship to the Pharisees. All this has disappeared in Thomas. The Q logion, in contrast, has a specific reference to a situation within the ministry of Jesus.[1]

Secondly, logion 78: 'Jesus said, Why did you come out into the desert? To see a reed shaken by the wind? And to see a man clothed in soft garments? (See, your) kings and your great ones are those who are clothed in soft (garments) and they (shall) not be able to know the truth.' (Cf. Matt. 11: 7–8 and Luke 7: 24–5.) The saying states that the 'great ones' of this world are hindered, by their dependence upon the world, from attaining to the truth and being saved.[2] The context does not aid clarification of the logion's meaning.

In Q the sayings are part of a comparatively lengthy passage on Jesus and John the Baptist; they are addressed to the crowds and follow Jesus' explanation of the nature of his mission in answer to the questions of John the Baptist's disciples. The verbal correspondence of Matthew and Luke is close. The Q form of the logion has definite links with a situation within the ministry of Jesus; it makes complete sense only when linked with other passages concerned with the relationship between Jesus and John the Baptist. The reference to the crowds going out into the wilderness to see John refers back to the earlier Q account of John's preaching (Matt. 3: 5ff. and Luke 3: 7ff.). Again the Q material has much stronger links with specific incidents, whatever the reasons which lie behind the particular form the comparable material takes in Thomas.[3]

Thirdly, logion 86: 'Jesus said, (The foxes) (have) the(ir) holes) and the birds have (their) nest, but the Son of Man has no place to lay his head and to rest.' (Cf. Matt. 8: 20 and Luke 9: 58.) The pattern already observed is repeated. The Gospel of Thomas logion has no 'setting'; the addition of

[1] The logion may possibly have come to Matthew and Luke independently; even if so, the main point being made here is not affected.

[2] So, B. Gärtner, *The Theology of the Gospel of Thomas* (London, 1961), p. 241.

[3] As a further example, cf. logion 46, Matt. 11: 11 and Luke 7: 28. There is no indication in Thomas that John the Baptist is a contemporary of Jesus. In contrast the Q logion and its context make clear Jesus' attitude to and estimate of John.

'and to rest' may be a deliberate alteration in a gnostic direction. The logion is merely a statement about the Son of Man; an application to the disciple or gnostic is not made explicit. The Q form, whatever it precise meaning, is closely related to discipleship and is linked to a specific situation in the ministry of Jesus. Although it is difficult to reconstruct the introduction to the dialogue in Q, the pericope did not begin at the point where Matthew and Luke first correspond closely: ἀκολουθήσω σοι ὅπου ἐὰν ἀπέρχῃ....[1]

This brief comparison underlines a frequently overlooked feature of Q: many Q logia are concerned with specific incidents in the ministry of Jesus, provide some information about the ministry and do not merely list teaching of Jesus. Indirectly some idea of the sort of person Jesus was is given. The Q logia discussed reflect Jesus' relationship with John the Baptist, the Pharisees, and the disciples in a way which is not found in the Gospel of Thomas. While Matthew and Luke have occasionally adapted and even altered the original setting, there is no question of their having provided a context of which there was no trace in the earlier stage of the synoptic tradition. This evidence must not be pushed too far, but it is significant that at the very point where the gospels seem to approach Thomas' lists of logia of Jesus most closely, the Q material's frequent reference, even if indirect, to a specific context and to a relationship of Jesus with others emerges clearly.

The logia in the Gospel of Thomas, whatever their background may have been, are meant to be understood as logia of the Risen Jesus and not of Jesus of Nazareth. The preface supplied by the author makes this clear: 'These are the secret words which the living Jesus spoke and Didymus Judas Thomas wrote.' In other gnostic documents where Jesus speaks to his disciples, it is as the Risen Jesus during the post-resurrection period, and this is the case here.[2] Luke's forty days are often

---

[1] Cf. logion 73, Matt. 9: 37f. and Luke 10: 2. In both Matthew and Luke, the words of Jesus are linked to his commissioning of disciples. The labourers are clearly the disciples; those whose task it is to pray are themselves sent. In Thomas the similar logion does not even indicate who the labourers are.

[2] See B. Gärtner, *Theology*, pp. 95–117. *Contra* E. Haenchen, *Botschaft*, p. 35. As Gärtner notes, we have to admit that the prologue's view does not agree particularly well with all the material itself (p. 112).

greatly lengthened and during this time Jesus gives his disciples the perfect teaching, the correct interpretation of his pre-resurrection sayings.

While the logia in Thomas have not lost almost every trace of a narrative framework or a specific situation in the ministry of Jesus simply because they are regarded as words of the Risen Jesus, the two factors are related.[1] The Risen Jesus, the Revealer, not Jesus of Nazareth, has become the focal point; hence there is little call for reference to the circumstances and people involved which would portray the character of the Revealer. All attention is focussed on the revelations and their interpretation.[2]

The same pattern recurs in most second-century material which has a post-resurrection setting. The longer ending of Mark and the Freer logion, for example, have virtually lost touch with Jesus of Nazareth and his ministry; the narratives are much more concerned with the disciples and are geared more explicitly to later times and later problems.[3] Many apocryphal documents, whether gnostic or not, begin with an appearance of Jesus who reveals *new* information to his inquisitive disciples.[4] The disciples and the new revelations are much more central than the continuity of the Risen Lord with Jesus of Nazareth. The canonical post-resurrection narratives have a very different perspective; Jesus' relationship with his disciples is much less artificial, for it is not merely a question of new information or new truths being revealed, but of a personal relationship being renewed.[5] The canonical gospels portray the Risen Jesus in terms of the Jesus of their pre-resurrection narratives.

[1] But see H. I. Marrou's protest (rather overstated) against the common assumption that the gnostic literature reveals no interest in the historical Jesus, history or time: 'La Théologie de l'Histoire dans la Gnose Valentinienne' in *Le Origini dello Gnosticismo* (Leiden, 1967), pp. 215ff.

[2] The role of Jesus in gnostic texts deserves a full study in itself, but this must await the publication of all the Nag Hammadi documents.

[3] John 21, unlike Matt. 28, Luke 24 and John 20, almost comes into the same category.   [4] E.g., *Ep. Ap.* 12.

[5] The rather general point being made here does not depend on a particular view of the origin and purpose of Thomas. For even if it is completely independent of the canonical gospel traditions, it still contains material related to Jesus, making the above comparison valid.

The contrast reminds us, from yet another angle, of the richness of the gospels' portraits of Jesus, for the Jesus of the gospels, including the post-resurrection narratives, is no mere revealer of heavenly secrets. If the Jesus of the gospels had been understood in the primitive church only as the Risen Lord of the community, with no interest in his life beyond the fact of his former existence on earth as a human, the gospels might have looked much more like the Gospel of Thomas than they do.

The gospels differ fundamentally from the biographical writing of the first centuries A.D., but, significantly for our purpose, the differences are least in evidence when the ways in which the character of a person was portrayed are considered. Even though the literary techniques of character portrayal must have been familiar to few, it is difficult to believe that on first acquaintance the gospels (or the gospel traditions) would not have been considered in the Hellenistic world of the first century A.D. to be 'biographical', to indicate what sort of a person Jesus was. Doubtless, continued acquaintance with the gospel material in a community conscious of the presence of the Risen Lord would add new dimensions to an initial understanding of the perspective of the gospels.

That the uniqueness of the gospels lies primarily in the impact of the resurrection on the primitive church is not in doubt; but the Gospel of Thomas reminds us that the resurrection faith has not transformed the gospel traditions about Jesus into mere revelations of the Risen Jesus. The uniqueness of the gospels also lies not so much in the ways they differ from Greek and Roman biographical writing, as many have insisted, but in the fact that there was no precedent in Jewish writings, from the Old Testament right through to the rabbinic corpus, for the gospels' concentration on the words, actions and relationships of one person. The Gospel of Thomas, however, is concerned with one person, Jesus, but at the one point where the gospels have closest affinity with the lists of logia of Jesus in Thomas, the Q material's frequent link with a specific context and a specific relationship of Jesus with others stands out. The wholly justifiable insistence that the gospels are not biographies has tended to hide the fact that when they are placed alongside comparable ancient writings, they are seen to tell us a surprisingly large amount about the life and character of Jesus.

Familiarity with the canonical gospels can easily blind us to their distinctive features. The early church need not have retained traditions about Jesus in the form in which they have come down to us: the traditions might well have looked rather more like *Pirqe Aboth* or the *Gospel of Thomas* than in fact they do. The gospels are kerygmatic documents, but their deeply embedded 'historical' and 'biographical' stamp is so unexpected against the background of comparable ancient documents that we are left with a problem: Why do the traditions about Jesus take this form?

CHAPTER 6

JESUS IN THE GOSPEL TRADITIONS

In the last two decades there have been several impressive attempts to show that the main outlines of the teaching of Jesus can be reconstructed by the modern historian: the outstanding authority with which Jesus taught, as well as the distinctiveness of much of his teaching, have been underlined most effectively. The so-called new quest for the historical Jesus has shown that we can know rather more about the historical Jesus than R. Bultmann had supposed and that the gap between the historical Jesus and the kerygma is not as wide as many had accepted. But most of the scholars associated with the new quest have accepted R. Bultmann's insistence that material in the gospels which is useful for the modern historian's reconstruction of the historical Jesus has survived *against* the primary intention of the traditions themselves.[1] The gospel traditions were not intended to be 'reports' about Jesus; they are not concerned with the 'past' of the historical Jesus, but belong to the church's proclamation of the Risen Christ.

A rather different approach is proposed in this chapter and in the chapter which follows: the gospel traditions which the church retained and used were intended, as one of their purposes, to sketch out the life and character of Jesus.

Some parts of the traditions which tell us a good deal about the character of Jesus, especially by recording his relationships with others, will be examined. But no attempt will be made to reconstruct all that can be known about Jesus, as, for our present purpose, the validity of understanding the gospel traditions in this way is the main point at issue. The teaching of Jesus tended to be singled out for rather more attention than the actions of Jesus by both R. Bultmann and by scholars associated with the new quest; this chapter argues that the words, actions and person of Jesus are very closely related to each other. This most important feature of the gospel traditions

[1] See, for example, R. Bultmann, 'Primitive Kerygma' in *The Historical Jesus*, eds. C. E. Braaten and R. A. Harrisville, p. 21.

turns out to have implications for the much-disputed question, taken up in chapter 7, of the *Sitz im Leben* of the traditions in the early church.

The Johannine gospel traditions are not set on one side, but are utilised in several places. A broad gulf separates the theological perspective of the Fourth Gospel from Matthew, Mark and Luke; but, nonetheless, the Fourth Gospel uses a cluster of traditions about Jesus which are not inconsistent with the traditions behind the synoptic gospels.[1]

The relationship between Jesus' proclamation and his conduct and actions is illustrated first from pericopae which record his concern for tax collectors and sinners. The attitude of Jesus to women and children is discussed, and the 'scandal' caused by Jesus' proclamation and actions, as well as his unpromising background, is stressed. Finally, the 'present' Son-of-Man sayings are considered, for if they are authentic, they confirm that Jesus made a direct link between his proclamation and reference to his character.

The Fringe of Society: Tax Collectors and Sinners

There is now a general scholarly consensus that Jesus proclaimed that God's eschatological rule was in some sense already present in his ministry,[2] although the relationship of the presence of the Kingdom to its future coming, as well as the precise nature of its presence, are still much debated.[3]

Jesus' proclamation of the Kingdom carried as an implication association with tax collectors and sinners and acceptance of them into table fellowship.[4] Tax collectors in Roman Palestine

[1] Similarly, J. Roloff, *Das Kerygma*, p. 48.

[2] The scholarly consensus has been attacked from two very different angles, by E. Bammel, 'Erwägungen zur Eschatologie Jesu', *Studia Evangelica* III (1964), pp. 3–32, and by R. T. Hiers, *The Kingdom of God in the Synoptic Tradition* (Gainsville, Florida, 1970).

[3] See, for example, W. G. Kümmel, *Promise and Fulfilment: the eschatological message of Jesus* (E.T. London, 1957); O. Cullmann, *Salvation as History* (E.T. London, 1967), pp. 193–209; E. Linnemann, *Parables of Jesus* (E.T. London, 1966), pp. 38f. and 132ff.; N. Perrin, *Rediscovering the Teaching of Jesus*, p. 67.

[4] In addition to the passages discussed below, see Matt. 8: 11; Luke 4: 16ff.; Matt. 22: 1ff. Perrin argues that Jesus' table fellowship with tax

were outcastes of society.[1] Even contact with tax collectors and sinners was an extraordinary step in Jesus' time, but Jesus included a tax collector in his group of disciples (Mark 2: 14 and par.).[2] Four passages which underline this important aspect of the character of Jesus and show how closely it was related to his proclamation are considered.

At Mark 2: 13–17 two originally independent units of tradition have been combined, one of which narrated the call of Levi, the other Jesus' table fellowship with tax collectors and sinners. The latter incident originally referred to Jesus as the host, and the meal took place either in Jesus' house or in some other house. Significance was seen in the fact that Jesus called Levi ἐπὶ τὸ τελώνιον, and another incident which revealed his concern for the outcastes of society was deliberately joined to verse 14.[3]

collectors and sinners has all but disappeared from the gospel traditions and that this is an indication of how far removed they are from historical reminiscence (*Rediscovering*, p. 102). But Jesus' mere association with tax collectors was almost as significant, and this is deeply rooted in the traditions (see, O. Michel, art. 'τελώνης', *TWNT* viii, 104).

[1] See Michel's well-documented article, *TWNT* viii, 88–106. The rabbis considered tax collectors to be especially unclean and comparable to thieves or robbers. The gospels themselves reflect customary attitudes; cf. Matt. 5: 46 and 18: 15–17.

[2] This is most unlikely to have been invented by the early church. Perrin, in *Rediscovering*, pp. 102f., and W. R. Farmer, in 'An Historical Essay on the Humanity of Jesus Christ', *Christian History*, eds. W. R. Farmer, C. F. D. Moule, R. R. Niebuhr (Cambridge, 1967), pp. 103ff., both suggest, apparently independently, that Jesus' table fellowship with the outcastes of society was an immediate cause of opposition which led directly to his death. But this is certainly an over-statement. Table fellowship was extended to Jesus by individual Pharisees (Luke 7: 36; 11: 37; 14: 1). John the Baptist also associated with tax collectors and sinners (Luke 3: 12 and 7: 29). And there were, of course, many other actions of Jesus which aroused indignation and opposition.

O. Hofius cites passages from the *Testaments of the Twelve Patriarchs* (Test. Sim. 6: 7; cf. the context of 6: 5 and 7: 1f.; Test. Asher 7: 3) which are, he argues, Christian additions which show that the significance of Jesus' actions was recognised in the early church. This is probably correct, though the origin of these passages is still not clear; *Jesu Tischgemeinschaft mit den Sündern* (Stuttgart, 1967), pp. 6f.

[3] R. Pesch attempts optimistically to distinguish not only Mark's redaction of pre-Marcan tradition in Mark 2: 15–17, but also the pre-Marcan tradition from the original form of the narrative: 'Das

Verse 16 introduces criticism of Jesus' conduct[1] in the form of a question, as in the pericopae which follow.[2] The tense of ἔλεγον may indicate that the criticism was sustained. Jesus replies to his critical questioners with two sayings. The proverbial logion in verse 17a raises few difficulties, but the οὐκ ἦλθον saying has been considered unauthentic, either because it is regarded as a later doctrinal addition, or because it is seen as the saying from which the whole incident was created.[3]

But the οὐκ ἦλθον logion is not as full of theological overtones as many have supposed. To ask why the Pharisees were not called is to miss the point. καλέω is used only four times in Mark; twice it is used in a straightforward literal sense without any possible 'theological' implications.[4] The

Zöllnergastmahl (Mark 2: 15–17)', *Mélanges Bibliques en hommage au R.P. Béda Rigaux*, eds. A. Descamps and A. de Halleux (Gembloux, 1970), pp. 63ff.

[1] Verse 16 introduces a new incident which probably, but not necessarily, followed the particular meal recorded in verse 15. ἰδόντες need not be understood literally; as elsewhere in Mark (e.g. 2: 5; 12: 15; 7: 2; and, possibly, 4: 12), the verb is to be taken as 'notice', 'become aware of'.

It is quite possible that Mark 2: 15–17 may have consisted originally not of two independent units, verse 14 and verses 15–17, but of three units: (*a*) verse 14, the call of Levi. (*b*) Verse 15 may have been a short narrative comparable to Luke 15: 1. The πολλοί of verse 15c may have referred to the πολλοὶ τελῶναι καὶ ἁμαρτωλοί of 15a and meant that many of the tax collectors to whom Jesus extended table fellowship followed him; or possibly the πολλοί of 15c was deliberately vague and referred both to disciples and tax collectors. If this is so, verse 15 would have been parallel to the preceding unit, which concluded with Levi following Jesus; verse 15 went further – many tax collectors and sinners (not just Levi), as well as disciples, followed Jesus. (*c*) Verses 16 and 17 could have been an entirely separate occasion.

B. M. F. van Iersel also finds three pieces of tradition here: 2: 14, 16–17a, 17b. Verse 15 is completely redactional: 'La Vocation de Lévi' in *De Jésus aux Évangiles* (Festschrift J. Coppens), ed. I. de la Potterie (Gembloux, 1967), pp. 212ff.

[2] Verse 16c is generally accepted as interrogative; Matthew and Luke both replaced Mark's ὅτι with διὰ τί.

[3] Cf. R. Bultmann, *Synoptic Tradition*, p. 18.

[4] Mark 3: 31 and 11: 17. Mark 1: 20 might possibly be interpreted with the deeper meaning. προσκαλέω is used nine times in Mark, frequently with strong 'theological' overtones.

rather surprising infrequency of the verb suggests that no deep significance was seen in it, such as is undoubtedly the case in Matthew and Luke. There are many examples of καλέω meaning 'invite' from the time of Homer; this meaning is common in the papyri and in the Septuagint,[1] it is found in Matthew and in Luke, and is almost certainly the original meaning here. The saying has a touch of gentle irony: Jesus has not come to invite to table fellowship those who consider themselves to be law-abiding, a cut above tax collectors and sinners,[2] but these much despised members of society. δικαίους need not be packed with Pauline theological connotations. The word is found elsewhere in Mark only at 6: 20, of Herod's attitude to John the Baptist; in both cases the meaning is to be understood in the literal sense – 'law-abiding'. Hence the saying is to be understood not as a 'theological' saying added by the primitive church, but as a self-characterisation of Jesus which is particularly appropriate when viewed against the background of his revolutionary action in extending table fellowship to tax collectors and sinners.[3] No doubt wider significance was seen later in the logion – the Lucan addition εἰς μετάνοιαν points in this direction – but this developed out of the original more restricted meaning.[4]

Why were these two incidents preserved? Surely one reason was that they showed clearly what sort of a person Jesus was.[5] The second logion was certainly used 'to call sinners',

[1] K. L. Schmidt, art. 'καλέω', *TWNT* III, 490f.

[2] *Contra* E. Schweizer, comm. *ad loc.*, there may not be any special significance in the absence of the τελῶναι in 17b; they are understood as part of the ἁμαρτωλοί. Luke 15: 2 provides a parallel: ἁμαρτωλούς clearly refers to the tax collectors and sinners mentioned in the previous verse.

[3] On οὐκ ἦλθον, R. Bultmann notes 'There can be no possible grounds for objecting to the idea that Jesus could have spoken about himself and his coming; that need be no more than befits his prophetic self-consciousness'. *Synoptic Tradition*, p. 153. However, Bultmann goes on to argue that individual sayings, including Mark 2: 17, rouse a number of suspicions. But see now O. Michel, '"Ich Komme" (Jos. Bell. III, 400)', *TZ* **24** (1968), 122ff.

[4] Retention of this criticism provided an explanation of the significance of Jesus' action, even for those outside Palestine who may have been unaware of the status of tax collectors.

[5] The second incident may have been retained partly because of the interest in the question of table fellowship in the primitive church; cf.

understood later in a more general sense, 'to repentance'; but the basis of this call was the action of Jesus during his ministry in inviting tax collectors and sinners to table fellowship and to follow him.[1] Whether Mark was responsible for linking the two incidents or not, the fact that they are juxtaposed is important and suggests that significance was seen in this aspect of Jesus' character. The two logia in 2: 17 are more than a reply to criticism; they expound the nature of Jesus' ministry and portray his character. Here the words and actions of Jesus go hand in hand.

The second passage, Matt. 11: 19 = Luke 7: 34 (Q), is a self-characterisation of Jesus; Jesus states that he has been accused of being

ἄνθρωπος φάγος καὶ οἰνοπότης
τελωνῶν φίλος καὶ ἁμαρτωλῶν.

The preceding parable and this logion probably belonged together in the tradition from the very beginning; both may well be authentic words of Jesus. 'Glutton and drunkard' and 'friend of tax collectors and sinners' are to be taken as two parallel phrases which supplement one another and refer to criticism not so much of Jesus' laxness in observance of fasts, as of his table fellowship with religious and social outcastes.[2] The parable paves the way for the application. The boys and girls sitting at the side of the street blame the other children for not falling in with their suggestion: God sends his last messengers, but 'this generation' is unprepared and offended

Acts 11: 3 and Gal. 2: 12. But later discussion centred on somewhat different problems. It is difficult to see any reflection of later discussions over the status of Gentiles in the synoptic accounts of Jesus' table fellowship with outcastes, however much the latter may have been seen as relevant to the later problems. R. Bultmann links this passage with controversy with Jewish opponents, but the retention of the curious phrase οἱ γραμματεῖς τῶν Φαρισαίων does not suggest stereotyped polemical material; *Synoptic Tradition*, pp. 18, 39f. The attitude of 'the scribes of the Pharisees' was one of critical inquiry, not dogmatic criticism; Jesus' reply does not contain polemical criticism, but irony.

[1] Cf. Barn. *Ep.* 5: 9, where Jesus chooses *disciples* who are exceedingly sinful, thus bringing out even more clearly the significance of Jesus' action in calling sinners.

[2] So also, H. E. Tödt, *The Son of Man in the Synoptic Tradition* (E.T. London, 1965), p. 115; *contra* R. Bultmann, *Synoptic Tradition*, p. 165.

equally by the ascetic John the Baptist and by Jesus who ate with the outcastes.[1] Again the character of Jesus is spelled out in terms of both actions and words, even if his actions are described here only indirectly. Jesus uses a parable to defend his own revolutionary conduct and to indicate the nature of his ministry. Even though the context is very different, this passage makes the same point as Mark 2: 13–17.

Luke 7: 36–50, which follows the Q passage just considered, also indicates that the gospel traditions present a rich and full portrait of Jesus of Nazareth and that Jesus' proclamation is closely related to his own conduct. The juxtaposition of the two passages is significant. In Matthew the enigmatic ἡ σοφία logion is followed by the woes pronounced on the Galilean cities, perhaps following the original order of Q; after including a lengthy block of Q material, Luke breaks off abruptly here[2] and records the remarkable story of the anointing of Jesus in a Pharisee's home by a woman 'who was a sinner'. No chronological or geographical link is provided[3] and there is no indication that Luke 7: 36–50 originally belonged to the material which follows at the beginning of chapter 8.

Why were the two passages placed together? Jesus' attitude to the woman was seen as a splendid illustration of how justified was the criticism of Jesus – φίλος...ἁμαρτωλῶν (7: 34). In both passages Jesus relates a short parable to defend his actions in associating with sinners, and in both the Q passage and the whole Lucan context actions and words of Jesus which reveal clearly his character are woven together. Luke 7: 31–50 demonstrates precisely the same process as Mark 2: 13–17: two originally independent units were linked together because they were both concerned with the same aspect of the character of Jesus.

This pericope (Luke 7: 36–50) also links a significant action of Jesus and a parable.[4] That the prostitute's act of devotion

---

[1] J. Jeremias, *The Parables of Jesus* (E.T. London, 2nd ed. 1963), pp. 161f.

[2] The woes on the Galilean cities reappear at Luke 10: 13–15 where they are not strictly relevant.

[3] It is at least possible that Luke understood 7: 36–50 as a partial illustration of the σοφία logion in 7: 35.

[4] Cf. H. Drexler, 'Die grosse Sünderin, Lucas 7: 36–50', *ZNW* **59** (1968), 167.

and Jesus' concurrence reveal a good deal about the character of Jesus needs no further comment. Is the pericope a Lucan composition and thus an indication of Luke's own interest in the character of Jesus? Has the parable been woven into the story artificially? However much the pericope may have been shaped stylistically by Luke, it is almost certainly independent of Mark 14: 3–9 and comes from the L traditions.

It has been suggested that the apparent discrepancy between the story in which love is regarded as the ground of forgiveness, and the parable, in which it is regarded as its result, is an indication that the two were originally independent.[1] However, the 'form' of the pericope does not necessarily suggest that two units have been combined.[2] Nor does the much discussed verse 47 support this hypothesis. J. Jeremias argues that as Hebrew, Aramaic and Syriac have no word for 'thank' and 'thankfulness', ἀγαπᾶν may bear the meaning of gratitude; in 47a, as in 47b and the parable, forgiveness comes first. The ὅτι in 47a indicates the evidence of forgiveness: 'Therefore I say to you that God must have forgiven her sins, many as they are, since she displays such deep thankfulness (grateful love).'[3]

The parable and the story go hand in hand; Jesus replies to Simon's unspoken criticism of his conduct and explains why he had allowed a woman who was a sinner to touch him. As in the preceding Q passage, Jesus' association with outcastes is criticised. Jesus' reply takes the form of a parable which declares God's concern for the lost in offering forgiveness to the undeserving.[4] As in the passages discussed above, we are told a good deal about the character of Jesus; in each case Jesus' actions are criticised and his reply shows how closely his message is related to his conduct.

[1] E.g., by R. K. Orchard, 'On the Composition of Luke 7: 36–50', *JTS* **38** (1937), 243ff. A. H. Dammers claims that verse 47 represents an illogical attempt to reconcile two points of view: 'A Note on Luke 7: 36–50', *Theology* **49** (1946), 78f.

[2] See C. H. Dodd, 'The Dialogue Form in the Gospels', *BJRL* **37** (1954), 60.

[3] J. Jeremias, *Parables*, pp. 126f. Similarly, H. G. Wood, who supplies references from Josephus and the LXX: 'The Use of ἀγαπάω in Lk viii (sic): 42, 47', *ExT* **66** (1954–5), 139f.

[4] Jeremias, *Parables*, p. 145.

In Luke 15 Jesus addresses parables to the scribes and Pharisees who are critical of his action in associating in table fellowship with tax collectors and sinners. Does the link between the parables and the criticism of Jesus' conduct in verses 1 and 2 represent the likely historical situation? The opening two verses are not a narrative introduction constructed by Luke in order to provide a context for the parables which follow, for there are traces of Luke's use of a source other than Mark. Although there are similarities of subject matter with Mark 2: 15-17, there are no signs of verbal dependence; it is not Luke's habit to rewrite completely his Marcan source.[1]

Even if it could be proved that Luke himself has supplied verse 3 in order to link the complaint of the scribes and Pharisees with the parables which follow in verses 4-34,[2] association of Jesus' own proclamation with criticism of his conduct is not an artificial Lucan construction, for the same pattern is found in the three passages from different sources discussed above. In each case, Jesus' defence of his conduct and explanation of the nature of his ministry are very closely linked to the criticism.

In Luke 15: 1f. as in Mark 2: 16, the comments of the scribes and Pharisees are to be understood as critical questions, rather than as overt accusations. Luke 15: 2, as well as Mark 2: 16c, is a question introduced by the interrogative adverb ὅτι. C. H. Turner noted a number of examples of this uncommon usage in Mark, Hermas and Barnabas and suggested that it belonged to less cultured Christian circles.[3] But it also seems to be found in Luke–Acts: Luke 15: 2, Luke 19: 7 and Acts 11: 3 can be interpreted similarly.[4] In Luke 15: 2

[1] Cf. the evidence cited by Jeremias, *Parables*, p. 100 n. 42. In addition, ἐγγίζοντες (15: 1) may be an indication of pre-Lucan tradition. Cf. F. Rehkopf, *Sonderquelle*, p. 93. W. R. Farmer notes as non-Lucan the periphrastic imperfect at the beginning of introductory sentences such as 15: 1: 'Notes on a Literary and Form-Critical Analysis of Some of the Synoptic Material Peculiar to Luke', *NTS* **8** (1962), 303.

[2] Farmer defends this hypothesis, 'Notes', *NTS* **8**, 302. But the linguistic evidence is not conclusive; the verse is too brief to allow a firm decision on its origin.

[3] 'Marcan Usage', *JTS* **27** (1926), 58ff.

[4] Some support, admittedly not conclusive, is provided by the textual tradition. C. H. Turner noted that some Latin versions of his examples

διεγόγγυζον leads even more directly to a question than to dogmatic criticism, for its suggests critical comments and does not carry the Old Testament overtones that γογγύζειν does in John 6: 41, 43. As in the previous passages, Jesus' table fellowship with tax collectors and sinners drew not so much damning criticism and outright rejection as shocked surprise and a genuine question, 'Why?'

These four passages each record Jesus' revolutionary conduct; the close link between Jesus' words and actions and the juxtaposition of similar incidents underline the significance of Jesus' actions. Interest in this aspect of the character of Jesus is not the prerogative of any one source, form of the tradition, or evangelist. Since there is no reason to doubt that Jesus' conduct was questioned critically by scribes and Pharisees, significance was seen in Jesus' behaviour during his ministry.

Jesus' own proclamation is closely related to his actions: both proclaim that God's rule is already being inaugurated. His proclamation is more than a defence of his actions, for although Jesus formulates his proclamation in such a way as to take account of the critical questioning of his conduct, he does not debate with those who asked 'why'. Their questioning only served to bring out even more clearly the radical nature of his conduct and his claims.[1]

The Fringe of Society: Women and Children

Jesus' attitude to women and children is just as significant as his relationship with tax collectors, for women and children were also on the fringe of the society of the day. Although the early church was undoubtedly influenced by the attitude of Jesus, its radical implications were not grasped; hence the

of ὅτι interrogative in Mark used *quare* or *quid* to translate ὅτι. Some Old Latin mss. read *quare* at Acts 11: 3 and Luke 15: 2; in the latter verse 1071 and ar. read διὰ τί. It is easier to envisage critical questioning of scribes and Pharisees at Luke 15: 2 being changed into rigid opposition than *vice versa*.

[1] Cf. E. Linnemann's observation that although almost all the parables are addressed to opponents, they do not reduce the opponents *ad absurdum*, but make it their aim to win their agreement: *Parables*, p. 22.

authenticity of this feature of the gospels' portrait of Jesus is established securely by use of the criterion of dissimilarity.[1] In addition, this trait is deeply rooted in the various strata of the traditions, with the exception of Q, and it is found in a number of different 'forms'.

The status of women was markedly inferior to that of men throughout the ancient world.[2] This is reflected in Philo and Josephus as much as, if not more than, in rabbinic writings.[3] Although Jewish scholars differ in their assessment of the rabbinic evidence, many accept that the attitude of Jesus towards women was very striking.[4]

During at least part of his ministry Jesus was accompanied by a group of women who ministered to him (Mark 15: 40-1; Luke 8: 1-3); this action is without precedent in contemporary Judaism.[5] Although Luke's account is similar to Mark's, there is little doubt that he had access to a tradition independent of Mark 15: 40.[6] Nor do the Marcan references to the women in 15: 40, 47 and 16: 1 arise from the evangelist's special interests, for the differences in the names mentioned point to pre-Marcan tradition.

In all four gospels women are witnesses of the crucifixion, visit the empty tomb, and, except in Mark, witness the appearances of the Risen Christ. The absence of the women from

[1] So also, for example, J. Leipoldt, *Jesus und die Frauen* (Leipzig, 1921), p. 105; *Die Frau in der antiken Welt und im Urchristentum* (Leipzig, 1955), p. 234; C. F. D. Moule, *The Phenomenon of the New Testament* (London, 1967), pp. 63f.

[2] See, for details, J. Leipoldt, *Die Frau*, pp. 10–16; P. Ketter, *Christ and Womenkind* (E.T. London, 1937); A. Oepke, art. 'γυνή', *TWNT* I, 776ff., and, especially, J. Jeremias, *Jerusalem in the Time of Jesus* (E.T. London, 1969), pp. 359ff.

[3] Cf. Jos. *Ap.* II, 24; P. Ketter, *Womenkind*, pp. 51f.; E. R. Goodenough, *An Introduction to Philo Judaeus* (Oxford, 2nd ed. 1962), pp. 126ff.

[4] See Strack–Billerbeck, *Kommentar* III, 611. Also, C. G. Montefiore, *Rabbinic Literature and Gospel Teachings* (London, 1930), pp. 47, 217; ed. C. G. Montefiore and H. Loewe, *A Rabbinic Anthology* (London, 1938), cf. pp. xviii and 656ff., 685; R. Loewe, *The Position of Women in Judaism* (London, 1966).

[5] W. Foerster, *From the Exile to Christ* (E.T. Philadelphia, 1964), p. 127.

[6] So M. Hengel, 'Maria Magdalena' in *Abraham Unser Vater* (Festschrift O. Michel), eds. O. Betz, M. Hengel, P. Schmidt (Leiden, 1963), pp. 245ff. This is challenged by J. Delobel, 'L'Onction par la Pécheresse', *ETL* **42** (1966), 415–75, but his evidence of Lucan redaction is not all equally convincing.

1 Cor. 15: 3ff. lies in the reluctance of Jewish law to accept testimony from female potential witnesses.[1] The gospel traditions forced their way through this barrier because the traditions of the extraordinary faithfulness of the group of women followers of Jesus, as well as his own attitude to women, encouraged the early church to insist that women were prominent witnesses of the very events which lay at the heart of its message.

The 'anointing' pericopae are the most striking accounts of Jesus' contact with individual women. The Marcan pericope (Mark 14: 3–9) and the similar Lucan narrative (Luke 7: 36–50) are basically independent, although the Lucan version appears to have attracted some motifs from the Marcan tradition. Matt. 26: 6–13 has retained the Marcan account; the Johannine tradition (12: 1–8) is more problematic. But traditio-historical questions have often overshadowed the significance of Jesus' acceptance of a public demonstration of devotion of a woman, a woman whose character is clearly placed in considerable doubt in Luke's account. In each case the action of the woman is criticised, but in each gospel we are aware that there is a veiled criticism of Jesus for allowing such an outrageous action – criticism which becomes explicit in Luke 7: 39. Jesus defends his acceptance of the woman's devotion in each passage. A strikingly consistent portrait of Jesus' attitude to women emerges.

Jesus taught women as well as men. In the Mary and Martha pericope in Luke 10: 38–42, the right of Mary (and by implication of other women) to listen to the teaching of Jesus is underlined, for Mary sat at the feet of Jesus as a pupil receiving instruction from a rabbi. Although it was not entirely unknown, it was very unusual for a woman to receive instruction in the law.[2]

A number of pericopae mark out the concern and compassion of Jesus for women. The incident concerning the widow of

---

[1] See R. Loewe's discussion of the rabbinic evidence, *The Position of Women in Judaism*, p. 24.

[2] See Strack–Billerbeck, *Kommentar* III, 468; R. Loewe, *Women*, pp. 28f.; E. Laland, 'Die Martha-Maria Perikope', *ST* **13** (1959), 73. J. Leipoldt stresses that the two sisters and Jesus were already well-acquainted; they belonged to the circle of Jesus' followers. Merely by staying in a house with two women, Jesus parted from the customary attitudes of the day; *Die Frau*, p. 125.

Nain is a good example; the detail that the dead man was the only son of a widow is irrelevant to the main point of the passage, but it indicates that Jesus' recognition of the particularly hard lot of a widow was seen to be significant.

The parables also reflect Jesus' attitude to women; almost without exception women are presented in a favourable light, while the opposite tends to be the case in rabbinic parables.[1] In several passages Jesus' attitude to women is made explicit in his teaching; again his teaching is consistent with his actions.[2] The juxtaposition of Mark 12: 40 and 41ff. illustrates Jesus' indirect teaching about women; the two pericopae have, in all probability, been placed together in order to point to the contrast between the attitude to women of the scribes and of Jesus himself.[3]

Jesus' unexpected attitude towards women is also found in the Fourth Gospel. At John 4: 9 the Samaritan woman is surprised that Jesus should ask her for a drink: οὐ γὰρ συγχρῶνται Ἰουδαῖοι Σαμαρίταις. D. Daube's elucidation of the meaning of this verb and the background of this sentence has established that Jesus here shows himself ready to disregard the customary hostile presumption respecting Samaritan women for the sake of a more inclusive fellowship.[4]

[1] Cf. J. Leipoldt, *Die Frau*, pp. 122f.; A. Oepke, art. 'γυνή', *TWNT* 1, 784. Matt. 25: 1ff. is an exception which proves the rule! When a woman is used in a rabbinic parable to serve as an example of an attribute of God, it is not a very ordinary woman, as in some parables in the gospel traditions, but a king's daughter! J. Leipoldt, *Jesus und die Frauen*, p. 26. But the point must not be taken too far; in some of the parables the fact that women are mentioned is either entirely incidental or completely necessary to the main point being made and hence can hardly be said to reflect Jesus' own attitude.

[2] See J. Leipoldt, *Die Frau*, p. 130, and C. G. Montefiore, *Rabbinic Literature*, p. 47.

[3] It has been suggested that these verses may have been transformed from a parable of Jesus (possibly based on a current Jewish parable) into an incident about him (M. Dibelius, *From Tradition to Gospel*, p. 261; E. Schweizer and D. E. Nineham, comms. *ad loc.*). While this is just possible, other clear-cut cases have not been cited; the alleged process does not seem to have been a feature of the transmission of the parable traditions.

[4] 'Jesus and the Samaritan Woman; the meaning of συγχράομαι', *JBL* **69** (1950), 137ff.; cf. C. H. Dodd, 'The Portrait of Jesus in John and in the Synoptics', *Christian History and Interpretation*, eds. W. R. Farmer C. F. D. Moule, R. R. Niebuhr (Cambridge, 1967), p. 196.

John 4: 28 implies that Jesus drank from the woman's waterpot; 'that was an act comparable to, and indeed more serious than, dealings involving contact with an Am-Haaretz'.[1]

Almost as revolutionary was Jesus' long conversation with a woman; at John 4: 27 the narrative itself draws attention to this.[2] The usual view that a woman's word and testimony are not reliable may also lie behind John 4: 42.[3] Why does John 4 refer to a woman? It is unlikely to be a Johannine invention, for this detail is far from necessary to the argument of the chapter. The attitude of Jesus to the woman is completely consistent with that found deeply embedded in the synoptic traditions. The evangelist was aware that Jesus was the sort of person who associated with outcastes and those on the fringe of society.[4]

John 5: 3ff. and 9: 8 reveal Jesus moving amongst and showing concern for the underprivileged in a way which has many parallels in the synoptic traditions. In John 9 the Pharisees accuse Jesus of being a sinner, but the context suggests that his infringement of the sabbath rather than his contact with the 'sinful' blind man lies behind the charge. However, the chapter as a whole reflects the customary attitude towards those with physical disabilities; Jesus' own attitude is contrasted clearly.

Although Jesus' association with women does not seem to have drawn overt opposition, Marcion's addition to the accusations against Jesus before Pilate (Luke 23: 2) is interesting:

---

[1] D. Daube, 'Jesus and the Samaritan Woman', *JBL* **69**, 138. The historicity of 4: 9b is a difficult question; but even if it is a later Johannine addition, the passage shows that the evangelist recognised that Jesus broke established conventions in his association with people who were regarded as sinners because they were unclean.

[2] Cf. Strack–Billerbeck, *Kommentar* II, 437; J. Leipoldt, *Die Frau*, pp. 120ff.

[3] Cf. Strack–Billerbeck, *Kommentar* II, 441.

[4] The history of the *pericope de adultera* (John 7: 53–8: 11) is an unsolved problem. The portrait of Jesus and the woman is not inconsistent with that found in John 4; in both cases Jesus is aware of the nature and implications of the woman's sins. Jesus does not simply overlook sinful conduct, but shows a concern for the woman which was unexpected. Similarly, the pericope is not inconsistent with synoptic traditions which portray Jesus' attitude to women.

καὶ ἀποστρέφοντα τὰς γυναῖκας καὶ τὰ τέκνα.[1] Marcion may well be following and not expanding an earlier text, but, whatever its origin, the addition shows that Jesus' attitude to women and the fact that a group followed Jesus did not pass unnoticed; it was seen as a distinctive feature of the ministry of Jesus which must have drawn the ire of opponents. Origen emphasises that women, as well as men, followed Jesus into the wilderness, 'forgetting the weakness of their sex and a regard for outward propriety in thus following their Teacher into desert places'.[2]

The gospel traditions which deal with Jesus' relationships with women are not confined to any one source or form. The naturalness of Jesus' relationships with women of all sorts is amazing. His attitude encouraged many women to take the very unusual step of following him and ministering to him. But the traditions insist that Jesus did not simply overlook the conduct of those who had erred. Jesus accepts women as they are and shows a respect which is distinct from the usual attitudes of the day.[3]

Although the evidence is less extensive, there can be no doubt that Jesus' interest in children is an authentic trait. There is some evidence, admittedly not conclusive, which indicates that Jesus' attitude towards children also differed from the customary attitudes of the day[4] and that its significance may have not been fully recognised by the early church.[5] Although Matt. 19: 14 and Luke 18: 16 omit the note in Mark 10: 14 that Jesus was indignant with the disciples, all three accounts stress that Jesus was anxious that children should be brought to him. Mark 10: 15 was probably an independent logion, for it is found in a different context at Matt. 18: 3 and may well lie behind John 3: 3. Hence Mark and Matthew (18: 2f.), or earlier traditions, link Jesus' actions and words, bringing out Jesus' distinctive attitude.

[1] See A. Harnack, *Marcion* (Leipzig, 1921), pp. 216f. for details. Some Old Latin mss. add 'et filios nostros et uxores avertit a nobis' at the end of Luke 23: 5, probably under the influence of Marcion.

[2] *Adv. Cels.* 3: 10.

[3] The puzzling final saying in the Gospel of Thomas, logion 114, provides a striking contrast.

[4] C. G. Montefiore, *Rabbinic Literature*, p. 258.

[5] Cf. E. Schweizer, comm. *ad* Mark 10: 13–16.

The history of the tradition in Mark 9: 35–7 and par. is more complicated, but these passages are consistent with Mark 10: 13ff. and par. and also show a close relationship between the words and deeds of Jesus. Accounts of Jesus healing children (e.g. Mark 5: 39ff.; 7: 24ff.; 9: 17ff.; John 4: 49) and Jesus' use of his penetrating observation of children playing (Matt. 11: 16–17 = Luke 7: 32) also reflect his attitude to children.

A clear and consistent portrait of Jesus emerges from the gospel traditions: his attitude to women was startlingly new, he was able to mix freely and naturally with women of all sorts, women followed and ministered to him, and he showed an unexpected interest in children. Jesus' concern for tax collectors and sinners, and for those shunned by society on account of bodily ills of various kinds was an implication of his proclamation of the arrival of God's kingly rule. Jesus' interest in women and children forms part of his concern for those on the fringe of society and thus is linked indirectly to his proclamation of the kingdom. The conduct of Jesus is 'message', as much as his words; they are inseparable and consistent.

The scandal of Jesus of Nazareth

Other aspects of the proclamation of Jesus also drew critical questioning. The final words of Jesus' reply to John the Baptist's inquiry (Matt. 11: 6 = Luke 7: 23) indicate that offence was given by the contrast between his claims that the prophetic promises were already being fulfilled in his words and actions, and the outward appearances which seemed to hold no such promise. The way the parables of contrast[1] are

---

[1] This is a more satisfactory term than 'growth', which suggests the unbiblical notion that the Kingdom gradually advances and permeates society. See the full discussion of these parables in R. Schnackenburg, *God's Rule and Kingdom* (E.T. Edinburgh and London, 1963), pp. 143–59; W. G. Kümmel, *Promise and Fulfilment*, pp. 124–40; G. E. Ladd, *Jesus and the Kingdom* (London, 1966), pp. 217–38; E. Jüngel, *Paulus und Jesus*, pp. 139–55; J. Jeremias, *Parables*, pp. 146–53; and, especially, N. A. Dahl, 'The Parables of Growth', *ST* 5 (1951), 132–66.

The parables of contrast include: the mustard seed (Mark 4: 30–2 and par.); the leaven (Matt. 13: 33 and Luke 13: 20–1); the seed growing secretly (Mark 4: 26–9); the drag-net (Matt. 13: 47–50); the tares (Matt. 13: 24–30); the sower (Mark 4: 1–20), in its original form, is added by

formulated confirms that the 'negative' aspect of Jesus' character was an issue during his ministry and that his pro- clamation of God's rule was framed against the scandal this caused.[1] For these parables insist that the Kingdom is indeed already being inaugurated in the ministry of Jesus, in spite of its apparent obscurity, and claim confidently that the Kingdom will come.[2] While these parables are primarily proclamation and not merely Jesus' defence of himself and his message against the scepticism of those who looked for more tangible and spectacular evidence, account is taken of such criticism.[3] Jesus accepted the surprise and scorn shown at the unexpectedly insignificant beginnings of the Kingdom, and turned it to good account by stressing the contrast between the beginning and the end. Again Jesus' proclamation arouses interest in and is related to the sort of person he was.

Gospel traditions which spell out the obscure personal back- ground of Jesus, his alienation from his family and his rejection also support these observations: as in the parables of contrast, the scandal of the 'negative' aspect of the character of Jesus is not glossed over.

Although Mark 6: 1–6 is primarily concerned with the related themes of the rejection of Jesus and his isolation from his family, these verses make the obscure origins of Jesus quite clear.[4] Those who hear Jesus in the synagogue are amazed at both his teaching and his deeds, but there is nothing striking about his background: his mother, brothers and sisters are all known. ὁ τέκτων was hardly the sort of person who might have been expected to speak and act as Jesus did.[5] Neither

some; N. A. Dahl includes the Johannine logion about the grain of wheat (John 12: 24).

[1] The individual parables in question need not be discussed in detail. The main points mentioned here are generally accepted.

[2] Cf. Dahl, 'Parables', *ST* **5**, 156 *et passim*.

[3] E. Jüngel denies that the parables are Jesus' defence against opponents or doubters: *Paulus und Jesus*, p. 154. But it is not necessary to draw a sharp contrast between defence and positive proclamation.

[4] *Contra* R. Bultmann, *Synoptic Tradition*, p. 31, there are good reasons for accepting the pericope as essentially authentic. Cf. V. Taylor, *The Formation of the Gospel Tradition* (London, 1933), p. 149.

[5] Origen denies that Jesus is described in the gospels as an artisan, *Adv. Cels.* 6: 36; this probably reflects later embarrassment over the apparently obscure origins of Jesus.

Matthew nor Luke makes any attempt to hide this very ordinary background, even though both have altered the pericope in other ways.

The obscurity of Jesus' background is also prominent in Mark's account of Jesus' baptism by John (Mark 1: 9), although here too it is not the main point of the pericope. If only the minimum detail had been retained, reference to Nazareth and Galilee could have been omitted. Neither Nazareth nor Galilee would have been understood in the primitive Christian communities as an appropriate background for the Messiah, yet both are firmly retained in the traditions. Nazareth certainly had no proud history. Even if the addition of ἀπὸ Ναζαρεθ τῆς Γαλιλαίας was made by Mark, it is still significant that such a specific comment should have been added. Luke brings out even more clearly that Jesus was brought up in Nazareth in Galilee (2: 39, 51; 4: 16), even though he was born in the city of David, Bethlehem (2: 4); Luke makes no attempt to link anything but Jesus' birth with the more illustrious town of Bethlehem.

The obscurity of both Nazareth and Galilee becomes explicit in the Fourth Gospel, where no attempt is made to hide Jesus' background or his alienation from his family. Nathanael asks, 'Can anything good come out of Nazareth?' (1: 46). Philip's reply accepts the obscurity of Jesus' background and stresses that this should not be a factor in Nathanael's evaluation of Jesus: 'Come and see.' Some of those at the Feast of Tabernacles ask, 'Is the Christ to come from Galilee?' (7: 41). Again Jesus' background is an issue.

Gospel traditions which underline Jesus' alienation from his family and their misunderstanding of him, also point indirectly to the unpromising beginnings of Jesus' ministry. Mark 3 provides striking evidence of Jesus' relationship with his family. Mark understood 3: 20 and 21 as linked to 3: 31–4; there could well have been such a link in the pre-Marcan tradition. In verse 21 we are told that οἱ παρ' αὐτοῦ ἐξῆλθον κρατῆσαι αὐτόν; close acquaintances, including relatives, are involved. It is quite possible that verses 22–30 have been included between verse 20 and verse 31 in order to modify slightly the harshness of verse 21. Matthew and Luke felt more keenly the aspersions cast on Jesus' family, even indirectly on Jesus, and omitted 3: 20–1. There is no direct link between 3: 21 and 22; since ἐξέστη does not round off the incident, further comment such as that provided in verses 31ff. seems to be necessary.[1]

The pericope obviously leads up to the saying of Jesus in 3: 34b and 35, but indirect information about Jesus and his alienation from his family is retained which is not strictly necessary. Hence the narrative is more than a frame for the saying of Jesus, especially if, as is probable, verses 20 and 21 originally belonged with 31–5. This pericope reminds us that a unit in the gospel tradition may intend to make more than one point, and hence have had more than one *Sitz im Leben* in the early church.[2] Jesus is alienated from his family; those who knew him best say, ἐξέστη. Again the Johannine traditions are complementary. Even if Jesus' use of γύναι in John 2: 4 is not discourteous, the preceding words τί ἐμοὶ καὶ σοί point to the same alienation of Jesus from his family as is found in Mark 3.

There is no need to demonstrate that there are many gospel traditions which point to Jesus' rejection by sections of the society in which he was active; these traditions also draw attention, indirectly, to the unpropitious outward circumstances of the ministry of Jesus. There is a striking contrast between the claims of Jesus and the response they drew.

The gospel traditions tell us a good deal about the background of Jesus, even though they do not satisfy modern biographical curiosity. In various ways the obscurity and scandal of the background and unpromising outward appearances of the activity of Jesus are stamped upon the traditions and are found alongside traditions which reveal Jesus' unique authority.

What role did these surprisingly full references to the 'negative' aspect of the character of Jesus play in the early church? No doubt they served to remind the Christian that he must also expect severing of family ties or even complete rejection. No

---

[1] So also, Bultmann, *Synoptic Tradition*, p. 29. Bultmann argues that the saying in verse 35 is original, while verses 20f. and 31–4 are secondary. This is most unlikely in view of the way Matthew and Luke are aware of, and therefore remove, the aspersions cast on the family of Jesus.

[2] This point is developed in chapter 7.

doubt the traditions more closely associated with the rejection of Jesus were used to explain why Jesus had been crucified. But was this their only *Sitz im Leben*?

Jesus' background and apparent lack of success had already been such an issue in his lifetime that he was forced to frame his proclamation accordingly – as the parables of contrast show. Since the proclamation of Jesus continued to be used by the early church, these issues were bound to arise again. The extent of the traditions which make this point in one way or another suggests that the early church also insisted that God's rule was being inaugurated in spite of appearances to the contrary, accepted the charge of 'insignificant origins', and made the scandal of Jesus of Nazareth part of its message. Interest in the past of Jesus is deeply rooted in the traditions on which the evangelists drew. Traditions are retained which answer questions and objections which must have been very common, 'Who was Jesus?', 'Where did he come from?', 'What sort of a person was he?'

The 'Present' Son-of-Man Sayings

In one group of Son-of-Man sayings Jesus speaks directly about his own character and the nature of his ministry; the 'present' Son-of-Man sayings can be called autobiographical in that however ὁ υἱὸς τοῦ ἀνθρώπου is interpreted, they refer to the pre-crucifixion period and cannot be taken as speaking of any other person.[1] The main sayings may be outlined: Matt. 11: 19 = Luke 7: 34 refers to the conduct of the Son of Man – unlike John the Baptist, he has come 'eating and drinking'; the context confirms that Jesus' extension of table fellowship to tax collectors and sinners is criticised. In Matt. 8: 20 = Luke 9: 58 Jesus states that while foxes have holes and birds of the air have nests, the Son of Man has nowhere to lay his head; the saying speaks of Jesus' homelessness, probably to be understood as his alienation from his family or his rejection by those among whom he moved. Mark 2: 10 speaks of the authority of the Son of Man on earth to forgive

[1] The term 'present' Son of Man is used simply for convenience; division of the Son-of-Man sayings into the three customary groups can be misleading.

sins, and in Mark 2: 28 Jesus claims that the Son of Man is lord even of the sabbath. Mark 10: 45 speaks of the purpose of the ministry of the Son of Man in terms of service and of the giving of his life as a ransom for many. In Luke 19: 10 the nature of the ministry of the Son of Man is summed up as seeking and saving the lost. Matt. 12: 32 = Luke 12: 10 states that speaking against the Son of Man will be forgiven, but warns against blaspheming against the Holy Spirit.[1] The diverse content of the sayings is immediately apparent; 'present' Son-of-Man sayings are found in Q, Mark and L.[2]

The 'present' Son-of-Man sayings are strikingly similar in general content to some of the aspects of Jesus' proclamation of the presence of the Kingdom and its implications for his actions which were discussed above; for also in these sayings Jesus refers to himself and his ministry in terms of his actions, conduct and unpromising personal circumstances. If the Son-of-Man sayings are authentic, they also indicate that Jesus' proclamation was very much bound up with his character. But their authenticity has been strongly attacked; many writers accept an origin in either the Palestinian or Hellenistic church, barely stopping to consider the possibility that Jesus used the phrase 'Son of Man' to refer to himself and his ministry on earth.

The most common objection stresses the apparent incompatibility of the 'present' and the 'future apocalyptic' sayings. Some of the latter are said to differentiate between Jesus and the Son of Man; the 'present' sayings expressly identify the Son of Man and Jesus, yet the Son of Man to whom they refer is very much devoid of the 'traditional attributes' of the transcendent figure of Jewish apocalyptic.[3] However, this general approach is not entirely convincing. On this view, why were Son-of-Man sayings formulated in which Jesus spoke of

[1] Matt. 13: 37 and Luke 6: 22 also refer to the ministry of the Son of Man on earth, but they do not stem from early tradition. So also, H. E. Tödt, *Son of Man*, pp. 123f. and 135. Mark 8: 38 par. (cf. Luke 12: 8f. = Matt. 10: 32f.) might be added, for 'it cuts across the trichotomy that is usually imposed upon the Son of Man material': C. K. Barrett, *Jesus and the Gospel Tradition* (London, 1967), p. 32.

[2] H. E. Tödt correctly accepts that Luke probably received 19: 10 from traditional material peculiar to him. *Son of Man*, pp. 133f.

[3] Cf. H. E. Tödt, *Son of Man*, pp. 125, 139 *et passim*.

his ministry, his conduct, his authority in such diverse ways?[1] Why did the early church not include any of the 'traditional attributes' of the Son of Man in these sayings?[2] The answer is, of course, that the church differentiated between Jesus' activity on earth and that still to come.[3] But if the earliest communities were able to avoid this anachronism, why did they press varied Son-of-Man sayings so strongly into the various strata of traditions, if Jesus had not referred to himself on earth as Son of Man? Why, on this view, did some of the Son-of-Man sayings created by the church fail to identify Jesus and the Son of Man unambiguously?[4] It is just conceivable that authentic sayings in which Son of Man was understood originally as an indirect reference to Jesus were reinterpreted later as more explicit claims of Jesus, but it is difficult to believe that the early church could have created Son-of-Man sayings which referred to Jesus as 'eating and drinking' in contrast to John the Baptist (Matt. 11: 19 = Luke 7: 34), or as having nowhere to lay his head (Matt. 8: 20 = Luke 9: 58).[5] But apart from such considerations, the validity of the basic premise is by no means self-evident, for the background material which is at all relevant does not necessarily indicate that the 'present' and 'future' Son-of-Man sayings are as incompatible as is often claimed.

A second line of attack on the authenticity of the 'present' sayings argues that at least some of them originated in Aramaic as a circumlocution for 'I', or as some

[1] H. E. Tödt claims that in all the 'present' sayings 'Son of Man' characterises Jesus in the *exousia* of his activity on earth: *Son of Man*, pp. 114ff. Some of the sayings, however, are forced rather artificially into this mould – e.g., Matt. 8: 20 = Luke 9: 58.

[2] If we accept the criterion of dissimilarity and if we assume that Son of Man was a transcendent individual figure in Jewish writings, the 'present' sayings emerge with strong claims to authenticity. Cf. E. Schweizer, 'Der Menschensohn; zur eschatologischen Erwartung Jesu', *ZNW* **50** (1959) (reprinted in E. Schweizer, *Neotestamentica* (Zürich, 1963), p. 74); E. Bammel, 'Erwägungen', *Studia Evangelica* III (1964), 20.

[3] So H. E. Tödt, *Son of Man*, p. 273.

[4] This point is relevant whether all the Son-of-Man sayings are taken as secondary (P. Vielhauer *et al.*), or whether only those which differentiate Jesus and the Son of Man are regarded as authentic (H. E. Tödt *et al.*).

[5] Many who sense this difficulty resort to the hypothesis of a linguistic misunderstanding.

other form of indirect reference to the speaker, or as a reference to 'mankind' in general; only on the basis of a linguistic misunderstanding did they receive a titular meaning. This approach has recently been revived and new evidence brought forward in support.[1] However, even if the underlying Aramaic phrase was widely used in any or all of these ways at the time of Jesus and not merely later,[2] there is still the possibility that Jesus used the phrase in a different sense, perhaps ambiguously.[3] Since the early church certainly did not understand the phrase merely as 'I', 'one' or 'man', from where did its understanding of Son of Man come? As F. H. Borsch notes, 'The linguistic argument cannot be based solely on the evidence from the slightly later rabbinic usage and thus conducted in a kind of vacuum. The Christian usage is evidence in its own right.'[4] Again the interpretation and relevance of Dan. 7: 13ff. and the passages in 1 Enoch are the key questions.

[1] See C. Colpe, art. 'ὁ υἱὸς τοῦ ἀνθρώπου', *TWNT* VIII, pp. 404ff. and 433ff.; G. Vermes, 'The Use of בר נש / בר נשא in Jewish Aramaic', Appendix E in M. Black, *An Aramaic Approach to the Gospels and Acts* (Oxford, 3rd ed. 1967), pp. 310–28; also J. A. Fitzmyer's critical discussion of G. Vermes' appendix in *CBQ* **30** (1968), 424ff. and M. Black's comments, *Aramaic Approach*, pp. 328ff.

[2] J. A. Fitzmyer raises serious objections to the relevance of the material cited by G. Vermes for the Son-of-Man problem in the Gospels, claiming that it is later than the first century and does not all come from Palestine: *CBQ* **30**, 424ff.

[3] J. Jeremias refuses to dismiss all the 'present' sayings as unauthentic and accepts Matt. 8: 20 = Luke 9: 58 as one of twelve authentic Son-of-Man sayings. Matt. 11: 19 = Luke 7: 34, Mark 2: 28, and, with hesitation, Mark 2: 10, are taken as philological misunderstandings (בר נשא = 'ein Mensch'). Jeremias argues that as the majority of the Son-of-Man sayings are also found in parallel formulations *without* the words 'Son of Man', the latter are original: 'Die älteste Schicht der Menschensohn–Logien', *ZNW* **58** (1967), 159–72. But a number of the alleged parallel formulations are unconvincing. To give but one example from the 'present' sayings, Luke 19: 10 is most unlikely to have been derived from Matt. 15: 24. See the discussion of Jeremias' article in F. H. Borsch, *The Christian and the Gnostic Son of Man* (London, 1970), pp. 5–28.

[4] *The Son of Man in Myth and History* (London, 1967), p. 26. On pp. 21ff. and 314ff., Borsch discusses the theory of a linguistic misunderstanding in some detail. He stresses that any attractiveness in the theory of a misunderstood idiom begins to lose much of its force when we are asked

Both objections to the authenticity of the Son-of-Man sayings turn on the relevance of passages in Jewish apocalyptic where Son of Man is used. If the 'present' sayings can be understood plausibly against the background of these passages, there is no need to postulate an origin in the early church for all of them, nor is there any need to insist they they can make sense only on some form of the theory of a linguistic misunderstanding. The widely held view that Son of Man was a transcendent individual figure linked with the eschatological hope of Jewish apocalyptic has rightly been called in question in a number of fresh investigations of the background material.[1] The crucial passage is Dan. 7, for 1 Enoch and 4 Ezra reinterpret or draw in some way on this chapter;[2] this is the only Son-of-Man passage to which Jesus himself clearly and directly referred.[3]

As a number of scholars have insisted, all three groups of

to believe that it was a part-time misunderstanding; Borsch asks whether Jesus used the phrase in both ways and yet neither he nor his immediate followers passed on any means of distinguishing between the two usages.

The majority of recent writers have rejected this theory. See, for example, H. E. Tödt, *Son of Man*, pp. 124, 138; A. J. B. Higgins, *Jesus and the Son of Man* (London, 1964), pp. 26, 123; M. Hooker, *The Son of Man in Mark*, p. 194. I. H. Marshall, 'The Synoptic Son of Man Sayings in Recent Discussion', *NTS* **12** (1966), pp. 328, 350f., cautiously allows the possibility of a circumlocution for 'I'.

[1] See, for example, M. Hooker, *The Son of Man in Mark*; N. Perrin, *Rediscovering*, pp. 164ff.; O. Betz, *What do we know about Jesus?* (E.T. London, 1968), pp. 109ff.; F. H. Borsch, *Son of Man*, pp. 43ff.; C. F. D. Moule, *The Phenomenon of the New Testament* (London, 1967), pp. 34f. and, more fully, in his review of Tödt's *Son of Man* in *Theology* **69** (1966), pp. 172ff.; R. Leivestad, 'Exit the Apocalyptic Son of Man', *NTS* **18** (1972), 243–67. These writers differ widely in the conclusions they finally reach, thus making their criticism of the widely accepted alternative view all the more important.

[2] 4 Ezra is later than the synoptic gospels. The date of 1 Enoch 37–71 is much disputed; Qumran specialists differ on the significance of the absence of this part of Enoch from the fragments of 1 Enoch recovered from the Qumran caves. Cf. O. Betz, *What do we know about Jesus?*, p. 110 and J. A. Fitzmyer, *CBQ* **30**, 428. Fitzmyer claims that the absence of these chapters is 'sheer chance'.

[3] This is not universally accepted. See, for example, C. Colpe's claim that Jesus' allusions to Dan. 7: 13 are secondary additions stemming from the early church: art. 'ὁ υἱὸς τοῦ ἀνθρώπου', *TWNT* VIII, 431; H. E. Tödt, *Son of Man*, pp. 23 n. 2, 35ff. *et al.*

Son-of-Man sayings do make sense against the background of Dan. 7. The Son of Man of Jewish apocalyptic, especially Dan. 7, to which the synoptic sayings must be related, is not a transcendent figure with 'traditional attributes',[1] for the one 'like a son of man' in Dan. 7 is identified with the saints of the Most High who suffer (Dan. 7: 18, 22, 27). This approach has been carefully defended by M. Hooker (among others), who concludes that

the Son of Man is not simply one who appears at the end of time to act as judge: rather it is because he is Son of Man now – i.e. elect, obedient, faithful and therefore suffering – that he will be vindicated as Son of Man in the future: the eschatological role of the Son of Man is based upon his obedient response to God now.[2]

This view takes seriously the most likely background passage, Dan. 7, and the main thrust of the different types of synoptic passages; weighty objections can be brought against views which dispose of one or more of the three categories into which Son-of-Man sayings are usually grouped.[3]

The 'present' Son-of-Man sayings fit in readily with an

[1] H. E. Tödt refers to E. Schweizer's insistence that in Dan. 7: 13 he who appears 'like a son of man' represents 'the people of the Saints of the Most High' (verse 27), but claims that the interpretation which follows 7: 13 probably explains the vision in a new secondary sense! *Son of Man*, p. 23 n. 2. R. H. Fuller dodges the implications of Dan. 7: 15f., 27, in a similar and equally unconvincing way: *The Foundations of New Testament Christology* (London, 1965), p. 36. Surely the interpretation provided by the Biblical text itself was taken more seriously by later readers of Dan. 7!

C. Colpe argues, admittedly with caution, that as neither Dan. 7, 1 Enoch 37–71 nor 4 Ezra explains satisfactorily the origin of the earliest synoptic Son-of-Man sayings, the latter must themselves be taken as evidence for a Jewish Son-of-Man tradition; thus Colpe is able to retain the existence of an individual transcendent figure with 'traditional attributes'!

[2] *The Son of Man in Mark*, p. 190. Cf. C. K. Barrett, *Jesus and the Gospel Tradition*, pp. 41ff., C. F. D. Moule, *Phenomenon*, pp. 34f. This general interpretation of Dan. 7 is defended by M. Delcor, 'Les Sources du Chapitre VII de Daniel', *VT* **18** (1968), 290–312; see esp. 302ff.

[3] Cf. F. H. Borsch, *Son of Man*, pp. 33ff.; M. Hooker, *The Son of Man in Mark*, pp. 182ff.; R. Maddox, 'The Function of the Son of Man according to the Synoptic Gospels', *NTS* **15** (1968), 45ff. Maddox rightly refuses to dismiss any one group as unauthentic *a priori*, but his discussion is marred by an inadequate treatment of the background of Son of Man.

interpretation of the background material which looks primarily to Dan. 7 and emphasises, not the supernatural-apocalyptic overtones of a traditional individual figure, but the Son of Man as identified with the saints of the Most High, a faithful martyr group who suffer, but who are vindicated by God. For the 'present' sayings point to a man (Jesus, the Son of Man *par excellence*) who lives a life characterised by authority, but also by 'obscurity', homelessness (understood as rejection), humility and service, concern for the outcastes of society.[1] The 'present' sayings merge into the Son-of-Man passion predictions, to which they are very closely related; Mark 10: 45 speaks of the nature of the Son of Man's ministry and his suffering.

The authenticity of the individual sayings need not be discussed here;[2] there is no reason to reject them *en bloc*.[3] In his teaching about the Son of Man, Jesus spoke not only about ultimate vindication but also about the nature and implications of his present ministry.[4] As has been shown, Jesus' proclamation about the presence of the Kingdom was also very much bound up with his actions, conduct, unpromising background and rejection. At this point Jesus' proclamation of the Kingdom and his teaching about the Son of Man correspond closely, although in other respects there are clear differences. The 'present' Son-of-Man sayings, like Jesus' proclamation of the Kingdom, point to the scandal, the 'unexpectedness' of Jesus' character, but they also reflect his authority and his concern for those on the fringe of society.

[1] Cf. E. Schweizer's interpretation of the 'present' sayings, 'Der Menschensohn', *ZNW* **50** (1959), 185–209; 'The Son of Man', *JBL* **79** (1960), 119–29; 'The Son of Man Again', *NTS* **9** (1963), 256–61. (The *ZNW* and *NTS* essays are reprinted in E. Schweizer, *Neotestamentica*.)

[2] Cf. F. H. Borsch's discussion, *Son of Man*, pp. 320–9; also I. H. Marshall, 'The Synoptic Son of Man Sayings', *NTS* **12**, 339ff.

[3] H. E. Tödt admits that Luke 19:10 must be an early saying, but claims that by analogy with the other sayings about the present activity of the Son of Man, it is not to be assumed that we have here an authentic saying of Jesus: *Son of Man*, pp. 133f. Rejection of the 'present' sayings by means of equally unconvincing arguments is common.

[4] The Johannine Son of Man sayings have not been mentioned in the preceding discussion; there are no clear examples of 'present' sayings (with which we have been primarily concerned) in the Fourth Gospel. Although the Johannine sayings raise rather special difficulties, they are relevant to the whole Son of Man question.

As P. Vielhauer's observations on the relationship of Son of Man and Kingdom seem, at first sight, to call in question the conclusions just drawn, a brief discussion is necessary at this point.[1] P. Vielhauer asks why Son of Man and Kingdom are brought together neither in the teaching of Jesus nor in Jewish background literature; he concludes that *all* Son-of-Man sayings stem from the early church and not from Jesus: Jesus' proclamation of the Kingdom was central and it was understood in such a way as to exclude the possibility that Jesus expected the coming of the Son of Man.

P. Vielhauer's starting points are so different from those just suggested that debate is not easy; Vielhauer presupposes, without discussion, that the 'present' sayings are not authentic and that Son of Man in the relevant background literature is a pre-existent heavenly being.[2] But even if these presuppositions are granted, his hypothesis is open to serious criticism. Vielhauer takes pains to emphasise that he does not contend that Son-of-Man sayings are unauthentic simply on the basis of an axiom that Son-of-Man and Kingdom sayings cannot both be authentic: this is the result, not the presupposition of his investigation.[3] Vielhauer's essay and his reply to H. E. Tödt's detailed criticism[4] are largely taken up with discussion of the authenticity of the 'future' Son-of-Man sayings,[5] for the validity of his hypothesis rests primarily on this question.[6]

[1] 'Gottesreich und Menschensohn in der Verkündigung Jesu' in *Festschrift für G. Dehn*, ed. W. Schneemelcher (Neukirchen, 1959), pp. 51–79; 'Jesus und der Menschensohn, Zur Diskussion mit Heinz Eduard Tödt und Eduard Schweizer', *ZTK* **60** (1963), 133–77. Both essays are reprinted in P. Vielhauer, *Aufsätze zum NT* (Munich, 1965).

[2] 'Gottesreich' in *Festschrift für G. Dehn*, pp. 56, 52, referring to Dan. 7, 1 Enoch 37–71 and 4 Ezra 13.

[3] 'Jesus', *ZTK* **60**, 138 and 153.

[4] H. E. Tödt, *Son of Man*, pp. 329–47.

[5] P. Vielhauer does allow that Matt. 10: 23 and Matt. 24: 37 par. may just possibly be exceptions and be authentic: 'Gottesreich' in *Festschrift für G. Dehn*, pp. 59ff., 67 and 71.

[6] Criticisms of P. Vielhauer's hypothesis which point to passages where Kingdom and Son of Man are found together in the traditions generally fall wide of the mark, for Vielhauer is prepared to accept that they are *juxtaposed* in the traditions or in particular sources, but asks for evidence that they were brought into a close relationship by Jesus himself. Vielhauer

Only if Son-of-Man sayings are accepted as unauthentic *in toto* does the fact that the two concepts are never fused in the traditions become a really pressing problem. If, on the other hand, some Son-of-Man sayings *are* authentic, then Kingdom and Son of Man must have been understood by Jesus and the early church not to have been mutually exclusive. This is one of the main criticisms Tödt makes. As Tödt shows, some of Vielhauer's exegetical conclusions on individual sayings are open to question.[1] But the method of *divide et impera* tends to hide more fundamental questions: Why was Jesus suddenly called Son of Man? Could all the very different references to Son of Man in the various gospel strata have been formulated *e nihilo*, as it were, in a short space of time by communities whose interest in and use of the expression Son of Man was soon to wane equally suddenly? Was the background literature really as formative and influential as such an hypothesis must assume?

But serious difficulties remain even if one concedes that all the Son-of-Man sayings stem from the early church. Vielhauer argues that Son of Man and Kingdom are very different concepts, having first excluded the 'present' sayings from consideration. But, on Vielhauer's view, the early church *also* formulated the 'present' sayings;[2] once they are included, a very different picture emerges. There are some strikingly broad similarities, as we have seen.[3] The early church transmitted both concepts; since there are similarities, why were

is thus unimpressed by Tödt's list of passages from Q where the two concepts are found side by side: 'Jesus', *ZTK* **60**, 96ff. This line of attack on Vielhauer's hypothesis is also used by M. Black, 'The Son of Man Problem in Recent Research and Debate', *BJRL* **45** (1963), 310. Cf. also J. W. Doeve, *Jewish Hermeneutics*, pp. 119ff.

[1] In his reply, however, Vielhauer does discuss the sayings Tödt considers to be authentic: 'Jesus', *ZTK* **60**, 142ff.

[2] P. Vielhauer denies that the 'present' sayings are circumlocutions for 'man' in general or for 'I'; Son of Man in these logia is a title: 'Gottesreich', *Festschrift für G. Dehn*, p. 56 and 'Jesus', *ZTK* **60**, 157ff.

[3] We need not demonstrate that there are even more striking differences. P. Vielhauer rightly accuses Tödt of tending to make Son of Man and Kingdom 'Wechselbegriffe'. 'Jesus', *ZTK* **60**, 152. E. Jüngel criticises Tödt for failing to stress that Son-of-Man and Kingdom sayings are found side by side because they are two concepts which must be differentiated: *Paulus und Jesus*, pp. 231 and 261f.

they not brought into a very much closer relationship? As Vielhauer has shown – and this can hardly be disputed – the two concepts are found side by side in the traditions, but are not combined. The answer can only be that both concepts are authentic, for if the earliest communities *created* a series of Son-of-Man sayings with some similarities to the Kingdom traditions which were treasured, then surely they would have been brought together at some points in the traditions.[1] The independence of the two concepts, so strongly stressed by Vielhauer, strengthens, rather than weakens, our case.

The interpretation of Son of Man and of Jesus' proclamation of the Kingdom which has been advanced does not involve an acute tension. The two concepts were juxtaposed but not explicitly fused either by Jesus, the compiler(s) of Q and the other strata, or by the evangelists, because they were concepts which could, but need not necessarily, have been linked together. Jesus saw himself as the obedient, faithful yet rejected and suffering Son of Man who would be vindicated by God; Jesus taught that God's rule was already manifesting itself in his ministry and person, even though it was also yet to come. We have sought to show that some of the implications of these two important themes in Jesus' proclamation bear striking similarities: both are related to Jesus' person, unpromising background, actions and conduct. At this point, these themes of Jesus' proclamation overlap – or, more accurately, run parallel; in other ways, of course, they differ widely.

---

[1] The background literature is not really relevant to the problem raised by Vielhauer. Vielhauer attempts to establish that Kingdom and Son of Man have nothing to do with each other in the Jewish background literature and that there was therefore no reason why Jesus should have linked them. Tödt contends that Vielhauer's case rests on only two texts at this point (*Son of Man*, pp. 232ff.); Vielhauer replies that such evidence as does exist, not silence, must be used ('Jesus', *ZTK* **60**, 137). Their debate serves to underline the paucity of references in the background literature either to Son of Man or to Kingdom; the relationship of the two concepts in the background literature would certainly not have discouraged the primitive church from linking the two concepts if they were seen to have some striking similarities. Nor is there any reason why Jesus could not have fused the two concepts even if they were unrelated in Jewish writings.

Neither the Son-of-Man sayings nor Jesus' proclamation of the Kingdom suggest that Jesus was merely an eschatological prophet; if that were the case, his message could be separated from his person. But that, as we have seen, is manifestly impossible, for two of the basic themes of Jesus' proclamation are closely related to the sort of person Jesus was. There is no need to demonstrate that this does not mean that Jesus made his own personality the basis of his proclamation.

As we have noted, criticisms of aspects of his 'biography', such as his 'obscure' background, his alienation from his family, and his extension of table fellowship to tax collectors and sinners, were made frequently, but Jesus insisted that the very features of his life to which objection was taken were part and parcel of his message, a message which must either be accepted or rejected.

Jesus made his most profound claims about his own person and ministry through his actions and conduct as much as, or even more than, through his words. Jesus' actions are not just illustrations of his message, they *are* his message. E. Fuchs' contention that Jesus' conduct was the framework of his proclamation is no exaggeration.[1]

The reply of Jesus to John the Baptist's question about Jesus and the nature of his ministry (Matt. 11: 2–6 = Luke 7: 18–23) provides striking confirmation of the conclusions we have drawn in this chapter. These verses undoubtedly stem from Q – this is particularly significant because, at first sight, the Q material seems to suggest that the Q community saw Jesus merely as an authoritative 'prophetic' or 'apocalyptic' teacher whose actions and character had little or no bearing on his words.[2]

In this passage Jesus says in effect that he who would understand who he is must pay close attention to his actions and to his proclamation and see them both as fulfilment of the prophets and as proof of the beginning of the Kingdom

---

[1] *Studies of the Historical Jesus* (E.T. London, 1964), p. 21.

[2] On Q, see below, p. 183 n. 1. The essential authenticity of the pericope is widely accepted; the ambiguous nature of the reply of Jesus supports this. See W. G. Kümmel's refutation of the suggestion that Matt. 11: 5f. was reshaped secondarily as an apologetic reply to the Baptist's question: *Promise and Fulfilment*, pp. 109ff. Cf. R. H. Fuller, *The Mission and Achievement of Jesus* (London, 1954), pp. 35f.

of God.[1] The ἐν ἐμοί indicates that Jesus' proclamation is linked inseparably with his person.[2]

Jesus' proclamation involves concern for those on the fringe of society; the groups of people to whom Jesus refers point not only to fulfilment of the prophetic promises of salvation in the last days, but also to Jesus' interest in those who, because they were considered to be unclean, were cut off from close contact with others and from the cultus.[3]

The sort of person Jesus showed himself to be caused a scandal (Matt. 11: 6 = Luke 7: 23). Jesus recognises that surprise is registered at his unpromising 'background' and says, 'Blessed is he who believes in spite of all present disappointing appearances.'[4] Jesus' background is already an issue during his ministry.

If the gospel traditions did intend to sketch out the character of Jesus of Nazareth, to show what sort of a person he was, how would this have been accomplished? As we saw in the previous chapter, the techniques of modern biographical writing were not those of the ancient world, where simple accounts of the actions, words and relationships of the subject were considered to provide at least as satisfactory a portrait as any character analysis or comment by the author. Hence there is no need to conclude that an investigation of the gospel traditions

[1] W. G. Kümmel, *Promise and Fulfilment*, p. 111. The last point is made more explicitly in Matt. 12: 28 = Luke 11: 20. It is significant that some of Bultmann's former pupils who have been unhappy with his insistence that the primitive kerygma was not concerned with more than the mere *Dass* of the historical existence of Jesus, have also criticised his view that Jesus proclaimed the imminence of the Kingdom, but not its presence. See, for example, G. Bornkamm, *Jesus of Nazareth* (E.T. London, 1960), p. 51.

[2] E. Linnemann's denial that the Kingdom is linked closely with Jesus' person is unconvincing; the distinction between Jesus' actions and his person is artificial: *Parables of Jesus*, p. 136 n. 29. Cf. W. G. Kümmel, 'the person of Jesus by his actions brings about already now what is expected from the eschatological future', *Promise and Fulfilment*, p. 111; also, R. Schnackenburg, *God's Rule and Kingdom*, pp. 117ff.

[3] G. Delling, 'Botschaft und Wunder im Wirken Jesu' in *Der historische Jesus*, ed. H. Ristow and K. Matthiae (Berlin, 1962), p. 397. Delling supplies a number of supporting references.

[4] This is Jeremias' paraphrase: *Parables*, p. 116.

which finds somewhat similar 'unsophisticated' methods in them, and which emphasises the degree to which they reflect the character of Jesus is based on presuppositions drawn from the modern world with its intense interest in personality and biography. The gospel traditions employ techniques of character portrayal which seem almost naïve to the modern reader and which can be and have been overlooked by scholarly eyes. A very simple and brief account of a person's relationships with others can reveal a good deal about the person concerned; the synoptic traditions need not be eliminated on account of their brevity. As long as such accounts referring to the same person cohere with one another, a few words can reveal a good deal about the character of the person concerned.

Our examination of Jesus' relationships with various groups and individuals with whom he comes in contact shows how clearly the traditions sketch out the sort of person Jesus was. These traditions provide many examples of a further essential requirement of an adequate portrayal of a person: coherence of words and actions.

Aspects of the character of Jesus which can be related in some way to Jesus' own proclamation, or which drew the attention or critical questioning of observers, by no means exhaust the richness of the portrait of Jesus found in the traditions, but they serve as convenient examples of the principle which we have emphasised. Jesus' relationships with other groups of people, such as disciples or opponents, could have been used in support. Particular traits, such as Jesus' perception and penetrating insight,[1] or his astounding sovereignty in dealing with situations according to the kind of people he meets,[2] or his compassion and humility might also have been considered.[3]

Although many irrelevant details did disappear in the course of the transmission of the traditions, many details have been

---

[1] Bornkamm correctly notes that such passages ought to be assembled without fear that this would be a merely sentimental undertaking and notes that this trait is confirmed by the nature of Jesus' preaching: *Jesus of Nazareth*, p. 60.

[2] Bornkamm, *Jesus of Nazareth*, pp. 58ff.

[3] Cf., for example, R. H. Lightfoot, *History and Interpretation in the Gospels* (London, 1935), p. 214.

retained which might seem to be of secondary importance to the saying of Jesus which is the main point of a pericope. Such details link with those in other pericopae to fill out our understanding of Jesus. For example, details of the places Jesus visited and the places in which he taught, and the way he constantly went to meet people, provide a portrait of Jesus which is quite different from that of John the Baptist or of the conventional rabbi.[1]

If the synoptic traditions are closely related to the life and character of Jesus, can the same be said about the traditions which lie behind the Fourth Gospel? A number of Johannine traditions have been shown above to be consistent with the synoptic portrait of Jesus of Nazareth. Behind the Fourth Gospel lie some traditions which, whether originally completely independent of synoptic traditions or not, recount incidents from the ministry of Jesus and his relationships with others which are broadly comparable to synoptic traditions.[2] Whether the Johannine theology alters the perspective of such material is another question, but many pre-Johannine traditions can be envisaged in a role in the early church similar to that played by synoptic traditions.

Many aspects of the gospels' portrait of Jesus are represented so widely in various sources, strata and forms of the traditions that their substantial reliability is established on the basis of the criteria of multiple attestation, coherence and consistency. Many others, some of which were discussed above, can be established on the basis of the criterion of dissimilarity.[3] While

---

[1] Bornkamm, *Jesus of Nazareth*, p. 57.

[2] See R. E. Brown, *The Gospel According to John* (New York, 1966), for a recent discussion of the whole question, pp. xli–li. Cf. R. Bultmann's comment, 'John gives all due emphasis to the humanity of Jesus, but presents none of the characteristics of Jesus' humanity which could be gleaned, for example, from the synoptic Gospels. The decisive thing is simply the "that".' 'Primitive Kerygma' in *Historical Jesus*, p. 20.

[3] This criterion is useful for confirming the authenticity of particular traits, but it leads to ridiculous and distorted results when it is used as the primary or sole criterion of authenticity. It requires us to assume that Jesus was completely at odds with the whole Jewish milieu of his time and that the primitive church totally misunderstood Jesus himself. See, for example, R. S. Barbour, *Traditio-Historical Criticism of the Gospels* (London, 1972), pp. 14ff.; M. D. Hooker, 'On Using the Wrong Tool', *Theology* **75** (1972), 575–81.

some individual logia and some pericopae undoubtedly were shaped or formulated in the early church, there is no reason to believe that the accounts of Jesus' relationships with various groups or the traits which are so deeply embedded in the traditions are secondary.

Only in the case of Jesus' relationship with his opponents would there seem to be possible grounds for suspecting that the primitive church has drawn the portrait.[1] Even here the traditions are remarkably consistent. But there is a significant inconsistency at one point: while Jesus' opposition to the Pharisees as a group is clear-cut, his relationship with individual Pharisees, especially as hinted at in Luke (e.g. 7: 36–7; 11: 37; 13: 31–3; 14: 1), is by no means bitter. If the gospel traditions' portrait of Jesus had been wholly stylised, it would be difficult to understand how such passages escaped unscathed, for Luke's *Tendenz* is not always in the direction of a softening of the opposition between Jesus and Pharisees (cf., for example, Luke 5: 30 and Mark 2: 16; Luke 12: 1 and Mark 8: 15).

When the gospel traditions are examined from a number of different angles without raising either the question of what was possible or impossible in the early church or what was their precise role in the church, one cannot escape the conclusion that they tell the reader about the character of Jesus of Nazareth. As we have seen, it was perfectly possible in sophisticated ancient biographical writings to sketch out the character of a person without a precise chronological framework. Hence the difficult question of chronology in the gospel traditions is irrelevant to the point we wish to emphasise; even if the 'loose' chronological framework in the gospels is secondary, the traditions can still be said to indicate the sort of person Jesus was. To this extent the gospel traditions may be described as 'biographical'. However, this expression has so many modern connotations (especially concerning 'personality') which are foreign to the ancient world, that (if it is not to be misleading) it can be used only with careful definition.

The early communities have retained traditions about Jesus

---

[1] On the whole subject, see H. Merkmal, 'Jesus und die Pharisäer', *NTS* **14** (1967–8), 194–208, and, for the opposite view, H. F. Weiss, 'Der Pharisäismus im Lichte der Überlieferung des NT' in R. Meyer, *Tradition und Neuschöpfung im antiken Judentum* (Berlin, 1965), pp. 89–132.

which provide such a rich and full portrait of him that we must conclude that the church began to look back to the past, or, to use the fashionable terminology, to historicise its traditions, at an early stage in its development. Interest in the past of Jesus is not solely Luke's prerogative, nor is this one of Mark's own distinctive contributions, for it is deeply rooted in the traditions on which the evangelists drew. A similar conclusion has been reached recently by J. Roloff in his *Das Kerygma und der irdische Jesus*. Roloff's monograph differs from this study both in method and in scope, but, with an impressive wealth of evidence, he argues that many parts of the gospel traditions reflect quite deliberately an interest in the past events of the ministry of Jesus.[1]

Interest in the life and character of Jesus was already present *in nuce* in the ministry of Jesus. Jesus' proclamation drew critical questioning: Who is this Jesus? Why does he behave in this way? Can God's promised rule really be associated with this man from Nazareth? But the earliest interest in Jesus, as later in the early church, was of a rather special kind: it was not curiosity about the physical features of Jesus, about his personality in the modern sense of that word, but interest in the sort of person he was – an interest which was aroused by the nature of his actions, conduct and claims.

[1] J. Roloff limits his study to the gospel traditions and concentrates on narratives about Jesus (pp. 48f.); he denies that the primitive church was interested in a character picture of Jesus (p. 247 n. 1).

CHAPTER 7

THE GOSPEL TRADITIONS IN
THE EARLY CHURCH

Why did the early church retain traditions about Jesus? How did the evangelists use the traditions on which they drew? Ever since the form critical 'revolution', most scholars have accepted that the gospel traditions were retained by the early church in order to meet its interests and needs. The traditions, form critics insist, are kerygmatic in the broadest sense of that term; they are not a neutral record of the historical Jesus, but were shaped and sometimes created in the light of the church's faith in the Risen Christ and were used to support and supplement the church's proclamation. Many scholars, following R. Bultmann's lead, have taken a further step and have denied that the gospel traditions intended to set out the life and character of Jesus: they are not concerned with the past, but with the church's present experience of and faith in the Risen Christ of the kerygma.

There is no need to quarrel with the form critical axiom that the traditions are kerygmatic. But, if the conclusions of the two previous chapters are valid, the kerygmatic role of the traditions has not smothered interest in the life and character of Jesus. The dual perspective of the gospel traditions is inescapable; they are kerygmatic and they intend to sketch out the life and character of Jesus. To by-pass or minimise either aspect is to miss the finely-held balance of the traditions themselves: they are neither purely 'historical' nor 'biographical', nor does their kerygmatic perspective exclude concern with more than the mere *Dass* of the historical existence of Jesus.

As our suggestions about the way gospel traditions were understood and used in the early church rest upon a cumulative case, we must summarise the main lines of the argument of the previous chapters at this point. Luke–Acts provides quite explicit evidence that in Luke's own day reference to the life and character of Jesus was part and parcel of the church's proclamation. Luke indicates that the church's initial missionary preaching must always sketch out the story of Jesus, unless knowledge of it can be taken for granted. In this respect, at least, Luke is not unique; he has not developed a new attitude to the life of Jesus and so parted company with Mark and earlier predecessors.

In order to minimise the risk of a circular argument which reconstructs the needs and interests of the early church solely from the traditions themselves, we then examined such evidence as there is outside the gospels for the early church's interest in the 'past' of Jesus. The speeches in Acts confirm that from an early period, well before Luke's own day, the church was interested in the life of Jesus and linked it closely to scripture. While it is impossible to be certain about the original *Sitz im Leben* of these pre-Lucan traditions, there is no reason to suppose that they were used in a setting very different from the one in which they have been placed by Luke: as part of missionary preaching – especially if we allow that this must have included a strong apologetic note.

The Pauline evidence is consistent with this conclusion. Paul was not uninterested in the 'past' of Jesus, indeed, he knew a good deal about the earthly life and teaching of Jesus, and his writings reveal that he had a rich character portrait of Jesus. Again, it was not possible to prove conclusively that Paul's missionary preaching included reference to the life and character of Jesus; this is not surprising in view of the nature of the evidence – in his epistles Paul does not rehearse the full contents of his initial missionary preaching. But his writings do not suggest any *Sitz im Leben* other than preaching for his interest in the life of Jesus; there is no evidence which refutes the strong probability that Paul referred to Jesus in his missionary preaching, whether or not he used traditions comparable to those on which the evangelists drew.

The evidence of the pre-Lucan traditions in Acts and of the Pauline material seems at first sight to be meagre, but it turns out to be exceedingly important. For form critics are often unable to reconstruct the needs and interests of the early church without calling upon the evidence of the gospel traditions themselves; they then jump directly from conclusions about the form of a pericope to its alleged *Sitz im Leben* in the early church.

When the gospel traditions are examined without any prior assumptions about their *Sitz im Leben* in the early church and are set against the background of roughly comparable material from the ancient world, we are surprised, not at the paucity of the material which the early church retained about Jesus, but at its extent. Scholars who deny that the church was interested in the 'past' of Jesus have awkward evidence to account for: if the early church was so completely dominated by her experience of the Risen Christ and by her apocalyptic expectations that there was at first no need for, and, indeed, no interest in the life of Jesus, why did the church retain traditions which have a deeply embedded 'biographical' and 'historical' stamp?

A further line of evidence for our cumulative argument was hinted at in the previous chapter and must now be explored more fully. It is usually and correctly accepted that the proclamation of Jesus was used by the primitive church to proclaim him: Jesus the 'proclaimer' became the one proclaimed.[1] If this was so, the nature of the proclamation of Jesus turns out to have important implications for any consideration of the early church's use of gospel traditions.

Jesus' proclamation was not taken up solely with the future; it was, as we have seen, related to the 'here and now' of Jesus and his ministry. Jesus claimed that God was already beginning to act decisively in his ministry; that claim was vindicated by the resurrection. The very fact that the church retained and used the proclamation of Jesus, even in the new post-Easter situation, meant that in its preaching it cannot have been indifferent to the past of Jesus.

Jesus' proclamation was, *in nuce*, a message about himself. Hence the transition from 'proclaimer' to 'proclaimed' was not a bridge over a chasm. Jesus himself had indicated that his significance was to be seen in his actions and conduct; even where these drew critical questioning, Jesus insisted that his unpromising background was part of the scandal of his

[1] See, for example, R. Bultmann's exposition of this point in 'Die Bedeutung des geschichtlichen Jesus für die Theologie des Paulus' in *Glauben und Verstehen* I, 205.

message. The profoundly 'personal' nature of the proclamation of Jesus was deeply embedded in the traditions retained by the early church; it could hardly proclaim Jesus by means of these very traditions without intending to indicate what sort of a person Jesus was, or without understanding the traditions as spelling out the character of Jesus of Nazareth. In particular, the church's proclamation of 'this man, Jesus of Nazareth' as Risen, as Lord and Christ, was bound to raise again the question of the unpropitious beginnings which the early church, no less than Jesus himself, insisted was part of its message.

Jesus' proclamation and his actions and conduct were linked inseparably; his teaching was not merely a series of prophetic propositions illustrated by his actions and conduct, for the latter were as much 'message' as his words. Similarly, as has been emphasised recently, Jesus' parables were intended neither to convey timeless truths, nor to illustrate the proclamation of Jesus; they themselves were 'message'.[1] The very nature of Jesus' own proclamation acted as a catalyst both towards the retention and use in the church of traditions which showed what sort of a person Jesus was and towards linking such traditions inextricably to the preaching itself.

At this point H. Schürmann's important article, 'Die vorösterlichen Anfänge der Logientradition', provides support.[2] Although it was published as long ago as 1960, Schürmann's article has not as yet received the attention it deserves; apart from the work of H. Riesenfeld and B. Gerhardsson, it is one of the few attempts in recent decades to reconsider some of the basic axioms of form criticism.[3] Schürmann argues that form criticism has unjustifiably limited its search for the *Sitz im Leben* of sayings of Jesus to the post-Easter community; their first *Sitz im Leben* is the pre-Easter circle of disciples – here

---

[1] Cf. E. Fuchs, *Studies*, pp. 130ff.; E. Linnemann, *Parables*, pp. 18f.; E. Jüngel, *Paulus*, pp. 120ff.; G. Bornkamm, *Jesus*, p. 69.

[2] *Der historische Jesus und der kerygmatische Christus*, eds. H. Ristow and K. Matthiae (Berlin, 1960), pp. 342–70.

[3] But see now E. Güttgemanns, *Offene Fragen zur Formgeschichte des Evangeliums* (Munich, 2nd ed. 1971). Unfortunately the present book was all but completed before this monograph became available to me. See also, H. Simonsen, 'Zur Frage der grundlegenden Problematik in form- und redaktionsgeschichtlicher Evangelienforschung', *ST* **26** (1972), 1–23.

they were first transmitted and used. In particular, the missionary activity of the disciples, which included proclamation of the Kingdom and of repentance, was extremely important: Jesus deliberately moulded his sayings and gave them to his disciples in order to assist their own proclamation.[1] In spite of all the obvious differences between the pre-Easter and the post-Easter communities, a clear line of continuity can be traced.

H. Schürmann limits his observations to the sayings of Jesus, but he does suggest in passing that the *Sitz im Leben* of part of the narrative tradition is also to be traced to the circle of disciples before Easter. Disciples who were sent out to proclaim, in the name of Jesus, the nearness of the Kingdom of God, were certainly asked about their authorisation and their Master.[2] This is a most important point which is confirmed by some of the conclusions we drew in the previous chapter. Critical questions about Jesus, his background, his conduct and his claims were bound to arise during his ministry. And, in addition, we have stressed that the actions and conduct of Jesus were as much part of his proclamation as his sayings.

As soon as we allow that there was some continuity between the pre-Easter and the post-Easter situations, and that the proclamation of Jesus was used by some communities in the early church to proclaim him, the nature of that proclamation becomes relevant to the question of the *Sitz im Leben* of the gospel traditions. Sayings and narrative traditions about the actions and conduct of Jesus may well have been used both in the disciples' proclamation and in early Christian communities.

There is one further argument which supports our suggestion that the early church referred to the life and character of Jesus in its missionary preaching – an argument which might be dubbed an appeal to common sense. The very fact that Jesus of Nazareth could not be fitted into any of the categories of the day meant that the early church could not simply make a theological pronouncement about him, and assume that no further explanation either of what sort of a person he was or

[1] H. Schürmann, 'Die vorösterlichen Anfänge der Logientradition', in *Der historische Jesus*, p. 362.
[2] 'Die vorösterlichen Anfänge', p. 366 n. 18.

of what sort of a life he had lived was necessary. In initial missionary preaching to those unfamiliar with Christian claims about Jesus, one could not say 'Jesus is Messiah' without very considerable qualification and explanation, for there was no one universally accepted portrait of Messiah. Nor could one simply say 'Jesus is θεῖος ἀνήρ', for, even if one makes the very doubtful assumption that there was such a fixed category in the first century A.D.,[1] Jesus was at least as dissimilar from as similar to contemporary miracle workers. Jesus broke all preconceptions about expected messianic figures in late Judaism; Hellenistic categories were no more adequate.

It must have been all but impossible to avoid sketching out the life and character of Jesus in missionary preaching. How could one claim that Jesus was the one person in the whole of history who fulfilled scripture in its widest and deepest sense, that Jesus was raised from the dead by God in a totally unexpected and unique way, and call for repentance and commitment to him without indicating who he was? How could one mention the crucifixion without answering in anticipation careful questioning about the events which led to the rejection of Jesus? Could one begin to mention the betrayal, arrest and trial of Jesus without arousing interest in the teachings and actions of Jesus?[2]

A number of different lines of evidence, when taken cumulatively, not only confirm that the early church was interested in the 'past' of Jesus, but strongly suggest that the primary *Sitz im Leben* for that interest was the missionary preaching of the church. The early church was a missionary church actively propagating its faith; hence the nature of its initial proclamation of the gospel is a relevant question. Gospel traditions were certainly used in the context of worship and of ethical instruction, but if there had been no initial preaching there would have been no worshipping community.

Can we be more precise and discover how gospel traditions were used in the church's preaching? As there is so little explicit evidence, any suggestions are bound to to be some-

---

[1] On this, see W. v. Martitz, art. 'υἱός κτλ.', *TWNT* VIII, 338.

[2] Cf. C. F. D. Moule, 'Jesus in NT Kerygma', in *Verborum Veritas*, pp. 24f.

what tentative. M. Dibelius envisages gospel traditions used as illustrations of the preaching.[1] Surely the strong kerygmatic thrust of many pericopae would be less prominent if they were only illustrations and were not making a particular point themselves. The evidence of the speeches in Acts suggests that reference to the past of Jesus of Nazareth was neither a mere appendage to the preaching, nor an illustration of the fact of the incarnation or some other kerygmatic statement, nor did it belong only to the instruction of those who had responded to the heralding of the good news, but it was an integral part of the preaching itself.

Nor do pericopae seem to have been used as 'texts' which were elaborated and expounded. This view is influenced unduly by modern preaching methods. Why were the 'text' and the elaboration ultimately kept apart? Were the former 'holy tradition'? It is possible that elaboration by the early church has intruded into the traditions at some points, notably into some of the parables, but, on the whole, the tendency was in the opposite direction – towards briefer units. Preaching was not a series of statements like news headlines which could be elaborated and explained with gospel traditions, nor was it a formal discourse in which one pericope, one theme, was expounded and its application drawn out.

Both views envisage the individual pericope as the basic unit in preaching, whether as a 'text' for a 'sermon' or as illustration of a statement. But were gospel pericopae normally used in isolation? Behind this assumption stands the very influential notion of M. Kähler that just as the light from the sun is reflected in every drop of the bedewed meadow, so the full person of our Lord meets us in each little story in the gospel traditions.[2] But this much-quoted statement is an over-simplification: why, on this view, have so many varied pericopae been retained if each makes essentially the same point? Some would be enigmatic if not set alongside others. Christians instructed by the church, involved in its worship and caught up in its experience of the Spirit might conceivably have been capable of understanding gospel pericopae in the way suggested

[1] *From Tradition to Gospel*, pp. 24ff.

[2] M. Kähler, *The So-Called Historical Jesus and the Historic Biblical Christ* (1896; E.T. Philadelphia, 1964), p. 81.

by Kähler, but it is difficult to believe that the traditions would be interpreted in this way by a person not yet committed to the message and life of the church.

Form critical study of the gospels has confirmed that behind the gospels lie originally independent pericopae which were used in the preaching of the church, but this does not necessarily lead to the conclusion that preaching revolved around an individual pericope. There is evidence in the gospel traditions, some of which was noted earlier, that pericopae were linked together at a very early stage; often such groups make a similar point or reinforce an aspect of the character of Jesus stressed in neighbouring pericopae. The full significance of many pericopae is seen only in the light of others. Many are so brief that it seems very likely that they were used in smaller or larger groups in preaching. Preaching in the early church was not a polished five-minute affair; even if it had been, several pericopae might have been fitted into such a brief period of time, whether as 'texts' or 'illustrations'.

The passion narratives offer assistance at this point. Individual passion pericopae were not used in isolation to illustrate the passion kerygma; nor were they 'texts' which needed elaboration; they were themselves preaching, announcement about Jesus of Nazareth. The earliest communities seem to have possessed a core of passion traditions which were later expanded or which, on occasion, were abbreviated. When used in the preaching of the church, a group of passion pericopae must have been understood not as a proclamation of the Exalted Christ, but as announcement about the past of Jesus – as portraying what sort of a person Jesus was. Why should not pericopae concerned with the ministry of Jesus have been used in a similar way?

There is no way of establishing with any certainty the extent to which gospel traditions were available at any given time or in any given place prior to the emergence of the gospels. Wherever gospel traditions were known and used – and it is probable that this was the case almost universally in the early church[1] – groups of pericopae related to the ministry of Jesus formed part of the initial preaching of the

[1] Cf. E. Käsemann's observation that the synoptic gospels belonged to the same Hellenistic communities as Paul and John: 'Sackgassen im Streit

179

gospel. No doubt the circumstances of the hearers dictated the number and even the content of the pericopae chosen on any given occasion. Pericopae which told about the arrest, trial, crucifixion and resurrection of Jesus were very probably linked to some kind of sketch of the ministry of Jesus. Announcement about the death and resurrection may even, on occasion, have preceded any reference to the character of Jesus. These suggestions are consistent with the summaries of the missionary preaching of the church in Acts, for there, too, reference to the ministry is linked closely to a summary of the crucifixion and resurrection; together they are declaration about Jesus. No doubt elaboration and interpretation of the theological significance of the initial announcement about Jesus followed.

Our suggestions about the role of the gospel traditions in the early church are a revival, with modifications, of M. Dibelius' well-known hypothesis.[1] In particular, we have emphasised, against Dibelius, the extent to which the gospel traditions are, by intention, concerned with the 'past' of Jesus. Although our case must rest primarily on the argument set out, we must take up briefly some of the criticisms which have been levelled against Dibelius' view.

R. Bultmann strongly attacked M. Dibelius at this point, even though, as form critics, they were in basic agreement. Bultmann claimed that Dibelius' view that 'in the beginning was the sermon' was a gross overstatement that endangered the understanding of numerous items in the tradition. Apologetics, polemics, edification and discipline must equally be taken into account, as must scribal activity. Bultmann accepted that biographical apophthegms were best thought of as edifying paradigms for sermons; they help to present the Master as a living contemporary, and to comfort and admonish the church in her hope.[2]

M. Dibelius' view was rather less rigid than Bultmann and many other critics supposed. He defined preaching in a very

um den historischen Jesus' in *Exegetische Versuche und Besinnungen* II, 55 and 47 (E.T. in *New Testament Questions of Today*, pp. 49 and 40f.).

[1] See, especially, *From Tradition to Gospel*, chapter 1.

[2] *Synoptic Tradition*, pp. 60f.

broad way: it included exhortation to a Christian community, missionary preaching, instruction of catechumens, as well as preaching during worship.[1] Dibelius stressed, as we have also done, that missionary preaching was primary: if there had not been any missionary preaching, there would not have been any other kind of preaching activity. Surely much of the church's missionary preaching included apologetic and polemics – unless we are to believe that early preachers adopted a 'take it or leave it' attitude.

But there is more at stake than a debate over definitions. Can individual sayings and pericopae be traced so confidently to a large variety of settings, some far removed from preaching, that our suggestions are undermined? The variety of settings proposed by individual form critics for the same pericopae strongly indicates that very often it is far from easy to draw conclusions about the *Sitz im Leben* of a pericope solely from analysis of its form and content. In addition, if the gospel traditions were originally used in a very large number of varied settings, none of which ever had anything to do with preaching, it becomes difficult to understand why the traditions were ever gathered together into documents called gospels.

There is a more important weakness in this position. Were individual pericopae used in only *one* setting? The evangelists had little difficulty in placing the same traditions in different contexts, often with quite minor modifications. Many parts of the traditions could have been used effectively in a variety of settings in the early church.

This is supported by recent research into the transmission of oral tradition. Hugo Kuhn has shown that the 'form' of an oral tradition is not necessarily closely related to its 'function'. Almost every form can be used in a variety of ways. Similarly, any one purpose or function may be served by traditions with very different forms.[2]

K. Stendahl, among others, attacks M. Dibelius on rather

---

[1] *From Tradition to Gospel*, p. 14.

[2] 'Zur Typologie mündlicher Sprachdenkmäler', *Bayerische Akademie der Wissenschaften, Philosophisch-Historische Klasse, Sitzungsberichte 1956*, Heft 5 (Munich, 1960), p. 21. See also H. Simonsen, 'Die grundlegende Problematik', *ST* **26**, 4.

different grounds. He notes that, apart from Acts 10: 38 and 2: 22, very little of the gospel material is found in the New Testament epistles or in the earliest non-canonical Christian literature. 2 Clement is the first Christian sermon, and 1 Clement and Barnabas may contain material relevant to the content of early Christian preaching; they all refer to words of Jesus but nothing is said of his deeds. Gospel material does not appear until the more scholarly work of Justin; it is significant that in the homiletic tradition we do not find any extensive material from the gospels.[1]

It is certainly true that gospel traditions are significant by their absence from much early Christian literature. But there are no extant examples of missionary preaching which are sufficiently early to shed any light on the use of gospel traditions within the New Testament period. Many scholars seem to assume that what is not known to us never existed.

Perhaps the most widely accepted alternative view links the portrait of Jesus, which the gospel traditions provide, with the need of Christians in the early church to be able to envisage the Risen Christ as a living contemporary. At first sight, at least, this explanation seems to account both for the kerygmatic perspective of the traditions and for the fact that they retain a portrait of the One they proclaim. But it is not easy to believe that the gospel traditions were understood solely in terms of the Risen Lord with no reference to the past of Jesus of Nazareth – especially if, as we have argued, the early church was not uninterested in the past of Jesus. If the gospel traditions were used in initial preaching, they must have been understood as declaration and explanation about Jesus of Nazareth, the One now proclaimed as Risen Lord. While a member of the fellowship of a worshipping community might well have been able to interpret in terms of the Risen Christ gospel traditions which were heard repeatedly, such a sophisticated theological interpretation would lie beyond the sort of announcement about Jesus required in evangelism.[2]

[1] K. Stendahl, *The School of St Matthew* (2nd revised edition, Philadelphia, 1968), pp. 13ff.

[2] The early church's need to know about the example Christians ought to follow is also often suggested as the *Sitz im Leben* for interest in the past of Jesus. This view is discussed above, pp. 7f.

There are, then, good reasons for suggesting that gospel traditions were used in groups in preaching; traditions which declared what had happened in the ministry of Jesus and what sort of a person Jesus was, were in themselves 'kerygmatic'. There is no dichotomy between the gospel traditions' concern with the life and character of Jesus and their use in preaching. The preaching of the church not only declared that the crucified Jesus was Risen and Exalted, but indicated what Jesus had done and what sort of a person he was, for the church claimed that in the actions and conduct of Jesus, God had begun to act eschatologically.

We have deliberately concentrated our attention on Luke's Gospel and on the traditions on which the evangelists drew. But what about Mark, Matthew and John?[1] Recent studies of Mark and Matthew which stress that both evangelists intend to look back to the ministry of Jesus confirm that the church was interested in the past of Jesus from an early period. S. Schulz vigorously contends that Mark, not Luke, writes the first life of Jesus; Mark intends to set out a continuous history of Jesus.[2] G. Strecker stresses the prominence of *Heilsgeschichte* in Matthew.[3] R. Walker argues that Matthew intended his gospel to be neither a 'new torah', nor a collection of pericopae for use in worship, nor a catechetical handbook, but a kerygmatic history, in which the ministry of Jesus is the centre point of salvation history.[4]

Mark, and following him, Matthew, as well as Luke, set

[1] For a discussion of the nature and purpose of the Q material, see G. N. Stanton, 'On the Christology of Q', *Christ and Spirit in the New Testament* (Festschrift C. F. D. Moule), eds. B. Lindars and S. S. Smalley (Cambridge, 1973), pp. 25–40.

[2] 'Markus und das Urchristentum', *Studia Evangelica* II (1964), 143f. Cf. S. Schulz, *Die Stunde der Botschaft*, p. 39. See also J. Roloff, 'Das Markusevangelium als Geschichtsdarstellung', *EvT* **27** (1969), 73–93.

[3] *Der Weg der Gerechtigkeit* (2nd ed. Göttingen, 1966), p. 186. Cf. also G. Strecker, 'Das Geschichtsverständnis des Matthäus', *EvT* **26** (1966), 57–74.

[4] *Die Heilsgeschichte im ersten Evangelium* (Göttingen, 1967). The existence of Acts is often said to confirm that Luke's Gospel has a perspective on the past which is quite different from that found in Matthew and Mark. R. Walker claims that Matthew's Gospel contains both a Matthean life of Jesus and an 'Acts of the Apostles' (p. 114)!

out the story of Jesus; in so doing the evangelists did not adopt a new attitude to the life of Jesus which was quite unknown in the earlier communities on whose traditions they drew.

John's Gospel is, in so many ways, a special case. But some of the traditions used by the evangelist do indicate what sort of a person Jesus was and can be envisaged in a role broadly similar to synoptic traditions. In spite of all its unique features, the Fourth Gospel is neither an epistle nor merely a collection of sayings of Jesus;[1] it is cast in the form of a life of Jesus and it does present a rich portrait of him, however much that portrait may be said to differ from that found in the synoptics.[2] If the evangelist did not intend, at least in part, to indicate what sort of a person Jesus was, why did he write a gospel which, when placed alongside, say, either the *Gospel of Thomas* or *Pirqe Aboth*, looks so much like the synoptics?

The precise purpose of the gospels is a vexed question. It is difficult, if not impossible, to identify the historical or theological situation which lies behind each gospel. But the gospels as they now stand would not have been inappropriate for use in evangelism. Luke, as we have argued, sees the life of Jesus as an integral part of the church's proclamation. And the Fourth Gospel declares that its purpose is evangelistic (20: 31).[3] Mark may well have anticipated that much of his material would be appropriate for his Christian readers to use in missionary preaching. Matthew is more clearly related to a catechetical purpose, but, as C. F. D. Moule notes,

it does not take much reading between the lines to recognize that a large amount of its material would be eminently suitable for pastoral instruction in a Christian community which had come out from Judaism but was still beset by antagonistic Jews at close quarters and therefore required both directly apologetic

[1] Cf. E. Käsemann, 'Sackgassen im Streit um den historischen Jesus' in *Exegetische Versuche und Besinnungen* II, 47ff. and 53ff., and R. Bultmann's reply, which dodges the force of Käsemann's point, 'Antwort an E. Käsemann', *Glauben und Verstehen* IV, 195.

[2] Cf. C. H. Dodd, 'The Portrait of Jesus in John and in the Synoptics', *Christian History and Interpretation*, eds. W. R. Farmer, R. R. Niebuhr, C. F. D. Moule, pp. 183–98.

[3] Although the precise meaning of John 20: 31 is disputed, few would deny that the Fourth Gospel is, broadly speaking, evangelistic in intention.

material and also the narrative of 'how it all began', which is indirectly of great apologetic importance.[1]

The gospels differ widely in their emphases and even in their theological perspective, but each contains material which would be appropriate in evangelism and each gospel has at least half an eye on non-Christians, whether Jewish or Gentile, who were either unfamiliar with the story of the life of Jesus or who held serious misconceptions about him.

[1] 'The Intention of the Evangelists' in *New Testament Essays: Studies in Memory of T. W. Manson*, ed. A. J. B. Higgins (Manchester, 1959), p. 169.

CONCLUSIONS

Several unfashionable suggestions have been made in this book, one of the most important of which is that the early church was interested in the past of Jesus.

This conclusion is supported by several lines of evidence. Neither the speeches in Acts nor Paul's epistles suggest that early Christian communities set no store by the life and character of Jesus. When set alongside roughly comparable material, the 'historical' and 'biographical' perspective of the gospels is striking; their rich portrait of Jesus cannot be brushed aside either as a misunderstanding of their intention or with the dictum 'the gospels are not biographies'. Jesus' words, actions and persons are very closely related; already in his own lifetime his conduct, claims and unimpressive background drew critical questioning. If we accept that traditions about the proclamation of Jesus were used in the early church to proclaim him, similar questions about Jesus were bound to arise: Who was this Jesus about whom so much is claimed? Why was he rejected and crucified? If the early church was uninterested in the past of Jesus, the emergence of the gospels becomes a puzzle. For, in spite of all possible qualification, the gospels, including John, look very much like lives of Jesus.

R. Bultmann's insistence that the kerygma of the early church was not concerned with more than the mere *Dass* of the historical existence of Jesus is no longer accepted without modification, even by scholars whom he has deeply influenced. It is now customary to argue that the gospels' concern with the past of Jesus was a complete reversal or a later development of the early church's attitude. A number of 'development' hypotheses have been suggested.[1] As we have seen, Luke's Gospel, a commonly suggested turning point, does not mark a new and unique attitude to the life of Jesus. Gospels and epistles can be seen to represent very different attitudes to the life of Jesus only if one assumes, quite unjustifiably, that they belong to the same *Sitz im Leben*. The traditions on which the evangelists drew do not take us back to a pristine period

[1] See above, pp. 3ff.

when the church was so totally absorbed in her experience of the Risen Christ and in expectations of an imminent *parousia* that the past of Jesus was of no interest.

Although a firm question mark must be placed against 'development' hypotheses, the significance of the life and character of Jesus was undoubtedly interpreted in a variety of ways: differing circumstances led to different emphases. It is just possible that different groups retained different portraits of Jesus.[1] But it is difficult to trace clear lines of development as far as interest in the past of Jesus is concerned. Even if interest in Jesus of Nazareth did not always take the form of gospel traditions, the early church did not overlook 'the story of how it all began'.

The only clear and important dividing line within the earliest decades would seem to lie at the point when the church began to preach to an audience unfamiliar with the story of Jesus – this is Luke's view in Acts, and there seem to be no compelling reasons to doubt its general reliability. Other dividing lines belong to the post-New Testament period. Some groups, especially those influenced by various forms of gnosticism, virtually emptied history of any meaning and dispensed with Jesus of Nazareth. Others set great store on tales about the miraculous powers of Jesus, especially as a child; these tales are quite out of character with the traditions on which the evangelists drew and blur the difference between the earthly and the risen Jesus.[2]

It is extremely difficult to discover to what extent the beginnings of such developments can be traced into the New Testament period.[3] The life and character of Jesus seems to have been of no importance in two interpretations of Jesus which stand at opposite ends of the spectrum; both were flirted with by some communities, but both failed to win the day. Some saw Jesus as a prophet or a teacher whose person

---

[1] Cf. E. Trocmé, *Jesus and His Contemporaries* (E.T. London, 1973).

[2] The *Infancy Gospel of Thomas* provides the classic example of this. It is significant that there are few apocryphal stories about Jesus which are comparable to canonical material; the canonical traditions seem to have satisfied biographical curiosity about the parts of Jesus' life they covered, or, at least, to have discouraged speculation about them.

[3] H. Köster, among others, is rather more confident. Cf. his 'One Jesus and Four Primitive Gospels', *HTR* **61** (1968), 203–47.

was not related to his teachings, while others regarded him as the revealer who revealed only that he was the revealer. If either view had been generally accepted in the earliest decades, we should now know almost nothing about the life and character of Jesus.

In order to establish that the early church was interested in the past of Jesus, it is necessary to find a plausible *Sitz im Leben*. This is by no means easy – mainly because our knowledge of the early church is not as extensive as we would like. We have taken as an hypothesis Luke's view that the church referred to the past of Jesus as part of its preaching, especially its missionary preaching. There are a number of reasons which, taken together, strongly suggest that Luke was not alone in recognising that the story of Jesus was an essential part of the church's proclamation.[1]

There are no good grounds for denying this strong possibility, and no equally compelling alternative explanation of the evidence. In particular, many parts of the gospel traditions have such a deeply embedded 'historical' and 'biographical' stamp that one is bound to ask why this is so: there was plenty of precedent for very different kinds of traditions about Jesus. No doubt gospel traditions were used in several different ways in the early church – but almost certainly a primary *Sitz im Leben* was missionary preaching. This hypothesis cannot be proved conclusively, but neither can it be shown to be false.

This suggestion will seem to some either to smack of liberalism's emphasis on the personality of the historical Jesus as the centre of the Christian message or to be an attempt to provide facts about Jesus as proof for faith. But the early church did not make the character of Jesus the focal point of its message. For his character is in a sense ambiguous: many traits can be paralleled in the lives of others.[2] Jesus

---

[1] These are summarised on pp. 172ff.

[2] E. Schweizer notes that Epictetus ate and drank with the socially lower classes, was a slave himself, and helped thousands of slaves to bear their destiny: 'Scripture – Tradition – Modern Interpretation' in *Neotestamentica*, p. 225. According to Luke 3: 12; 7: 29, John the Baptist associated with tax collectors and sinners; Matt. 21: 32 notes that harlots, as well as tax collectors, liked to go to John to do repentance. The soldiers

himself recognised that his own background and the unpromising outward appearance of his ministry were scandalous
when placed alongside his claims. Any attempt to stress the
noble qualities of Jesus or to make Jesus into an appealing
hero must always neglect the scandalous nature of his character
– and this lies at the heart of the gospel traditions and of Jesus'
message.

We know nothing about the personality of Jesus in the
modern sense of his psychological make-up. But our ignorance
is not to be taken, as it so often is, as confirmation that the
early church was uninterested in Jesus of Nazareth: we know
next to nothing about the personality of any figure in the
ancient world; ancient writers did not indulge, in the manner
of modern biographers, in psychological analysis of personality,
in description either of character development or of the influence
of external events on character. But the gospel traditions'
accounts of Jesus' actions, words and relationships reveal a
good deal about his character. M. Kähler was over-confident
when he claimed that the synoptists' portrayal of Jesus evokes
such an undeniable impression of reality that one might venture
to predict how he might have acted in this or that situation,
or even what he might have said.[1] But we do have a sufficiently
clear portrait of Jesus in the gospels to enable us to say that
certain things would be inconsistent with his character. Indeed,
we can go further and suggest that the historicity of certain
events and at least some aspects of the portrait of Jesus are
essential to faith, for if historical research were ever able to
prove conclusively that the historical Jesus was quite unlike
the Jesus of the gospels, then faith would certainly be eroded.
The gospel is concerned with history: not in that it stands
if its claims could be verified by the historian, but in that it
falls if the main lines of the early church's portrait of Jesus of
Nazareth were to be falsified by historical research.

These conclusions carry implications which run in all
directions, though we can do no more than note briefly several
which are particularly important. We have twice found it
necessary to place a firm question mark against the assumption

of Luke 3: 14 might also be added to the outcastes with whom John
associated.

[1] *The So-called Historical Jesus*, p. 78.

that Christological reflection gradually moved 'backwards' from *parousia* expectations to the life of Jesus: first, we noted that the life of Jesus was interpreted in terms of scripture from a very early period, and, secondly, we stressed that it is a mistake to explain the Son-of-Man Christology in this way. If our suggestions about the church's interest in the life of Jesus and about the nature and purpose of the gospel traditions are plausible, the church's traditions about Jesus were very probably more influential on early reflection about the significance of Jesus than is often supposed.

It is frequently assumed that an assessment of the degree to which the gospel traditions or the gospels are historical must accept that this was not their intention. While our suggestions do not prove their reliability, they do provide a broad hint that the early church was much more aware of the distinction between the 'past' and the 'present' of Jesus than is often allowed, and therefore less likely to confuse its own understanding and experience of the Risen Christ with its account of who Jesus of Nazareth was.

As we have seen, the actions of Jesus are to be related closely to his teaching and both together seen as message. If so, there would seem to be strong reasons for refusing to regard the narrative traditions in the gospels as less likely to be authentic than the sayings. Incidents and narratives were not spun out of sayings as frequently as R. Bultmann suggests,[1] for the church had a stake, from the earliest period, in preserving traditions about the actions and words of Jesus which were seen to be consistent and interrelated.

What are the implications for the church today? We need to know what sort of a person Jesus was in his earthly life if the kerygma of the New Testament is to be comprehensible. As E. Schweizer insists, it is important that Jesus is, for us, no mere ghost, but a man with specific features. But he also suggests that a theology in which the kerygma of the first church is the centre must be corrected by this insight.[2] If our suggestions are valid, no such correction is necessary, for the early church reached similar conclusions about the importance of the life and character of Jesus.

---

[1] *Synoptic Tradition, passim.*   [2] *Neotestamentica,* pp. 229f.

Any understanding which modern man has of the ministry and character of Jesus is more often than not a misunderstanding; Jesus breaks modern preconceptions about his person just as in the first century. Hence it is as necessary today as ever it was to sketch out the life and character of Jesus as an essential part of evangelism. The church must ensure ever anew that the scandal and the uniqueness of the life and character of Jesus are held together and that both are linked to the scandal and uniqueness of the cross and resurrection. The resurrection faith of the church did not obscure the past of Jesus. On the contrary, the resurrection acted as a catalyst which encouraged retention of traditions which told about the past of Jesus, for the early church claimed that Jesus was neither a mere teacher nor a mere revealer of heavenly secrets whose character was irrelevant: Jesus of Nazareth, who went about doing good, was crucified but was raised from the dead by God; in spite of the scandal of his conduct and background, he was vindicated and exalted.

I INDEX OF PASSAGES CITED

II INDEX OF AUTHORS

Note: Italics indicate that a new title appears for the first time.

III GENERAL INDEX

Acts 10: 34–43 19ff., 67ff.
U. Wilckens' interpretation 19ff.
Acts, speeches in; *see also* Luke *and*
Missionary preaching
circumstances of hearers 15ff.,
20ff., 25ff., 30, 67
Jesus of Nazareth in the speeches
13ff., 115ff.
origin of the speeches 13ff., 67ff.,
173f.
Semitisms 68ff.
tradition and redaction 67f.
use of the Old Testament 70ff.,
77ff., 189f.; abbreviations of
Old Testament citations 71ff.

Biography 117ff., 167, 170, 189; *see
also* Hellenistic biographical
writing
Gospels as biographies 117ff.,
124ff., 135f., 170, 186
Jewish biographical writing 126ff.

Character portrayal 46f., 52, 99ff.,
121ff., 146, 167ff., 189; *see also*
Luke as literary artist *and* Paul
and character of Jesus

Form criticism 2, 9, 117, 172ff.,
175ff., 179ff.; *see also* Biography
circular argument 11, 173f.
Sitz im Leben 6, 9, 138, 156, 173,
176, 177, 180ff., 186ff.

Gospel traditions; *see also* Character
portrayal
chronological framework 170
historicity 146f., 169f., 189
juxtaposition 141f., 143ff., 179,
182
perspective 137ff., 167f., 170f.,
172, 174, 178f., 180, 186, 188

use in the early church 6ff., 175ff.,
177ff., 181ff., 186, 188
Gospels
perspective of 117ff., 183ff.
reasons for emergence in the early
church 3ff., 186ff.

Hellenistic biographical writing
118ff.,
character portrayal 121ff., 125ff.
chronological order 119ff.
descriptions of personal appearance 124
historical context 123ff.
topical presentaton 119ff.

Jesus of Nazareth; *see also* Son-of-
Man Christology
actions and words: inter-relation-
ship 166, 168, 174ff., 189
associations with tax collectors
137ff.
attitude of children 151f.
attitude to women 146ff.
character traits 9f., 99ff., 168ff.,
188f.
example of 1, 7ff., 31
parables of contrast 152ff.
proclamation of the kingdom 138,
152f., 157, 162ff., 166f., 174,
176
relationship with opponents 170ff.
scandal of his obscure origins
152ff., 162, 167, 174, 189
Johannine traditions 138, 149f.,
154, 169, 184, 186

Luke; *see also* Luke's Passion narrative
as biographer 31, 47ff., 52ff., 54,
66
chronology 37, 54

206